C.O.N.F.L.I.C.T

*An Insider's Guide to Storytelling
in Factual / Reality TV and Film*

C.O.N.F.L.I.C.T

An Insider's Guide
to Storytelling in
Factual / Reality TV and Film

Robert Thirkell

methuen | drama

METHUEN DRAMA

1 3 5 7 9 10 8 6 4 2

First published in 2010

A & C Black Publishers Limited
36 Soho Square
London W1D 3QY
www.methuendrama.com

Copyright © Robert Thirkell 2010

Robert Thirkell has asserted his rights
under the Copyright, Designs and Patents Act, 1988,
to be identified as the author of this work

A CIP catalogue record for this book is available
from the British Library

ISBN: 978 1 408 12909 8

Typeset by Country Setting, Kingsdown, Kent CT14 8ES

Printed and bound in Great Britain by Martins the Printers,
Berwick-upon-Tweed

TO MATTIA

and all who have worked and put up with me,
thank you

CONTENTS

FOREWORD

How wonderful – one of the best TV makers in the world gives you all of his secrets and advice in film-making. Warning: this book may possibly make you feel inadequate and will certainly make you paranoid about your work, but you will probably make your best film ever from reading it. Personally I think that Robert is mad giving away all of his TV trade secrets. So make the most of it, learn from one of the TV greats about his ethos in exceptional television making.

C.O.N.F.L.I.C.T is the recipe book of great television that means something or matters, and Robert Thirkell is the master of C.O.N.F.L.I.C.T.

JAMIE OLIVER

ACKNOWLEDGEMENTS

I would like to thank the many talented friends I have worked with, whose influence has helped me to make better films. I would particularly like to thank the entire production team of *Jamie's School Dinners*: Andrew Conrad, Dominique Walker, Guy Gilbert, Lana Salah, Zoë Collins, Louise Holland and not least Jamie Oliver, who had the big idea. And a particular thanks to all the many other directors who sweated making films for me – it was demanding! I sometimes think my mistake was to think every film had to be a winner, which can be tough on directors. But then I think pushing people to exceed what they had dreamed of is what it is all about. This book will, I hope, do that for you. I have tried to acknowledge the people who did the real work, especially when you gave me wonderful material to work with. If it gnarls that I am telling it from my point of view, it is because it is the one I know, and makes the learning point: the directors were the ones who got the brilliant material, put it together and have their names at the ends of the films.

I would also like to thank all the many friends who have bravely let me quote them. I am hugely grateful to all of you: Alan Hayling, who also pushed me to publish when I was scared it was a load of self-indulgent tosh; Alex Graham, Andrea Wong, Axel Arno, Bo Tengberg, Cecile Frot-Coutaz, Charles Wachter, Charlotte Black, Dominique Walker, Hugh Dehn, Jan Tomalin, Jane Root, Jo Ball, Jon Rowlands, John Smithson, Julie Uribe, Lana Salah, Matthew Robinson, Michele Kurland, Nick Mirsky, Nick Stringer, Patrick Collerton, Peter Moore, Roy Ackerman, Simon Dickson, Stephen Lambert, Stefan Ronowicz, Thomas Breinholt, Thomas Heurlin, Victoria Dummer and Zoë Collins. Thank you every one for your courage in taking part. It is like being a contributor.

Also I could have done none of it without my legendary agent Anita Land, all at Capel Land, and Jenny Ridout (and her team), who was actually willing to publish this and put up with me. I have driven her mad trying to make it accurate. I always thought it was tough for writers making the transition to film; now I have found just how tough it is the other way round, as I have stumbled along.

Finally I would like to thank friends, family and especially my partner who has put up with me rewriting this ever since we met in 2006. It seems writing is just like making a film, but even more exasperating for lovers, who suffer book as well as TV neglect. Mattia wanted the title to be 'Pushy Bastard', but the nice publishers thought better of it.

Phew, what a lot of thanks – it's a very handy word for TV producers. You can never use (or get) enough!

In this book I have used the job titles for people who have given top tips, as at the time of writing. These are not necessarily formal titles, but descriptions of what they do, to suit the context. I hope that they are correct, as also my recollections of many programmes over a long career. I have driven many people mad, as usual, trying to check accuracy, so if some detail of a film, its making, or your job title has slipped through the net please bear with me. People move fast in TV so many job titles will be outdated anyway – sorry.

MY ANGO-AMERICAN TV DICTIONARY

Like so much that looks similar between Europe and America, there are many differences. Having been lucky enough to work in both, I have attempted to cover some of those differences in factual film-making, as each has so much to learn from the other. Given some varying terminology, here is a brief glossary of different terms as I see them.

UK	US
Assistant Producer/ anyone else	Producer
Back story	Previously on
Channel/Broadcaster	Network
Commentary	Narration (Talk in Scandinavia)
Commissioning Editor	Network Executive
Contributor	Contestant/Cast/Participant
Current Affairs	News
Cutting room	Edit bay
Episode 1, 2 etc.	Episode 101, 102 etc.
Executive Producer	Executive Producers (usually lots)
Factual/Documentary	Reality/Unscripted/Docuseries
Part	Act
PD (Producer/Director)	This one person usually replaced by many: Supervising Producer, Producer, Segment Producer and a Director
Pre-Ad Break	Tease
Pre-Title/Front	Cold Open
Presenter	Host
Production Manager	Executive in charge of production, Line Producer
Researcher	Assistant Producer
Runner	PA/Runner
Script sequence	Beat
Series	Season
Series Producer	Show Runner (Executive Producer responsible creatively)/Co-Executive Producer
Series setup	Super Tease
Taster DVD	Sizzle/Promo/Presentation Reel

INTRODUCTION

When Jamie Oliver and his wife Jules burst into my hotel bedroom, on a small island between Sicily and Tunisia early one Sunday morning, and told me the film was off, I wondered which rule of television I had broken this time. However, there was a near hurricane blowing. The ferries tried to get into harbour but turned back, defeated by huge seas; Jamie, Jules and our film team were all stuck on this tiny remote island with just two restaurants and one simple hotel. I would have plenty of time to think about it.

Making films is tough. It's not a science, but I thought there might be rules that can help make it a bit easier. This book uses my experience of nearly thirty years in TV to try to identify the tools that have helped me. I have used first-hand experiences of making programmes, some of them with Jamie Oliver, as case studies to illustrate how these rules can help.

What continually surprises me is that mostly it isn't the big obstacles that defeat films – often the films that are toughest to make turn out to be the best – instead, it is often a host of small and obvious things that could easily be avoided. There is on TV now a proliferation of factual output that fails: reality shows, features, documentaries, factual entertainment, specialist factual and far more. The shows fail because they have ignored the basic principles of authentic storytelling, which is so easy to do when you get too close. I'm lucky; it gives me a job!

As a director and then head of the BBC's Business Documentary Unit I was responsible for creating many hit formats such as the BAFTA winners *Troubleshooter* with Sir John Harvey-Jones, *Back to the Floor* and *Blood on the Carpet*, as well as some shows I prefer to forget about. When I announced that I would be leaving the BBC, I was asked to join independent production companies, and the broadcasters encouraged me to set up my own. However, I asked TV bosses in the BBC and

Channel 4 if I could follow a different direction, in a job not done before. I wanted to become the TV Troubleshooter. Having developed a reputation for storytelling through over a hundred films, I wanted a new challenge: to see if or how I could apply what I had learnt to many other people's work, and even come up with a toolkit that could be used in my absence, to help directors avoid the many pitfalls I had seen.

As a TV Troubleshooter I have visited many different independent production companies and broadcasters, sometimes to help create the structure of factual series which are about to be filmed, more often to help sort them out in the cutting room, to make the director's dream programme come true. In the rush of modern television it is very easy to start filming without asking the right questions. When filming it is easy to get so close to the material you can miss the most important points. And in the cutting room it is easy to forget some basic rules that make factual programmes work.

While troubleshooting dozens of films each year for broadcasters all over the world – from ABC and Discovery in the US, to all the UK terrestrial broadcasters, and all over Europe and Australia – I have been lucky to have an unparalleled view of the nuts-and-bolts working of factual television. So, since those waves lashed off Italy five years ago, I have attempted to work out a toolkit to help avoid messes in the first place, and to get out of them when, as is almost inevitable, they strike.

This toolkit is initially assembled from my experience in the BBC's Business Documentary Unit, spending many years with Britain's leading businessmen, and time with hundreds of companies, making hundreds of films, including many dozen *Money Programmes* and *Trouble at the Tops*. Some of the tools are influenced by the world of business, and although concerning television, should be of use in any job. These tools are combined with others which have been developed during my career, first for getting on in the snakes and ladders of the TV world (you climb the snakes and tumble down the ladders where the rungs are cut), and more recently the fruitful years helping hundreds of factual programmes and working closely with chefs Jamie Oliver and Heston Blumenthal on how to think creatively and originally, from the start, to win. There are even a few tips on how to stay sane and happy in the crazy world of television. These tips go right through the film-making process from finding stories and characters to structuring scripts and filming; from editing and the all-important finding of motivation for characters and sequences, right through to delivery, titles and getting people to watch. They are the rules I have found useful when in doubt; if you disagree with them and find your own that work for you, all the better. I hope reading about mine may help you do that.

As I travel the world helping to format new ideas and troubleshooting TV series that aren't working out quite right, I find that the strong storytelling outlined in this book is becoming increasingly necessary for programmes to sell, survive and win out, not just in Britain but in country after country. The US now imports a long list of 'unscripted' factual programmes from Europe, and is creating more and more reality shows of its own. The tips I outline here are spreading round the world. A decade ago on the BBC we originated *Back to the Floor*, a hit series in which bosses experienced their own shop floor. Now that programme idea has resurfaced, imaginatively reinvented as *Undercover Boss*, and is playing to huge audiences in the US, revealing a vast and unsatisfied appetite for factual programme with content in America. The art of narration, unpopular in the US for a long time, is making a comeback and the principles of casting strong characters and highlighting jeopardy are becoming increasingly important everywhere.

Wherever you are, the tips outlined here are designed to help you jump ahead of the game. They come from long experience of working out just what enables programmes to break through, and developing the **C.O.N.F.L.I.C.T** toolbox.

Storytelling has always been important, but it depends on us following people we care about. So first we need to find the right '**C**haracters' and concept. Then think '**O**ut of the box' as we construct a strong script. As we go filming we need to sustain a strong **N**arrative drive, always remembering the questions of the film and sequence. In the edit, if we can get the all important **F**ront right and work out the motivation for characters and sequences, the rest will follow. All along we have to **L**ove and deal with our contributors and presenters, and turn them into people. Then we have the question of how to mix **I**nterview, actuality and commentary. Finally, when we have finished the film, we have to get it on the air in a way that will make the audience **C**are, and we have to make the commissioners care about our projects too. And that means getting the right **T**imeline and title – I have probably seen more films wrecked by getting these wrong than anything else - and, above all and most important, keeping it authentic, remembering the Truth.

All these letters spell **C.O.N.F.L.I.C.T**, and it is what this book is all about. When I ran the Business Unit at the BBC, transmitting dozens of films each year, I was renowned for saying only three things mattered in our film-making: conflict, conflict and conflict. Storytelling is about revealing characters under pressure leading to their transformation and, ideally, redemption. The pressure, or conflict, is necessary for the characters to reveal themselves and change. If it works, we are moved, understand ourselves better, and are better able to construct stories for ourselves out of the many chaotic aspects of our existence. So let's start with the first letters, and finding those **C**haracters and the concept.

One

CHARACTERS
AND CONCEPT

GETTING STARTED

Marooned with Jamie and the film crew on the small island off Sicily, as the seas continued to rage, I thought back to the moment eighteen months earlier when I had first met the star chef. It was shortly after I had left the BBC and I had just been asked to take on his latest project, on school dinners. It appeared to have big downsides. Jamie had been hugely successful in his previous hit *Jamie's Kitchen*. He had risked his own money to build a restaurant: there were fifteen memorable characters in the kids he was trying to help, and a coherent story with plenty of jeopardy. I was hardly likely to better that, particularly with what seemed to be a dreary political subject rather than a real story full of drama and conflict. So I thought, 'No, I won't do it.' I was trying to establish myself outside the BBC after many years working there, and it would be too risky a first series. Still, I was intrigued, so began to think about it.

Making TV can be misery at the best of times, but you forget the pain if you have a success – you don't if you have a failure. In advance of making the programme, I needed a toolkit designed to do as much to prevent failure as possible, and I would need to stick limpet-like to every rule I had picked up during my career.

This chapter is about the first of the tools in the **C.O.N.F.L.I.C.T** toolbox, which starts with the letter '*C*' – finding the right CHARACTERS and the concept. It is all about choosing the right story, with sufficient ambition or twist, peopling it with heroes, and persuading them to take part. Your film and all your hard work can live or die as a result of this; get it right and you have a Heston Blumenthal up against Ian Peglar, boss of Little Chef in *When Big Chef Met Little Chef*, Ben and Jerry fighting the founder of Haagen Dazs in *Blood on the Carpet: Ice Cream Wars*, Gordon Ramsay and the restaurateurs in *Kitchen Nightmares*, Donald Trump and his apprentices in *The Apprentice*. Get it wrong and you could waste a year or more making something no one watches.

Getting it right is sometimes a matter of good fortune, but there are some key things that can help: first of all having the right character, and then making sure they are involved in a struggle, a journey or a mission, however great or small. Which is what most good storytellers have realised, and just what I wanted.

Finding characters is tough. When *The Apprentice* came to the UK, and I was asked for my advice, I thought it would be near impossible to find a replacement for Donald Trump, the unique and outspoken businessman who had made it such a success in the USA. Many people were looking for a British Trump-lookalike, but I knew that was impossible. The British team needed to be brave enough to look for someone very different.

PETER MOORE

Former Head of Documentaries, Channel 4,
first Executive Producer of *The Apprentice* in the UK

I was looking for someone who would make you feel very afraid when you went into the boardroom — be very, very afraid. I remembered Alan Sugar from a film on Tottenham Football Club and I just knew he was outspoken. I had been told before I met him by his PR man that Alan was the rudest man he had ever worked for. So the combination of a very bright, very sharp individual, but also very frightening. A recipe for conflict.

The BBC didn't want Alan Sugar — they wanted someone much bigger like Philip Green or, failing that, Richard Branson. I just repeated he was the best person for the job, he had the visceral qualities that would make him a star on screen. And when they saw the result they were completely won over.

The British Apprentice *was far less ritzy than the US version, and filmed much more for real. We decided to be less fawning about our central character on screen. We weren't interested in seeing his largesse, his wealth, his chandeliers and so on. Our boardroom looked modern and contemporary, there was no make-up and it was shot in a more documentary style with fewer cameras and angles, so it felt more real.*

Choosing characters is so important because many of the best films reveal people reacting to and transforming under pressure and show us universal truths about people: they contain genuine conflict (which is what this book is all about). But unless you are lucky enough to take over something that already exists like *The Apprentice*, finding characters is often like opening a Russian doll.

So in this chapter first we will look at how to identify a subject area in which to begin your search, then how to find a story within it, then how to recognise a fairy tale within that – all of which make the concept – and only then look at that most important part of film-making: discovering the characters who people it.

AN ARENA FOR THE STRUGGLE

So first to identifying the best arena in which your characters can conflict. I worked for many years in a small outpost of the BBC Science Department, making films about business, and I was always envious of my colleagues' subject matter. Potential death is a great reason to start watching a film, and they could make films about diseases that threatened to kill loads of people, earthquakes and volcanoes about to kill loads of people, animals that did kill loads of people, air crashes, crashes at sea, car crashes, medical disasters – and even the psychology of killer people who kill loads of people. It is great to be able to start a film with high stakes: 'These people will die unless . . . ' It is a staple of Hollywood drama. But business doesn't have much looming death, except perhaps in southern Italy and the Bronx. Luckily, however, there are other things that create conflict: for instance relationships. Just look at RDF's *Wife Swap*, Firefly's *The Family* (an updated fly-on-the-wall following a family, with dozens of cameras rigged in their house) or the American *Real Housewives*, created by Scott Dunlop.

What all these share are different mindsets banging into each other like the tectonic plates that underlie a country colliding. If you can hit these fault lines you may be on to a winner. In Britain the fault lines could be geographic (North *vs* South), historic (modern *vs* old-fashioned, financial (rich *vs* poor), or best of all to do with class, which still encompasses the lot. In America, while class may not be quite so important, money works very well, and so does young *vs* old. These plates banging together are of course just what is really happening in *Kitchen Nightmares* with Gordon Ramsay, or its forerunner *Troubleshooter* with Sir John Harvey-Jones. The advantage here is that you have the potential for humour too.

However, it is hard to care about a subject, easy to care about a story, so in my experience the first rule of coming up with good films – and selling them – is to make them into a story, rather than about a subject.

Over my years as a commissioner, so many people came to me and said, 'Let's make a film about takeovers' – or twins, or trains – and I always replied, 'Where is the story?' A subject on its own is not a potentially moving film: you need the story to have a chance. It needs to be a story that the people involved in really care about, and are hopefully passionate about too; it also helps if it is one that has an easily understandable challenge or quest. But unless you are lucky enough to read about the perfect story in a newspaper, or hear it at a dinner party, subject areas do have a use: they can narrow down your area of search, particularly if you identify an area that is likely to contain good stories.

IDENTIFYING A SUBJECT AREA

Before talking about how to find the fairy tale and the characters, I want to lay out a few examples of successful stories which we explored in my BBC unit, and how the subject areas were found. In my very first series, *Troubleshooter* (the original expert makeover show, and father to so many series), top businessman Sir John Harvey-Jones set out to transform failing companies, saying just what he thought. As I searched for a story for the pilot I had a salutary shock about the importance of finding the right subject area for strong character and conflict to play out. Sir John was then Britain's leading businessman, having just been voted industrialist of the year three years running. One evening he had bumped into BBC TV boss Michael Grade at some function, and asked if he could do something to popularise business on TV. It was 1987 and business was still a slightly dirty word in Britain. I was at the time an assistant producer on magazine shows, with no apparent prospect of advancing anywhere else. At the same time I had a Saturday job in Portobello Road selling coats, and I was thinking of leaving TV to pursue the market full-time, as it appeared to offer better prospects.

Luckily for me, everyone else in the corporation rejected the challenge of turning an elderly, plump, long-haired, unkempt businessman into a TV star; most people hate ideas that come down from bosses, and back then most people in the BBC particularly hated business. The idea was even rejected by the Documentary Department, so my editorial boss in Science took a gamble: I was an obscure assistant producer who had never made a film, and was about to leave, but I had been a researcher on a not very successful business series, so I might be the ideal person to make a pilot for the Managing Director's pet project that no one wanted. It turned out to be an unbelievable bit of luck on which I built an entire career.

I knew that on the success of this rested my one chance of ever becoming a director. But when I began work I had little idea how television programmes were actually structured, for although I had shot inserts, I had never directed a whole film. I was to work with the 'reject' Sir John Harvey-Jones, within the 'reject' subject area of business. Although I had directed no programmes I had read a lot of fairy tales, and felt that somehow, just as with Jamie Oliver so many years later, I had to portray Sir John as an archetypal hero. And I hoped that business, like any human struggle, could contain heroic stories, with heroic characters and larger-than-life opponents, though nobody had put business like this on TV before.

Television always changes what it looks at, just by virtue of filming it, but at the time the convention was never to acknowledge this. I didn't realise this, so along with executive producer Richard Reisz I accidentally came up with a plan not only to accept that television changed what it looked at but, taking that idea to its logical end, to use television to try to change reality on a grand scale. Sir John Harvey-Jones, the hero, would charge into companies, see what was wrong and suggest changes – such as selling half the company or even sometimes sacking the boss.

However when I made my first recce visit to see what Sir John actually did, it seemed this concept would prove disastrous. He took me with him to a heat-exchanger factory he was visiting in Herefordshire. When we arrived all he did was say hello, look at the accounts for twenty minutes, and leave. It was even more boring than watching paint drying. My career was on the line. I vowed never to make films in an engineering subcontracting factory. But besides a far better subject area, I would need to find far better characters for Sir John to come up against. This is real detective work. You need to search everywhere – from print to the internet, trade organisations, experts, whoever and whatever you bump into, even that *Apprentice* football match. I called contacts on *Tomorrow's World*, a very popular science magazine that filmed with hundreds of companies, interrogated colleagues and friends, and even got diary pieces in the newspapers about the show I wanted to make. I went through hundreds of companies to try to find the right characters, who might conflict engagingly with Sir John. But none was quite good enough for me. Putting it off and putting it off, I continued to work on other films while I searched for a strong character for my star to come up against — someone who was risking a lot, was at a real break point, and for whom something needed to happen. And they had to be working in an interesting business.

Staring failure in the face, I decided to search in areas that the public interact with and which can annoy them. I started with stores and supermarkets, the police, consumer goods from toys to pottery, transport (which has the added merit of being visual), and best of all services where people get most tense: restaurants and hotels, holiday companies and housebuilders; after all, going on holiday or buying a house can be particularly stressful. These subject areas ended up as just the ones that give the best audiences, and we took most of our stories from them.

As I have continued beyond *Troubleshooter* — searching for stories for series as far apart as *Blood on the Carpet*, the original business battles show, and *Back to the Floor*, the original hit which followed bosses back to the shop floor for a week, and predecessor to *Undercover Boss* — I have discovered a few basic rules for finding an arena for your characters: first, the audience love seeing behind the scenes of places we see and use every day, as long as they are seen from a new angle.

CECILE FROT–COUTAZ *and* JULIE URIBE

Respectively CEO and Senior Vice President
Unscripted Development, Fremantle Media, North America

Thom Beers with Original has successfully taken you behind the scenes (from Deadliest Catch *following trawlermen, to* Ice Road Truckers*). Discovery and Nat Geo go behind the scenes of carp fishing, oil rigs, smoke jumping.* American Idol *took you into the hidden back stage of that music world — it's a bit of a fantasy world and that was part of the appeal of it. We are exploring stuff in a butcher's shop, an auction house . . .*

LOOKING IN HIDDEN WORLDS

Many successful factual programmes work well just by taking the audience behind the scenes of a very familiar world we all know from the outside: inside the police in *The Force*; into stores like Selfridges in *The Shop*; a hospital in *Hopkins* (the Johns Hopkins hospital in Baltimore); a hotel, in the aptly named *Hotel*; or a restaurant – a great subject in many countries. All of these have made successful series because each reveals how, in reality, much of the familiar world was hidden because we only knew it from the outside.

I have used all of these subjects to find stories again and again. So in *Trouble at the Top*, which followed exciting business stories over many months, two of our best-rating and most entertaining programmes were on Marks & Spencer, and Weisfeld's, a big Scottish department store. Sainsbury and House of Fraser were two of the most watched in *Back to the Floor*. I also always return to hotels, and one of the best *Blood on the Carpets*, which followed historic business battles, was about a vicious hotel takeover battle.

These subject areas work so well that they have each spawned their own *Troubleshooters* – for restaurants with *Kitchen Nightmares*, hotels with *Hotel Inspector* – and even shops with *Mary Queen of Shops*, which successfully follows larger-than-life Mary Portas as she sorts out failing stores. All have made multiple series and won awards. There are more *Troubleshooter*-style series to be made in other popular areas, especially in the USA, where *Kitchen Nightmares* proved extremely popular.

Public institutions can make good arenas too. Both police forces and the army featured in *Back to the Floor*, and many other factual/reality series too. Do persevere even if it is often a lengthy process to gain access, particularly if it is inside a political area, as was *The Dome: Trouble at the Big Top*, which followed the Labour Government building the Millennium Dome, or, like *The System*, inside a government department – or, if you're very lucky, even inside a secret organisation like MI5 or MI6.

Film technology can also help in taking us into unfamiliar worlds. It could be secret filming as in *Undercover Britain* or *MacIntyre Uncovered*, or new photographic techniques which take us under the sea, documenting life as we have never seen it before, as in *Blue Planet*. It can even involve using endoscopic photography to take us inside our own bodies, something with which we are self-evidently familiar on the outside, but with a completely new perspective, as in *The Human Body*. CGI (computer-generated imagery) can re-create past worlds, and take us inside them (but even *Pompeii*, *Rome* and *Dinosaurs* have their heroes). More recently it has been huge, remote, hidden camera rigs, complete with the house-next-door turned into a TV gallery, that have taken us further than ever before into the hidden world of *The Family* and, in *One Born Every Minute*, a maternity ward.

There are many institutions that we feel we all know well, but which, in reality, we know from the outside only; a film can take us to a hidden inside. Anything that serves the public works well. It is well worth thinking of ways of revealing such hidden worlds if you can.

I also like anything that moves – cars, boats, trains or planes. They are easier to film than heat-exchangers! I first learnt this on *Tomorrow's World*, on which I had to follow new inventions in short five-minute films. I survived by making endless transport films, including a Sinclair electric bike, a Second World War submarine, a ship that opened in the middle to eat up oil slicks, a Maglev train, many planes, and a car that steered itself down a German motorway with no one at the wheel. For that I had to find a motorway under construction, and pray.

Later, on *Troubleshooter*, Sir John Harvey-Jones took on Morgan cars and Norton motorbikes, and in *Back to the Floor* I featured episodes around Anglia trains and Unijet's airline, all of which rated well. Transport doesn't have its own TV troubleshooter yet, though there have been series like *Airport* and *LAX* and Britain's top-ranked chef Heston Blumenthal takes on food as served in all means of transport in his latest series for Channel 4.

Even factories making products we know can contain interesting hidden mysteries. One of the most successful *Trouble at the Top*s was *Kinky Boot Factory*, which took us inside a traditional Northampton shoe factory, though in a slightly quirky way. And the highest-rated *Blood on the Carpet* was *Ice Cream Wars*, which took us inside the food business with the added twist of hippies against the corporate. In both, we – the public – use and have an opinion on the end product.

But at all costs avoid boring arenas for your heroes – which usually means computers, electronics, widgets, parts that go into something else – and heat-exchangers! Most of all avoid anything that smacks of being about a subject rather than a story – for example, school dinners as a subject without a story, without a clear quest peopled by individuals – and especially the right heroes.

Recently I went to visit Stephen Lambert, who created *Secret Millionaire* and *Wife Swap* and was now making his *Back to the Floor* successor, *Undercover Boss*, at his new company Studio Lambert. Like *Back to the Floor*, this follows bosses as they go to work as ordinary workers on their own shop floor. But Stephen had added two key extra elements. Having made *Secret Millionaire*, he would keep the boss incognito in every episode, something we had successfully tried but didn't follow in most episodes as we worried about its effects on trust and our ability to keep making the series year after year. And he would also formalise the recognition of good employees, making the thrust of the conclusion a reward – promotion, a pay rise or even money for something personal they needed – rather than big changes in the business structure: in other words, a more personal and emotional denouement.

Back to the Floor was a big hit over many seasons in Britain; in fact my BBC colleagues became quite annoyed with me as boss Jane Root kept going on about how she wanted everything to be like it. But *Undercover Boss* has been huge in the US, breaking through more than any other recent show, finally proving that intelligent British factual formats can do just as well, or even better, across the Atlantic. I went to visit Stephen Lambert with a list of the highest-rating *Back to the Floor*s of the many dozen we had made, the subjects that had worked for me. These were on stores, including big department store chains, well-known holiday companies such as Carnival Cruises, Butlins and Unijet, and one, surprisingly to me, on extra-big housebuilders, such as Berkeley and Carillion – but then the public love houses and have lots of dramas buying and repairing them. 'Funny, that,' said Stephen. 'Those are exactly the subjects we are already making for *Undercover Boss*.' The first series of just two in the UK featured a holiday group and a construction company. And the first US subject, one of our biggest *Back to the Floor* hits, was garbage men. The subjects that work best go on being the same.

In fact, looking back at past original hits can be a brilliant way of coming up with new ones. Look at all the talent shows that come round like buses, from *New Faces* in the 1970s to *X Factor*. And think of the ever-growing number of makeover shows *Troubleshooter* has spawned, calling experts not only to your business (*Undercover Boss*, *Kitchen Nighmares*, *Hotel Inspector*), or your life (*Life Laundry . . .*), but to your home (*Supernanny, How Clean is Your House?*). But best of all is to take an earlier hit to a country that has never seen it. So read those old TV guides!

PETER MOORE

Former head of Channel 4 documentaries and in at the start of Studio Lambert, makers of *Undercover Boss*

Back to the Floor *was a bloody good show — how do you do that for the twenty-first century? What could be different, how do you improve it, and how could you restage it? Some people I've worked with are particularly good at that. If you are a businessman it's a great idea.*

In the world of documentary, producers have been remaking the classics from Grierson to Wiseman and Flaherty. If you think about it Grierson filmed Drifters (*about trawlermen, in the 1920s*), *Jeremy Mills made* The Skipper (*a big early-1990s hit*) *and now we've got this* Deadliest Catch *— three generations of fishing and three different styles.*

JON ROWLANDS

Former Head of Development BBC Factual,
Creative Director, Renegade

As technology changes, the way in which you can make programmes changes. Deadliest Catch *uses multi-cameras because cameras are cheaper and smaller, so you can film it more like a drama. So the content has stayed the same, but the form has changed.* The Family *from the 1970s and* The Family *from 2009 both observe a family going about their daily life. The idea is identical, the title is identical, but the form in which it is captured changes because you can have slave remote cameras, you can have thirty cameras in a house, you can get rid of the portable single camera and the 16mm camera of the past and just let people go about their lives.*

Subject/story selection may seem obvious but, as with so much TV, it is the obvious that is easiest to overlook, and most worth remembering – which is why you are reading this. The best subjects areas in which to search include these I have mentioned, and any other areas of stress and conflict which people care about, from hospitals to jungles to history series about the Nazis. Unless you are lucky enough to light directly on a compelling story, it just helps to find a subject area to narrow your search, and then never forget you are looking for a story within it.

ENTERTAINMENT PLUS CONTENT

To tell a successful and believable story it helps to have what I call 'entertainment plus'. This means making an entertaining and engrossing story which is also underpinned by meaning and content, and backed by really good research – a product that does something for you, but is fun with a good wrapping! Much modern TV has been based on the notion that entertaining programmes need no content, and – even worse – that programmes with content should never be entertaining. However, the audience is more intelligent than many programme-makers think, and has a huge appetite for programmes with both entertainment and meaning.

Many entertainment programme-makers think that no one will watch if they add any content or meaning, and so do little research. But if you just have entertainment without content or meaning, you may end up with yet another version of the derided reality shows that we see so many of on TV today. Conversely, there are still documentary-makers who are scared that their programmes might be entertaining, and so not real documentaries or sufficiently worthy. But if you have content and meaning, without entertainment, you have many of the dreary, worthy factual programmes that happily for me seem to be appearing less often now on our screens, but still dominate much public service broadcasting around the world. So whatever the latest clothes your programme is wearing, ask yourself every time whether you have both necessary bits to make it work. I don't become fixated dividing factual programmes up – it is now a continuous genre from documentary to factual formats in which everyone can benefit from everyone else.

JANE ROOT

Former President, Discovery Networks,
and Controller BBC2, now CEO Nutopia

You know how we came up with I Love the 1980s: *the* Rock and Roll Years (*broadcast from the mid-1980s, each week concentrating on a single year*). *David Mortimer and I got* Rock and Roll Years *out of the BBC archive because I'd remembered it from when I was a child. A lot of the younger BBC team had never seen it and I showed it to them in my office and said, 'What could we do that could bring this show back?'* I Love the 1980s, *the hit the team went on to create, turned out to be even bigger in America, where it ran on VH1 for years.*

Another one like that is Birds' Eye View *which I really remember from my childhood; I was about ten when I watched it. Ever since then I've had a love of aerial photography as a way to enliven any show and give it more energy, so when we did* Restoration *we put all those aerial shots in.*

But if you are going to come back or you're doing a second series or a spin-off series it's got to be bigger than the first. It might be bigger in what happens or the level of emotions or more cameras. You have to say to the audience, 'You liked that, now you are going to like this even more.' Sometimes I think modern audiences, and modern commissioners, are like two-year-olds learning to talk, and one of the first words they learn to say is 'More – more more more!' So embrace your inner toddler!

STAR QUALITY IN THE STORY

John Cadwell, once the inspired US salesman for BBC Science programmes, told us that to succeed in the US it helps if the story has a star. It needs to feel big, either because it has a star presenter, a star concept or more usually a star subject area – not easy with the films about business I was making. Big names interest an audience more, so should get better numbers, especially in America.

But big companies and institutions can be far harder to get inside and, even if you do, far harder to get a handle on because of their size. Given these difficulties I decided instead to follow companies or institutions that were relatively small, but appeared big because of their names, unique stories with big meaning. So I needed companies that the public thought were big, but which were small enough to allow identification with the main characters, and not so small that no one would care. This principle can be applied to looking for stories in any subject area.

In selling stories, superlatives help to create a 'star' subject, something unique or special. My final list for *Troubleshooter* included small subjects where we had found something special – from cars (Britain's 'oldest' car company, Morgan, also one of the most famous, even though employing just a few hundred people) to Tri-ang toys ('once the world's biggest' toy company, though again now just with a few hundred employees). You might think they don't sound that star-like, but we had created a series with a 'star' presenter in Sir John, a 'star' concept in making over firms, sacking bosses and transforming lives, as well as 'star' subject areas. Most important of all, we had identified strong stories within 'star' firms that were small enough to film.

The firms also needed to be at a crossroads with something about to change, and to have charismatic bosses. The series won many awards,

---

VICTORIA DUMMER

Senior Vice President of ABC Alternative Series,
Specials and Late Night, USA

Well, first come up with unique, clear ideas that are both focused and for us very broad, like Undercover Boss *– tackling issues that everyone can relate to, but doing it in a big way, which* Undercover Boss *did by having national companies and national brands.*

And be really clear storytellers and have clear protagonists and clear antagonists, so you have an arc to the story that is really going to engage the audience. Often we'll receive pitches that go from point A to point B pretty much in a straight line, which is not as interesting to us.

Remember for broadcast TV we have to be 'broad' casters, and that means we can't be small; if it is a singular idea it needs to be big – for us they can't be small singular ideas.

including the seldom-awarded BAFTA for originality, a nomination as one of the British Film Institute's TV programmes of the year, and even best science-based programme of the year, which seemed decidedly odd. I was exceedingly surprised, and very relieved, not knowing quite what had hit me. But how to do it again?

My quest for strong subject areas in which to search for strong stories continued. Despite the success of *Troubleshooter*, my bosses were still not convinced, and said that to prove it wasn't a fluke I needed to make a series without Sir John Harvey-Jones as presenter. My next format, *Trouble at the Top*, which was to go on for many seasons, followed stories from the world of business over a year, as bosses tried to transform their companies; but with no star presenter it needed to attract even more with its subject matter. Imagine my pleasure when a hungry assistant producer, Michele Kurland, who had yet to make a film (my favourite sort of director — most of my hits have come from them) approached me with not one but two films, one of which was from the unlikely subject area of the traditional British shoe industry. Within it she had found a very quirky story. A family-run shoe manufacturer had handed power over to the next generation. The business was old-fashioned and made traditional gents' shoes such as brogues in a single old red-brick factory in Northampton, and it was losing money, as foreign imports adversely affected the British shoe business.

It turned out that the son, who had taken over the factory even though his old dad was still very much around, had had a brainwave. With time running out, he would try to save the factory by making high-heeled fetish footwear for men. Now *that* was an ambitious idea! You could hardly make it up. The audience really cared. There was real jeopardy and a real question of survival. There was family struggle — would the young hero surprise his father and succeed? The heroic son was willing to do anything to save the jobs of his workers, whose futures were on the line. With plenty of real conflict and the important added extra of the potential to be very funny, one could really engage emotionally. It was full of those tectonic plates, with new and old, north and south, banging together — plus seaside humour, as the traditional workers turned to making fetish wear, which, lacking cash, the boss had himself model for photographers.

We called the film *The Kinky Boot Factory*; it got our highest ever *Trouble at the Top* audience, and beat the big launch of *Sex and the City* that had been heavily advertised on billboards round the country. It turned out to be such a good story that a successful cinema drama was recently made from it, using the same title that had helped to sell the TV film. It is interesting how first films from young directors are often so successful. *Kinky Boot* director Michele Kurland went on to great things, running the hugely successful *Apprentice*.

MICHELE KURLAND

Executive Producer, *The Apprentice*, Director, *Kinky Boot Factory*

The thing with new people is they want to prove themselves and they're not stuck with 'You can only do it my way.' When you're new you don't think you know it all. We knew what we knew, we knew we loved doing what we knew, but we didn't know how to make it better. When you're a beginner you want to learn, and do what you are asked, whereas when people have been doing it a long time they think, 'I've always done it this way, and that doesn't work and this doesn't work.' Often they're not open to new ideas.

My next boss, Jana Bennett, said *Trouble at the Top* was all very well but it was still actuality, and it often took expensive time to get access. She wanted us to diversify into historical conflicts, thinking they might be easier, so I developed *Blood on the Carpet* with Nick Mirsky, and we decided to follow big-business battles of the recent past from both sides. While all my rival executive producers were competing for the most seasoned directors, I believed that I needed hungry new ones again if I was to succeed. It had worked with *Troubleshooter* and Michele and those kinky boots.

And one of the best films in the first series did come from a fresh, new, and truly talented young director from educational TV. It was a new area of documentary for him, and the subject he chose, ice cream, was again a consumer subject, with potential to appeal to the audience by revealing a hidden inside to something we are familiar with. However, *Ice Cream Wars* was not a documentary 'about' the subject of ice cream, but a story of one war that illustrated it. The story was the battle between two hippy ice-cream-makers, Ben and Jerry, and the behemoth

Haagen Dazs. It was a fairy-tale story of how the two heroic hippies won despite all the obstacles. The resulting film got the highest ever *Blood on the Carpet* audience, and contributed strongly to it winning us yet another BAFTA, the British Academy Award. Simon Dickson, its witty director, not surprisingly went on to become one of Britain's most innovative documentary commissioners at Channel 4.

Hollywood drama is, of course, also all about stories, not subjects, and so is much successful American documentary. *Supersize Me* isn't about McDonald's but our hero Morgan Spurlock experiencing it. When Michael Moore wants to make a film about American gun laws he does it through a single story, *Bowling for Columbine*, a dramatic story about how two kids shot other kids at school.

ALAN HAYLING

Michael Moore's Commissioning Editor, Channel 4,
now Editorial Director, Renegade Pictures

I couldn't at first see how Columbine *could make a funny but powerful film — it was about kids shooting kids, after all. Then Michael Moore described the story arc to me. Michael's narrative centred round one story. He would try to recruit hundreds of thousands of his supporters to join the National Rifle Association, elect him President and turn it into an anti-gun organisation, 'like the National Cancer Association is against cancer'. It was a compelling storyline which, combined with the tragedy of Columbine, clearly had great potential — a film in which Michael Moore would be the central character. Then many other things could be hung off it.*

Feature documentries for the cinema such as *Bowling for Columbine* depend even more on a strong and well-researched storyline. In Hollywood feature dramas they can write whole backstories for characters who may say only a few lines, just to get those few lines and so their story right. To sum up, I have always encouraged producers to search for subject areas the public can interact with or that have great drama with potential heroes and conflict, but also to look for areas with the added extra of those tectonic plates in modern Britain banging into each other. Then, having identified the subject area, to find one story. But there is something else that the Greeks came up with, and that helps too.

JOHN SMITHSON

Executive Chairman, Darlow Smithson,
and Producer, *Touching the Void*

Feature documentaries can be incredible fun. Lots of nice festivals, the prospect of awards and the chance to really make an impact and have a film that lasts in people's memories.

The hardest thing is finding a story that works on the big screen. Most TV docs, even really good ones, simply won't work in the cinema. There has got to be something extra to persuade people to pay good money to watch your doc in a cinema or on DVD. The story is crucial. You can't do it on visuals alone. One clue – I think there's something about big, close-up, intimate stories that illustrates a bigger point that seems to work well theatrically. Only a handful of British feature docs have ever been both a creative and commercial success.

TIME AND SPACE

Many of the best stories are shot in limited time and space. This can make it easier to care. The action of the hit feature documentary *Touching the Void* followed two climbers having to cut their rope on the descent of a Peruvian mountain, and one of them having to crawl back from a deep crevasse with a broken leg, over three days – it was limited in both space and time and a mythic single story. *The Dome: Trouble at the Big Top* may have been two years in the making, but it was essentially contained in one building site in south London as we followed New Labour's dream of changing Britain through constructing the Millennium Dome.

Similarly a school or a factory can make a great location, as can a hotel, a shop, a restaurant or even a tower block – as in the award-winning series *The Tower*, in effect a soap opera set over eight episodes in one rough tower block in south London. *Nightmare at Canary Wharf*, which followed the setting up of L!ve TV by Janet Street-Porter, also took place in a tower block. In fact the location was even tighter: almost all the action took place on the twenty-fourth floor. Or of course there's *Big Brother*, taking place entirely in one house.

Limiting time can help too. This can be reduced to a week, which makes it more intense, as in *Back to the Floor*, *Wife Swap* or *Extreme Home Makeover*. Or you can speed it up even further as in *Trading Spaces* (*Changing Rooms* in the UK), which transforms a house over a couple of days, or further again like *Troubleshooter*, in which the action took place pretty much in a day. The drama *24* is the ultimate example.

CREATIVE SPARKS

It is good to be on the lookout for as many stories as possible, talking to other people and avidly scouring newspapers, magazines, the trade press and, especially now, the internet.

JON ROWLANDS

Former Head of Development, BBC Factual,
creator at Renegade Pictures of hit formats such as
Don't Tell the Bride for the BBC and BBC America

The internet is the new source of mining people's personal feelings about life, so now you can enter 'getting married blogs' and read streams of first-person anxieties and worries. Previously everything had been filtered through journalism, which is trying to make a point, whereas the internet gives direct access to human beings, so you can write to them immediately: 'Hey, Clare, you think this about your wedding, why is that?' And you can dig down and research your audience directly now, so it's really important to keep up to date with blogs, with thirty or forty different websites. Load up all the Google alerts, with all the key words, so you read them every morning and then see the nugget you can build your show out of.

The more stories you find the more likely it is that you will trigger another helpful aid to creativity – for instance, an article that says something, and then perhaps a person who says something else which you link it to, and which together then fizz into an idea. Many of the best inventions come when different ideas bang into each other, and start something new – this is the act of creation, a eureka moment.

As you research, hopefully you will get the same insight from two directions. For instance, when it eventually came to *Jamie's Return to School Dinners*, I was away in the Far East, where I got talking to an aid worker. She used to be a headmistress and wanted to know how the huge sums of Tsunami aid money had been spent. This made me wonder where the hundreds of millions the government had promised for school dinners in the UK as a result of the original series had gone. It was what the update programme should have been all about, but it is so big and obvious I had forgotten it. So I called the director in London from a crackly mosquito-ridden phone box.

It is often the biggest and most obvious thing of all that you forget. I learnt this in my very first assistant producer job. It was on a series that had, at the time, one unique attribute: each of the stand-alone episodes was filmed over a whole year. Yet we forgot to tell the audience about this – its biggest selling point. I still believe it was partly because of this that it never really broke through or was much noticed by the public. You never know who will tell you something that reminds you what your film is really about, so listen to everyone.

Sometimes the best creative sparks fly when two creative people bang ideas into each other. This is how the franchise that began with *The 1900 House* and spread around the world started. Sarah Ramsden, Commissioning Editor at Channel 4, and Alex Graham of the independent production company Wall to Wall had a meeting. Alex had read an article in *New Scientist* magazine on how our lives have changed because of advances in domestic products over the last century. In the meeting he tried to sell Sarah something based on the idea. But it didn't sound very interesting, so Alex went away and almost forgot about it. However, it continued to bubble around in his brain. Remember slow burners – if ideas don't come to fruition for a while, don't forget them. Many ideas need slow cooking, and if you let them bubble away, even for a few days, the ingredients will come out of your brain served up as something else.

The following year Alex was visiting his mother in Scotland and, seeing a few ancient appliances, wondered what it must have been like to live without them. This brought to mind the series idea from his lunch six months earlier, but he still couldn't think how to do it. Then later in the year Sarah Ramsden invited Alex to lunch. Between courses she mentioned a series that had been on television years earlier, *Living in the Past*, which put a group of fifteen young volunteers to live as though in the Iron Age. Suddenly they both saw how to enliven the boring subject of changes in domestic living – to put individual people through it. They would follow the story of an individual family. Even better, it was genre-busting, putting documentary and drama together, as the family really acted the part. Like so much of successful modern

---

ALEX GRAHAM

Chief Executive, Wall to Wall

People see The 1900 House *as groundbreaking, but in one sense it was a remake of* Living in the Past *– the same basic idea moved on, taking something that has worked well in one context and using it in another. My contribution was to go away and work out how you did it. I think it's 1 per cent inspiration, 99 per cent execution. When people say 'I've got a great idea,' my response is 'Join the club.' The question is, can you turn it into telly; that's what really matters. You could have had ten different production houses doing* The 1900 House, *you would have had ten different versions, and probably most of them would have been crap.*

With Who Do You Think You Are? *in 1989 I read a magazine article in which Billy Connolly described his and his father's experiences as welders in the shipyards of Glasgow, and halfway through it suddenly struck me that you could find many other celebrities whose history was the embodiment of big historical stories, like Connolly's was a history of Glasgow and its shipyards.*

We pitched it to the BBC and it went into a bottom drawer. Twelve years later Jane Root [then controller of BBC2] *came for a glass of wine. She had just done* Great Britons, *and* Restoration, *and I asked why didn't Wall to Wall do one of these big ideas, but she said really big ideas don't usually come from producers but from marketing, who start from what people are doing, not what makes the programme.*

Genealogy had become huge on the internet, and we remembered we had this big idea from twelve years ago. Good ideas are good ideas and never completely go away, they are just out of their time.

factual television, it was experiential. And so *The 1900 House* and its many offspring which combined drama, transformation and experiential history was born. It spawned a host of follow-up living history series, from *Frontier House* on PBS to *The 1940s House* and *The Edwardian Country House*. Alex followed it up with another huge international hit, *Who Do You Think You Are?*

Stephen Lambert told me that the inspiration for his first format hit *Faking It* came from his wife saying one night why not try *Pygmalion, My Fair Lady*, for real. It is fashionable to say these moments don't happen, and you need endless committee meetings to come up with good TV ideas. However, they do happen, as long as clever people are open to new ideas. Highly authored and opinionated television can prove beguiling and popular. Strong authorial voices, not committee-driven TV, win most awards.

I often wonder why so many series that break through in Britain such as *Jamie's School Dinners* and *Too Big to Walk* (*Fat March* in the US) don't do so in such a big way in the US. Many say it is because of the different cultures, and it is certainly true US programmes are cut quicker and have less commentary. But in my experience it can also be because so many more people get involved that there is no one vision driving the programme. It is often strong authorial voices like Michael Moore that have won through, making their opinionated one film again and again, debunking received wisdom.

ALAN HAYLING

Former Head of BBC Documentaries, and
Commissioning Editor for Michael Moore, Channel 4

The best programmes absolutely don't come from committees, they come from authored voices. I just don't think you can make a good factual programme by committee. You need a good authored voice, which could be the presenter, it could be a director, but you need a singular vision.

While a committee is the death of creativity, a brainstorm, a group of people firing off one another to come up with a great idea, can be the opposite. Michael Moore has a big team around him, and brainstorms even stunts within films, but he makes the ultimate decisions. He uses brainstorming as a creative tool, but ultimately it is his vision.

There are many ways to make strongly authored pieces such as *An Inconvenient Truth*. Across the Atlantic Adam Curtis has had a big success with his own highly iconoclastic, archive-driven series on recent history from *Pandora's Box*, debunking science, to the *Mayfair Set* debunking business and *Power of Nightmares*, debunking the PR industry – and winning BAFTAs every time.

But there's more to a story than finding it and having creative sparks. The most successful stories have layers of meaning below the surface. When commissioning I ask producers of a film not only about the main story but also the subtext. The main story may be three brothers struggling and competing to run a pottery factory, the subtext how Stoke on Trent hasn't kept up with changing Britain. The more subtext the better. So it helps if as well as conflict, and tectonic plates colliding, your film can delve right behind the scenes. It might be showing us what it must have been like to live in the world of 1900, the truth behind al Qaeda, inside a government department or a store chain, or deep inside everyday ice cream – all winners.

GAINING ACCESS

With access, it pays to persist and follow slow burners. In 1996 I had another piece of luck when the Science Department asked me to attend a dreary dinner at the Royal Institution. It's a bit like parties you don't want to go to – it is almost always worth attending 'just in case'. Even if it's rare to find Mr or Ms Right there, you just might – or you might meet someone who leads you to that hard-to-find person. At the dinner I was placed next to Jennie Page, newly appointed by the then Conservative Government to be Chief Executive of the Millennium Commission.

It turned out that she had a 'Dome' to build and fill, if the government approved. An election would be coming up and it would cost hundreds of millions of pounds, so it would be a very political decision, but she was full of enthusiasm. I filed it away as an idea that, if it bumped into something else, might be great – although no one else seemed much interested back then. In May 1997 New Labour won the election and came to power. Shortly afterwards they announced that they would indeed go ahead and build Jennie Page's Dome. The Dome would now be a symbol of New Labour success, headed by the government minister Peter Mandelson. What a symbol, what a film! Suddenly two things had banged together. I immediately asked for permission to make the film, but the interminable cogs of government ground on for ever. As 1997 moved into 1998 I worried that I had missed my chance, but you must hold your nerve. Many of the best films take time and patience. Like ideas, they too are slow burners.

It took nearly two years of long, slow courtship from first meeting before the Dome film finally got going. It took just as long to court Marks & Spencer, as the firm went through its endless rough patch before we finally got access. Both projects were highly worthwhile in the end. So always try to keep some films that take a long time to negotiate up your sleeve. If you finally get access, and particularly if something happens, as with time it is likely to, the broadcasters will be highly likely to commission it and, best of all, no one else will have it.

AMBITION

There is one final, and most important, requirement for your story: ambition. This could be getting inside something huge, or difficult, or special, or more often it could be adding to the stakes. So rather than just following a restaurant we find participants who compete to win one, as in *The Restaurant*, or we take the staff of a huge supermarket to the top, as in *I'm Running Sainsbury* (soon to be reformatted in America). It could be ambitious in what it is trying to change, like *Jamie's School Dinners*, which set out to change the whole nation's school meals. But ambition will help you sell, around the world.

VICTORIA DUMMER

Senior Vice President of ABC Alternative Series,
Specials and Late Night, USA

We'd rather fail spectacularly than succeed in a mediocre way. If people come in with big ideas that have really interesting twists in them, and surprises for the audience – surprises for us – that's what we are looking for: really unique ideas. Something one may have seen as a smaller cable show might succeed incredibly, as did Undercover Boss, *because it was able to bring in those national brands and is a broadly relatable idea.*

However, these conceits are tough to pull off, as we will come to see later. They need not only to be ambitious but authentic – to have a real and genuine point. Programmes with a unique and credible ambitious conceit – *Wife Swap, Faking It, Don't Tell the Bride* – can be winners. But the absolute secret with these, and the hurdle at which so many fall, is authenticity. They need to feel real, and the characters need to follow trajectories that we feel they might do for real. Perhaps *I'm Running Sains-bury* didn't do as well as it might have in the UK because the company was just too big and PR savvy, so the audience didn't quite buy into it.

Often, however, you don't have the chance to sell your own story, in fact you may not even want to, but need to decide whether to take on someone else's. A lot of success in TV comes from choosing the right stories from others to work on. All that you have read so far may help you make up your mind, but let's look a little more at how to decide what you should take on, especially if it is not your idea.

TAKING ON OTHER PEOPLE'S STORIES

On leaving the BBC in 2002, when I first set up on my own as a TV Troubleshooter, I asked the BBC and Channel 4 to let me know of any problem programmes they might need help with. The first series they called about was *Jamie's School Dinners*. Jamie Oliver wanted to leave the big production companies and make his new series alone through his own tiny TV company, but Channel 4 was worried that first series by new companies can be risky. So they persuaded Jamie to take me on as a 'grown-up'. I agreed to meet him, but was still reluctant.

TV is a fashion business, and what is in vogue now is likely soon to become less so. It would, for example, be a bad idea to take over head-ing the twenty-five-year-old *Tomorrow's World* at its peak, to risk becoming tarred with its death – the last editor is now long forgotten. It would have been a bad career move to work with Jeremy Clarkson after the success of the original *Top Gear*. There followed a series of programmes that passed by without memory, from his chat show to his journey round Europe. It was the producer who 'saved' Clarkson after these, and reinvented *Top Gear*, who won out and became a hero at the BBC.

It can be most dangerous of all to take over a department, company or channel that is 'flavour of the month': you'll have a hard job doing better and the downside risks are high. So if possible don't take over the successes of others; take over their failures! If you fail too you can say it was an inevitable disaster anyway. If you succeed (even a little) you can play the saviour card for all it's worth – and it's worth a lot.

But Jamie was no disaster, quite the opposite. As we have seen, his two previous series, *Naked Chef* and *Jamie's Kitchen*, had been mega-hits: they had been highly entertaining and won many awards, including the prestigious RTS for both, and the BAFTA for Best Features Series, an exceptional achievement. Now with some of the press having turned, and in a truly British way having a field day getting at him, and even some of the public beginning to tire of his success, with his heavy exposure and all the Sainsbury ads, Jamie seemed to have peaked. Worse for me, *Jamie's Kitchen* had been near perfect and seemed impossible to live up to, let alone better, for a number of reasons. First, it had a classic ingredient that is becoming ever more prevalent in hits, and is one of my cardinal rules for creative success: to create winners get different genres to collide.

COMBINING DIFFERENT GENRES

Jamie's Kitchen combined not just two genres but three, and worst of all from my point of view, three of the best at that! First there was choosing which kids would join, and which be thrown out – the classic *Pop Idol* genre, but then still fresh in other factual/reality formats. Then there was the countdown, tension-building genre, in this case following the build-up to the opening of his new restaurant, Fifteen. It's a genre I have used often, and works with the opening of anything from a new hotel to a new TV station, as everything heats up to the climax of the opening and beyond. Finally the series featured the human soap story of Jamie and Jules's relationship at the crunch moment, as they had their first baby, and Jamie puts their money and their house at risk. And each one of these three storylines contains the most important thing of all: *conflict*, which is what this book is all about.

Combining genres is a key to success in modern TV. *Top Gear* was a long-running, tired car review magazine show till host Jeremy Clarkson left and tried other TV genres, including becoming a chat-show host. When he returned he and his producers created a new genre-busting magazine show that has become a worldwide mega-hit, estimated to have 350 million viewers. It is the show magazine programmes around the world now try to emulate.

JANE ROOT

Former President, Discovery Networks
and Controller BBC2, now CEO, Nutopia

I often think that shows are sort of marriages, so Top Gear *was a car review show with an enormous amount of entertainment. It was really a hybrid of the car review show it had been and Clarkson's chat show. It was a car review show that became an entertainment show – we took it from one genre to another. Clarkson came back with that confidence to be with a live audience and take a big audience with him rather than just talk to camera. It was daring for everybody because it was a show that didn't look like a success.*

Top Gear had the key ingredients of successful modern factual magazine shows, inspired by entertainment. They have a toolkit of parts: an audience, humorous challenges, games, an interaction between presenters you want to be with, and a twist or two – in *Top Gear*'s case The Stig, a secret car tester, and celebrity interviewees who also attempt to drive faster round the test track than other celebrities and other crazy stunts.

EXPERIENCING, NOT JUST LOOKING

To see people, even celebrities, experiencing is also becoming more and more important. If you look at a traditional consumer magazine show like *Basta* in Denmark, much like the traditional *Watchdog* in the UK, what it misses is experience. In modern and successful consumer shows, like *Rogue Traders*, presenters use hidden cameras to show up rogue builders and confront them – we are on a scary journey of conflict. *The Real Hustle* does something similar showing (not telling) confidence tricks from Poker to ATM machines, like a thriller as our protagonists proceed. Magazine shows have to take on these tricks. More and more are doing so.

The F-Word in Britain is now trying to do for food what *Top Gear* did for motoring, making the same jump. Just when people thought magazine shows were dead, reinvention has made them hits again. Hosted by Gordon Ramsay, *The F-Word* also takes place with an audience, but not

---

JULIE URIBE

Senior Vice President, Fremantle Media North America

We have so many magazine shows on cable networks that cover that consumer space – whole datelines are devoted to con men and things like that. They have a news staff that can support those kinds of investigative programmes. They don't need the same releases, they can go under news. CNBC, MSNBC, CNN can do those troubleshooting things.

---

in a conventional studio. Like *Top Gear*'s airfield hangar, it has a restaurant where fifty people have to be fed, celebrities and the public can be included, and there are humorous and experiential filmed challenges. And a presenter, or host, people want to be with.

JON ROWLANDS

Former Head of Development BBC Factual,
Creative Director, Renegade

When it comes to feature shows, you want people you would like to spend time with, that you find interesting. Talent is someone you want to be your friend, somebody you'd like to spend an hour of your day with. The Top Gear *presenters are a prime example of that. They are three blokes that most people in Britain would like to go and have a beer with. That sense of them being your TV friend is very very important.*

A gardening show format might be great, for instance, but if you don't love the gardener then you are not going to stick with it. If you put in someone like Alan Titchmarsh, he's an avuncular character who people just adore, so you want to spend time with him.

So the keywords of magazine shows are 'attitude', in terms of location and presenters; 'experience', in terms of both presenters and guests doing something; and 'interaction', between the contributors and celebrities.

FINDING THE FAIRY TALE

The new series that I was being asked to run, *Jamie's School Dinners*, might have a wonderful presenter – Jamie again – but after a long hard think it still appeared to have those three problems in making the story come alive successfully. First it would be near impossible to better the success of *Naked Chef* and *Jamie's Kitchen*. Second it appeared to have none of the genre-busting characteristics of *Jamie's Kitchen*, and instead of trying to transform fifteen characters as in that show (which is already a lot), it needed to transform the nation's kids. Third, it was about what appeared to be a worthy subject, and a political one at that – what the government says Britain's kids should eat at school. And to make matters worse, Jamie, who had taken big financial risks with the restaurant Fifteen, staffed by his disadvantaged chefs, appeared to be risking nothing this time. The series to me had potential failure written all over it. Indeed, persuading anyone else that it was a good idea later proved even tougher. The first series producers I sounded out had seemed already convinced of my first rule ('never take on something that has been successful') and could see only downsides. No one wanted to be the person to turn Jamie into a failure and, this being my first series out on my own, without the BBC, I was still really scared of failing. So before searching for more characters it was out with another tool: what could the structure of this story be? Where was the fairy tale?

MYTHIC STORIES AND THE HERO

Over my career, my story structures have been stolen from what has worked from the beginning of time, the storytelling of folklore and legend, the Greeks, Shakespeare and Hans Christian Andersen. The tried and tested can be best in any line. These are stories that hit your heart and have a universal theme, with which people can identify as they struggle to make something of life, against the inevitability of decay and death. Whenever a story is being pitched to me I say, 'What is the fairy tale?' When we are stuck in the cutting room I say, 'Tell it to me like a fairy tale.' Unless you can write a dozen sentences that sum up your film's sequences, and flow like a fairy tale, you probably do not have a film.

I specialise in telling one main classic story – the hero with a quest – again and again, all the way from *Troubleshooter* through *Back to the*

Floor to *Blood on the Carpet*, from *The Boy Whose Skin Fell Off* to *When Big Chef Met Little Chef*. In each film we follow the hero through successive hurdles, as he (or she) fights other characters and obstacles. Things look tougher and tougher until he wins through, in the process revealing his true character under pressure, leading to transformation and ideally redemption. For a film to succeed best, the lead characters should be in a position they almost couldn't even envisage by the end.

There is one other main story structure I use, more occasionally. This is based on *Icarus*; classic tragedy. In this story structure the characters get bigger and bigger, or more and more pleased with themselves, but, as in Punch and Judy, we are hoping for them to get their comeuppance. Such were the films I worked on about Robert Maxwell, following his ultimately doomed takeover of the *Daily Mirror* and its aftermath. Although it took longer than the making of our films for the tragedy to play out, it seemed inevitable to me at the time. I don't follow tragedy all that often, but the British and Northern Europeans love it, though American networks tend to prefer 'feel-good' happy endings, and European broadcasters are going the same way.

Just as in the myth of the hero with a quest, the audience can see the end coming from the very start, but are made to doubt it en route. This time they are thrilled, but hopefully slightly surprised as, by the end, our central character is transformed and resoundingly fails.

There is a third story I use, but it is really just a combination of the other two. In this you have two sides struggling against each other, but usually one is heroic and one is tragic – and the hero wins! So try to find a fairy tale that suits you: you are lucky as a director if you do. There are other mythic stories – *Little Red Riding Hood*, in which someone disobedient gets what they deserve; *Cinderella*, where someone from nowhere gets discovered (the clever extra twist at the end of *Undercover Boss*), and plenty of other morality tales.

If you look at many Hollywood directors or writers, they find one good story and stick to it, just giving it different clothes. It is surprising how easy it is to identify different directors' films. However, in TV, as in much of modern life, appearing to do the same again and again is considered very old-fashioned, so a key part of the job is to disguise your endlessly repeated story as innovative television!

Most times a new TV boss arrives they make a similar opening speech outlining a strategy they consider novel and surprising and well worth

CECILE FROT-COUTAZ

CEO, Fremantle Media, North America

*The thing that always works well here is rags to riches, because it's
the American dream. It's why those performance shows like* Idol *and*
Got Talent *do so well, because they work on that basic level. It's your
unknown – the girl next door – who will have a go at stardom, the
notion that anyone can be famous, anybody can be rich, anybody can
turn round their lives. These competition shows have done very well in
this competitive landscape. Any show that goes back to this basic
premise, whether it's an* American Inventor *– which was successful,
though we could never figure out the middle portion – or an* Idol *or*
Got Talent *or potentially a* Master Chef *if they get it right.*

the salary: they want films that make a noise, that lots of people watch
and are innovative. Well, strike me down, do they really think every
other boss before them wanted programmes that no one talked about
or watched? What everyone wants is the programme *everyone* is talking
about, and in TV 'innovative' is a synonym for just this. As in many
modern industries, TV likes the word 'old-fashioned' even less than it
supposedly disdains the 'rip-off', but the big advantage we have is the
ignorance and hypocrisy of many TV executives happy to call almost
any hit 'innovative' TV. So as long as your repeated story is successful
you will be called a pioneer, and may even win awards for innovation,
and nobody will notice it's the same old thing again.

So most of my films have followed heroes with a quest, from *Back to
the Floor* to *Jamie's Ministry of Food* and *When Big Chef Met Little Chef*.
It is not surprising that although there are other structures, many other
factual award winners also follow this storyline, right from the wonderful *Meet the Natives*, in which the inhabitants of a remote Polynesian
island are desperate to meet their God, Prince Philip (with another twist:
each week they have to live with and survive a different class of British
family), to *Faking It* (the same structure but with a touch of *Cinderella*
and an extra twist: will the character faking the job convince a panel
of experts at the end, and succeed in not being found out?). I decided
that despite my worries *School Dinners* might fit my classic quest, but

first it would require some new clothes, a new story! These would need to feel authentic to Jamie and the subject, since unless the story feels true to the character the audience won't believe it. I was lucky to have a month from being asked to take on the challenge to making my decision. But going through the downsides, as you wrestle with the decision, is important in helping you make it work in the end.

KEEPING THE STORY UP TO DATE

As long as you find up-to-date clothes to fit your archetypal story, then nobody should notice the ancient story inside – they will just appreciate it. These new clothes also need to fit the time; you need to sense what is just about to spring into fashion. Over my career I've luckily been blessed with many awards, but the terrible truth is that they are nearly always awards for the same old stories – and no one noticed as yet again I was being told how innovative I am. Because those same old stories continue to work. This is how I have been retelling them.

In the eighties the field of business was my raw material, making films about transforming business, a surprisingly rich territory, full of heroes under pressure. After all, apart from relationships, work is the area that for most people creates the biggest conflict. It's where we live out dreams and fantasies, try to change our bit of the world and to make meaning out of life. The office has become the modern village where as often as not we now meet our partners.

If I had been a medieval film-maker I might have made films about heroic knights in shining armour riding off to the Crusades. Back in the eighties I could follow heroic businessmen leading a Thatcherite crusade to transform Britain and make money. So *Troubleshooter* was hard-edged and tough. But this soon changed. Genres are cyclical: as some go down, others rise. I remember Jane Root – BBC2 boss from 1999 to 2004 before she took over Discovery – saying that cookery was dead, it was so overdone on UK TV, just before it was reinvented by Jamie Oliver and Pat Llewellyn with *Naked Chef*, the series that added the adventures of a lively young cook to the recipes.

So just when cookery looked as if it was down was the moment to seize cookery series again, but in a new way. After a short decline it made a big comeback, in Britain with Jamie Oliver, Gordon Ramsay, Heston Blumenthal, Nigel Slater and Hugh Fearnley-Whittingstall – but

JANE ROOT

Fromer President, Discovery Networks and Controller BBC2, now CEO, Nutopia

I tell you what I thought was dead. People used to use television to give information. The Travel Show, which I cancelled, used to tell you how to book a ticket on a plane. Now even if you watch Delia [Delia Smith, a British Julia Childs/Martha Stewart since the early 1970S], *queen of the recipe, you expect to go to a book or online site in order to find the actual recipe. Now you enter the world of an expert to see them transforming something, to marvel in the expert's prowess. Television is a great medium for enthusing you, for giving you jeopardy and emotional engagement with something; if you want practically to learn how to do something, there are loads of other ways to do that.*

all of them now doing something more than cooking, from changing the way we eat to changing our attitudes to food, from transforming school dinners to setting up their own supermarket. With that reinvention cookery has become an even bigger hit, and around the world there are successful TV food networks with dozens and dozens of chefs on air. And Gordon Ramsay and Jamie Oliver have moved on to primetime US network TV. As Warren Buffett says of shares, buy just when everyone else is giving up.

Business dipped at the end of the nineties, times were getting a little softer, Thatcher was already gone, New Labour was in, and I felt that we were even about to care a bit more about people. So I began to make the same story, but now about transforming people rather than businesses. Even my business programmes became a bit more caring – as in *Back to the Floor*, where the caring boss would try to find out what life was like for the workers. But even the caring bosses were still under pressure, and most came out of the process transformed.

In the new century, and under New Labour, it was changing society that many people cared about. My story needed yet another new set of clothes. So I worked on series like *One Last Job*, following a group of ex-prisoners as they tried to seek redemption setting up a florist's shop; and *The House of Obsessive Compulsives*, following a group of Obsessive

Compulsive Disorder sufferers who were hoping to seek redemption and cure with a radical new treatment. Now, while business takes off on TV in the US (keep looking at what was a hit a decade ago across the Atlantic from either side) it may be community that is about to take off in Britain, changing society together when politicians can't, or won't.

In *Gerry's Big Decision*, Sir Gerry Robinson replaces the banks that won't lend and uses his own cash to save ailing firms. Even in the US *Oprah's Big Give* follows a group of good people to see who can raise most for charity, in a knockout show. Of course some, like these two, don't win through, partly because the time isn't right in their market, but also in the case of *The Big Give* because they don't have strong enough characters for us to care about, or sufficiently clear, simple, believable narratives. But my advice remains that unless you are brilliant enough to be able to do more, stick to one thing but keep adapting it to how the audience wants it delivered. It also makes it much easier to find jobs, which we'll come to later, as those in a position to give jobs get to know what sort of programme you do.

When I received the summons inviting me to do *Jamie's School Dinners*, it was just as I was pursuing this changing society set of clothes for my traditional story, and also just as I was wondering again if maybe now I should give up television. But Channel 4, and Jamie's TV managing director, the charming Andrew Conrad, had now tickled my tummy, the insecurity button most producers have, and used extreme flattery to win me over. I always think TV producers run on the dual rocket fuels of arrogance and insecurity – but if one gets too big you explode; you need both to function. So, as full of insecurity as the next producer, I believed them when they said I was the only man for the job! It is that unique moment when employers are lovely to you just before you sign the contract, then mostly they forget you again.

I had now convinced myself that my hero story – the film I always make – might work, and an email correspondence from an internet café on a South African beach led to my flying back to meet the famous chef in a pub in Hampstead. It was just after Christmas and I had a collection of new Global kitchen knives I had been given as a present in my briefcase, plus a cookbook my granny had written, to try to establish contact. The interview wasn't what I expected. It turned out not to be Jamie interviewing me but the other way round. The famous chef had a huge heart, but appeared to be at a stage of questioning where he was in life, at the age of twenty-eight. The approach of thirty is well documented as a moment of transition, a time to question a life path that has only been played at in the twenties. Jamie felt as if he was at just such a moment – the cheeky chappy transforming into the dad who cared about the world. I thought he had the potential to be truly heroic, because the best heroic stories are also coming-of-age epics in which the hero sets off as one person, then – as he confronts demons, trolls and collapsing rope bridges – grows up and comes to terms with the real world, returning transformed, older and wiser, from boy to young man, or young man to maturity.

So although it first seemed utterly crazy to take on *School Dinners*, there is one very counter-intuitive rule, which can overrule all others in any line of business: follow your gut – which is actually made up of all your experience. Despite the danger of the subject, and Jamie's previous successes, my gut told me more and more that it was an intriguing idea, partly because of Jamie's own passion for it. Although following your gut in TV might get you into some terrible pickles, more likely it will lead you to some wonderful places. Because TV is essentially an emotional medium. I decided to take on the challenge.

However, there was one upside: no one else thought it would be the winner it became, so I was able to do just what I wanted. I had the full backing of Channel 4, and a trusting commissioning editor in Peter Dale, who would let me do what I liked, with an occasional incisive pointer or deep question – the best sort. But if I was to serve him well, and the series was to have a chance of big success, it was clear that I would need more of my survival toolkit, starting with perhaps the most important tool of all: casting the right characters.

FINDING THE CHARACTER

You might say that we already had a great character in Jamie, though some of the press had become hostile, and according to the Channel 4 marketeers even sections of the public were turning cooler, with some viewers beginning to think that he was not for real – despite the fact that he is, for the caring person you see on TV is what you get in reality. But the press had been getting at him, and there were those Sainsbury ads – which might be misread as money-seeking overexposure. Jamie would need to be turned into the public's hero again.

NICK STRINGER

Marketeer for *Jamie's School Dinners*, now at ad agency BBH

There had definitely been a cooling off on Jamie. In Jamie's Kitchen *he'd done an amazing job, but it was too soon after that, plus all the Sainsbury stuff made people weary. Jamie was felt to be absolutely everywhere, and on his book covers his face had gone from happy-go-lucky cheeky chappy having a go to looking a bit earnest and serious.*

I had decided that, with all the dangers around, *School Dinners* should be based on my main story model of the fairy-tale hero struggling against tremendous odds to achieve the impossible. But how could we show Jamie as a fairy-tale hero? To be truly heroic he needed someone to fight against, not just a government that does not feel very human to start with. I decided the series just might work if he was up against a strong opposing character who would, ideally, be at a real breaking point. It's the next key point in the rulebook.

ANTAGONISTS AND PROTAGONISTS

To create dramatic structure in a documentary every hero needs something to oppose — it could be a mountain or something physical, but more usually this is personified in an opponent of some sort. An out-and-out adversary is the most obvious solution. Giants and ogres work well in fairy tales because it is satisfying when they are slain at the end — remember those *Troubleshooter* bosses who were fired near the end of the programme. But there is an alternative: to give the hero a 'number two' with whom he can argue, someone who can stay with us through the programme or series. Many fictional characters have such followers. From Don Quixote and Sancho Panza to Captain Kirk and Spock, from Robin Hood and Friar Tuck to the Lone Ranger and Tonto, or Batman and Robin, the hero and his 'number two' always need to have opposite traits for the drama to work. Usually we have a flighty, dreamy creative leader as number one and a more prosaic, down-to-earth character as number two. But they stay with each other till the end, when part of the transformation is that they see each other's point.

This works well for real-life characters too. It may not be surprising that Jeremy Clarkson's series *Speed* is little remembered, since although it was Clarkson experiencing fast machines, he was doing so alone. But the addition of two sidekicks, chosen to be able to tease and conflict with him, helped the new *Top Gear* to become a huge international hit.

So what would be the opposite of Jamie? Self-evidently no one even slightly dull, or boring, because television reduces people so you need characters with potential to be larger than life while still being true to themselves. To seem large on TV, characters need to be much bigger than you'd generally find in real life, and in order to seem normal on the box they need to be persuaded to speak with slightly more hyperbole, more outrage, than they would in day-to-day life.

STEPHEN LAMBERT

Creator of the hit formats *Wife Swap*, *Secret Millionaire* and *Undercover Boss*

To find good characters, employ good people and then persuade them to ask nicely. And then when you're looking at what they've found, trust your judgement over whether this is the person who engages you.

You haven't got the luxury to keep looking, but it is the most worthwhile place you can spend money. With both Wife Swap *and* Undercover Boss, *it took much, much longer to cast almost anybody, never mind about good people, than we expected, so both the first series of* Wife Swap *and* Undercover Boss *went over-budget because we kept having to delay shooting because we couldn't cast. If I can see that a format has the potential — if it's well executed at the beginning — to become a hit, which is to do with how excited one is about the idea, one makes the commercial decision that the reward is great enough to take the financial hit of delaying shooting and keeps on investing in it.*

In America, the network pores over the casting of everybody, so you're required to get a performance out of people, even on the casting tapes. One of the tricks is that you want the best stuff to come out when you're doing the proper filming, which means that people haven't already said what they wanted to say in the best possible way on the casting tape.

YOU HAVE TO LOOK BAD TO LOOK GOOD

The important thing is to turn your presenters or main characters into heroes. This is why that opposing 'number-two' character can be so useful, but to be heroic, our hero also needs to be up against big challenges – the bigger the better. Most contributors, and many presenters or hosts (excluding the outward-bound Bear Grylls types) don't want to be pressed so hard they might fail. In fact they would like to look as boring as possible till they see the results on TV. Then they wish you had made them look better by showing their true selves, which is why you have to push them while filming. Being challenged is just what keeps us watching and makes contributors heroic – they have to look bad to look good.

After I had completed the hit series of *Troubleshooter*, the Science Department finally turned my official title to producer! After another two hit series with Sir John Harvey-Jones, they finally even made me an executive producer, but first they didn't want more business (*Back to the Floor* and *Blood on the Carpet* had yet to be invented). Instead they wanted me to concentrate on making real programmes, the first about engineering, and called *The Limit*. One of the directors on the series was stumped by a particularly dangerous double-whammy – a Danish bridge builder who spoke accented English on one monotonous note, and also proudly proclaimed that he never ever took risks. I flew over to Denmark to try to persuade him to be livelier. His daughter told me that she was embarrassed, even at school, to say her father was an engineer. This, I told him, is what engineers have to contend with. I appealed to his vanity to do something for his profession.

There's no harm in flattery or asking people to make programmes for the good of their profession or passion. Or telling them you'll show the world the wonder of what they are doing. You need to use every means to encourage your contributors to seem as heroic as possible. However, this tack was not enough to enliven our very dull Dane, who had made a profession of saying that nothing worried him about bridge building, even when it did. So I told him that the programme was a big break for the director, his first film, and a first for me as an executive producer – both true. I told him that both our careers were on the line, which is always the case, and that if he couldn't become a bit more interesting we would both fail and, TV being what it is, risk our promising futures. When even this failed, I used the line that if his job was really so easy (and so lacking in difficulty, danger and doubt) then presumably even my mother could do it. Was he really so pleased with himself that he never ever worried at all about his bloody bridge? He finally broke down, admitting that indeed he did, and engineering became a tiny bit more interesting. You never know which approach will work, but at least I didn't need to go to tears – the ultimate stage in convincing a reluctant contributor.

I frequently use tactics such as these with other reluctant, or unlively contributors, who are not keen to say what they really think. It is an effort to make them look better. With business leaders I lament that the country doesn't really value or understand the sort of thing they do, often thinking of them as wicked rather than wealth creators. I tell them they owe it to their colleagues to show how fascinating, interesting and wonderful their profession is, and therefore implicitly how wonderful they are themselves. It's surprising how often this works – but you have to believe it: if you think that most people do most things because they believe in them, contributors will sense it. It even persuaded Peter Mandelson to let me make *The Dome: Trouble at the Big Top*.

If all else fails, appeal to their charity. Tell them it is too early in your career for you to be fired. And always push for the best because in the end the thing that will upset your contributors most is putting all that effort into a programme no one watches just because they look so dull.

PERSUADING PEOPLE TO TAKE PART

The negotiation for access and performance is a tender dance – in essence a courtship ritual, so don't ask contributors to marry you, and sign up, too fast. I find two hours is about the right time for a first meeting with a contributor. Three-quarters of the conversation can be about life and just finding common ground – which you can find with anyone, if you have to. Then when we come to talking about the programme, if I feel the contributor is hooked I reel them out again.

In fact the more I want them the less I commit, saying I will need to sell them to the TV station or my boss. For it is most important they feel that they want it too. Or they can fail to bite and it can be just the start of a long ritual. Some access negotiations, like winning some lovers, or fishing for salmon, can take years of persistence and strategy.

MICHELE KURLAND

Executive Producer, *The Apprentice*

You have to give them a reason for doing it — they're never going to do it because your programme is going to be better. It could be anything: sharing a problem, a passion, something that matters to them. I always talk them through everything that is involved.

The key thing is when I come home that night, or if I went out for a drink, would I tell you about it? The kinky boots you would tell anyone you met that evening — that's how you need to react if it is to come all the way through the screen to the viewer. They move you in some way to make you laugh or care about them and their passion If you are reading about them they have to jump off the page, if you are in a room with them you don't want to leave them.

In 1998 we embarked on *The Dome: Trouble at the Big Top*, the series that would follow the building of the Millennium Dome and the organisation of the exhibitions that would take place within it. The negotiation turned into one that would take not committing, as a tactic, to the extreme. After months of negotiation we were finally allowed to begin filming, although we still didn't have any written agreement. Eventually, after much discussion, the Dome team finally got round to sending us the 'wedding' contract some months after filming had begun. But it was impossible for me to sign: they wanted a degree of editorial control, something I am never willing to concede. As negotiations continued we paused filming and played chicken. It was a scary time, and barely a year to the opening, when we were finally able to agree and go ahead, with us retaining editorial control. Many felt that we had missed key moments, but the audience never knows what you haven't filmed, and more important neither does the film editor! In my view editorial integrity is more important than missed footage.

A careful and gradual approach, not scaring contributors off, can be very important, especially with bigger and more difficult subjects. When the courtship is properly under way, and they are hooked, you can afford to take more risks. Tell them that there will be bits that make them look bad, and point out more downsides. Acknowledge and discuss what could go wrong in your relationship, and what they are

JAN TOMALIN

Former Controller, Legal and Compliance, Channel 4,
MD, Media Law Consultancy

*Never cede editorial control to a contributor. The secret of getting and
retaining great access is trust. However, the wording of the access agreement
is of vital importance if there is ever a disagreement. Some disputes can
even end up in court, with the contributor seeking an injunction to stop
the programme, and you need to be sure the wording works for you, not
against you, and you have foreseen the issues that are likely to arise.*

*A clear and consistent programme description of about three sentences,
agreed upfront with the broadcaster and used by the whole team in all
approaches to any potential and actual contributor, will go a long way in
protecting you from a claim later that the contributor was misled about
the programme.*

*Resist the temptation of writing rude or otherwise pejorative things
about your contributors or the subjects of your film in emails etc., as
these may need to be disclosed later if there is legal action or a complaint
to the regulator. It has even been known for the contributor to be
accidentally copied in on an email chain containing sarcastic remarks
about them — with explosive results.*

worried about in relation to taking part. The fact you have thought it
through, and are willing to mention the downsides, should make them
feel more secure, not less! Remember it is all about trust.

Whenever you are asking too much of a potential contributor, and
feel a 'no' coming your way in this elaborate courtship ritual, I advise
quickly changing the subject. Once people have said 'no' it is hard for
them to change their minds and say 'yes' again; but if they haven't
uttered the syllable, they won't lose face by changing tack later. Like
lovers, they need to want it too. So courtship needs to be gentle. As soon
as you feel them biting, start winning their trust by backtracking, giving
them the reasons why it might be a boring film — why they shouldn't
do it. This way they will also feel it is more their idea, and you will also
be thinking through your film and why it might not work — if you
recognise the downsides. the upsides will take care of themselves.

SIMON DICKSON

Deputy Head of Documentaries, Channel 4, and
commissioner responsible for many award-winning programmes

*One of the things I do is find out, by pushing the contributors quite
hard at the beginning, whether they are suitable for the programme we
are asking them to do, as in* The Family *or* One Born Every
Minute [following a maternity ward, with a similar multi-
camera rig]. *I go to meet these people with the production company,
and go through what I would call 'The Talk of Doom'.*

*'The Talk of Doom' is where I cut through that feeling of apprehension,
excitement and nervousness that is the prelude to an observational series,
and say to the contributors, have they thought about the possible outcomes?
Have they given real thought, as a group and as individuals, to what
people will think about them in the final analysis and what sorts of
things might happen to them during the filming period? And I take the
contributors, with the production company, through a process of thinking
about the best things that might happen as a result of being on board
a particular project – and also the worst things that might happen.*

MICHELE KURLAND

Executive Producer, *The Apprentice*

I've had people say to me every year, including Apprentice *candidates –
even the parents in* Junior Apprentice *– 'Are you trying to put me
off?' I never want people to feel that I have charmed them, talked them,
conned them into it. Television is the easiest thing to stitch people up
with, and that's what's happening too much in TV. The viewer can feel
it, and you just end up with a very unhappy contributor who doesn't
trust you.*

*If you don't go though all the doubts with them you may be sure,
when you've gone, after the first or second recce, all their family and
friends will go through them, so it's much better if you raise the
elephants in the room and resolve them.*

Don't lose heart in this game of cat-and-mouse, because you are missing the story, for it never matters starting a film a bit late. When I was employed to begin filming *Jamie's School Dinners*, a development team had been researching for many months. The tiny team had already come up with one school in Islington. Filming was imminent, Jamie's hectic diary filled in, other dates would be hard to find, money was being spent. We needed to begin immediately. But I was still worried whether the characters would be exciting or real, and also about the story arc and ambition. So I stopped everything. What a bastard!

Never compromise on characters; it is always worth searching for better ones; adequate isn't good enough. But it's also important only to reject the merely adequate contributors at the last possible moment – you never know whether you might need to fall back on them. So the first school they had found was kept going, while I was rethinking what the series could be about, and wondering how we could find better characters. The original school wasn't bad, but I felt it was a bit 'Stoke Newington' – right on, and over-keen to take part. They even had someone from 'No. 10' advising them on PR.

I am always suspicious of anyone who is instantly keen to take part in your film. It's a bit like sex – if they are too keen they often become less attractive. But remember the corollary – that when you strike gold and really want someone to take part in your film, at all costs don't let them know. Tell them that you are too busy to meet when they next want to meet, and keep saying that you'll need to convince your boss.

With the time and money clocks ticking, we appointed a series producer, Dominique Walker, who spent ages driving the team on as they toured the whole of London, visiting boroughs from Enfield to Camden. The team were becoming demanding as she was convinced that we still needed a great antagonist to make Jamie heroic. We finally found a school that seemed very good, and was thinking of changing its meals. It would be open and convincible, but the dinner ladies were again not good enough to make it a hit.

It was scary for Jamie, embarking on a series with his own new company, money going out of the door and nothing happening, dates put aside in his busy schedule, and then being ignored. The pressure on me was increasing, but I held my nerve until finally Dominique Walker and her team found Nora Sands, the loveable, natural and outspoken dinner lady at Kidbrooke School in Greenwich. She had huge charisma and believed in her way of doing it. Originally Irish, she had the real gift of the gab, and to top it all said whatever she thought. We had at last found a strong second character, and plenty of potential for conflict.

We still needed to get the public to remember her, so we would put her in the pre-titles (the cold open), and intercut her with Jamie post-title, as they anticipated meeting each other. 'Nora' would become a big, and strong, 'number-two character', who would help Jamie on his mission, but keep it fun and full of conflict. You need to be demanding all down the line, expecting only the best in everything.

DOMINIQUE WALKER

Series Producer, *Jamie's School Dinners*, now
Commissioning Editor, Factual Entertainment, Channel 4

You have to make the team respect you enough to be scared of bringing you anything that is mediocre. If they had come back and said the dinner lady was OK, and I went to see her and thought she was mediocre, I'd be really pissed off, because I'd just wasted the day going to see someone mediocre that they'd told me was good. For me the one job I had to do was cast someone who would stand up to Jamie. That came from traditional documentaries where you live or die by the characters that you put in your show. With other shows that have talent at their heart, there isn't generally the push to find that other brilliant character.

NAMING CHARACTERS

It is surprising how often characters aren't built up from the front of a film, or given memorable characteristics. In the first cut of Jamie sorting out school dinners in America, *Jamie's Food Revolution*, based on the original *Jamie* series from the UK, the dinner ladies were not named till well into the first cut, appearing as just 'dinner ladies' till then. It was a situation we quickly remedied on first viewing. *Jamie's Ministry of Food* was transformed, at the end of the edit, by finding two strong characters in the rushes we could set up from the off, complete with their own monikers: Natasha, 'who has never cooked her children a meal', and Clare, 'who eats twenty-seven packs of crisps a day'.

Monikers are vital: the more you can do to mark out and popularise your main characters the better.

No one called Harvey-Jones 'Sir' John – even his driver called him John. But I used 'Sir John' at every opportunity, and then everyone who heard me would call him that too, on camera as well as off. It helped to underscore his character – to identify him as a rotund, guffawing, witty, outspoken Sir Toby Belch-like figure. The boss of the Tri-ang factory, Sidney Orchant, was known to his workforce as 'Mr Sid' and I made sure I called him this at every opportunity too. We even wrote an opening line together, for 'Sir John' to voice, in which he described his first impressions of Mr Sid as a 'rather old-fashioned and slightly autocratic chief executive', filling in the characterisation before continuing with points about the company and its problems of diversifying and buying expensive new machines. All this made Mr Sid memorable.

There were two other leading characters in this pilot show for *Troubleshooter* – Sharna, daughter of the giant 'Mr Sid', with a factory named after her, huge letters on its top, and responsible for sales; and the 'city accountant', a frosty new investor from London who had just bought a large number of shares in the company. A clash of characters looked inevitable, and fireworks duly happened, as 'Mr Sid', the Chairman, was forced out following 'Sir John's' tough advice. Although still an assistant producer I was commissioned by the boss of BBC2 to make the winning series, helped by naming the characters in the pilot. As a film doctor one of the most common ailments I find when called in is that the characters have not been brought out.

Even in a series like *Too Big to Walk*, where I only helped at the end, it was important to make the characters even stronger, so you cared from the beginning. The series followed a group of obese people as they walked the length of Britain to lose weight, and was based on an American idea in which the real key, the subtext, was to build self-esteem through the march, for these people were obese for a reason. We made the programme engaging by beginning post-title with one character's worries and expectations just as she was about to leave her home and two small children for two months – a pretty dramatic situation. By caring about her, as she brought us to the big day of the march's start, we were ready to understand the worries and stakes for some of the other key characters as they too got ready, and immediately set off with a very strong timeline. Mark Rubens's UK series worked well.

The US version *Fat March* added the competition, challenges and voting out that are the mainstays of factual network primetime. That also meant a decision to introduce all the characters in the pre-title, with a still photograph and caption, and again soon thereafter. Maybe it didn't break through partly because somehow the audience didn't care enough about the characters from the off. But this can be a challenge in US primetime where there is an expectation of pace, action, competition and knowing as many participants as possible, as well as the proposition, which can be a lot when it is not a familiar competition like an *American Idol*. Casting and character introduction are vital.

So let's draw all this together. Finally you have found the right character, you have used all your wiles to get them to join up, and made clear who they are. But before you invite everyone to the wedding you need to make sure it will be an interesting marriage. You need a story, not a subject, peopled by a few key characters. And you've given it a twist or an angle, an extra challenge for the heroes, something big and ambitious for the characters to overcome.

On *School Dinners* we would restrict our range of characters by beginning our quest transforming just one school. We would then give it a twist and scale by using the conflict between our two key opposing characters, Jamie and Nora, to try to transform a whole borough feeding 20,000 kids. We wanted to keep our story simple, but to make it big. Finally we hoped Jamie would come of age and seem more caring, while Nora, who at first thought he was a TV plonker, would come to see value in the new Jamie and become a zealous supporter of his mission. By the end of the series the humble dinner lady would be talking on the stage, inspiring thousands of dinner ladies, in a posh suit, and even going on to write her own cookbook, with Jamie's support, and adoring him. That was real transformation and something that at the start she couldn't have started to envisage.

We also now had two genres: first transforming one school, secondly a political programme about changing a borough, convincing politicians, the Minister and even the Labour Party. To have our third genre we would seek to film more of the ongoing Jamie and Jules saga, as he struggled with school dinners, with his restaurant and with the press.

We had a quest, the ambition had become big and multifaceted, and we had our two strong opposing characters. We were on our way.

Two

OUT OF THE BOX
AND SCRIPTS

GETTING READY TO FILM

You have found your characters and concept; now it is time to go filming. Two apparently contradictory skills are required for good film-making. First you need to be the sort of organised person who can write a very clear script, the route map of the film. But second you need to be able to think OUT OF THE BOX and depart from this route map if things turn out differently – which is virtually always – when it comes to factual scripts.

There are three kinds of directors: one who writes a very detailed script, complete with storyboard, and then whatever happens in the real world tries to stick to it. Often these directors come from an advertising background, but although this approach might work well in drama, documentary is very different – in fact it is surprising (or not as we will discover) how few directors successfully make the leap from drama to documentary and factual/reality, and even fewer the other way round.

The second kind of director, often from the world of 'reality TV' and often inexperienced, believes in shooting first, and thinking later, if at all. Here the idea is to turn the camera on as often as possible and shoot everything that moves (and even a lot that doesn't) in the hope that out of this morass of material they'll be able to find the story in the cutting room.

However, to succeed in factual TV you have to be a third kind, an amalgam of the two, writing a very clear script and embarking with a very clear storyline, but using this as a springboard to adapt to changing circumstances, changing your script as you go, and being willing and able to think OUT OF THE BOX.

This chapter is all about thinking out of the box as you set out to film. This key maxim applies first to finding or joining the right team, and being brave enough to realise that a bit of conflict, even within a team, can be creative. Then there is research, which requires a particularly open-minded ability to think out of the box, get rid of preconceptions and see what is really there. Finally we get to how to write the all-important script itself – a road map if you like, but one you will be willing to depart from. But first to the team.

FINDING YOUR TEAM

As a TV Troubleshooter, I often consider the most important part of my job is neither sorting out films in the cutting room, nor at the initial script stage, but being a glorified employment exchange. For if you employ the right team there will be very little sorting out to do. However, employing the right team to make original TV is not as obvious as it might seem; nor is joining the right one either.

Back when I was in the BBC Science Department there were two competing strands fighting for the best talent, run by two strong women. Both would use any tactic, including bursting into tears, to get the best directors from the BBC Science staff pool and were sometimes furious at having to employ inexperienced talent. But, as we have said, in the right mix inexperience (and hunger) can be the most useful of all. When I eventually became a series editor too, it gave me the edge.

So when it came to *Jamie's School Dinners* I wanted a series producer who had never made anything like it before. Many of the most successful businesses in the world follow this strategy, giving hungry new talent challenges in areas they do not know, but with very clear tasks and guidance. Television does this far too seldom, employing 'old hands', and then interfering with them far too much, which only pisses them off.

This time, with my first network series since leaving the BBC (and all its support), I wanted to prove myself and do everything the way I had always wanted – to make as near perfect a series as I could from all I had learned. The team was vital. With the project on hold I spent three months searching, and holding countless interviews. Many potential series producers declined the job. Finally I found what I thought was the right series producer for the project. She appeared eminently *unsuitable*, her two previous films were hardly popular factual entertainment, one following Muslim women to Mecca, and one following recently released convicts being mentored. But she was lively, inquisitive and best of all hungry. I employed Dominique Walker without seeing a thing she had made; I nearly always employ directors without seeing a single film they have made, just impressed by their sparkle and references – you never know who did what in TV!

EMPLOY BY RECOMMENDATION

I always think the best way to employ is by recommendation. For in television it is often almost impossible to tell who made a film successful, unless it is someone like Adam Curtis who does so much himself, with series like *Power of Nightmares*, even editing and narrating, or someone experienced, with a long track record. Otherwise how do you know how much the success is really the work of the director? Or was he or she rescued by their film editor, series producer, executive producer, or perhaps even their assistant producer who shot most of it? You have to ask these questions. So cultivate fellow directors, series producers and executives, and just ask them to name the most talented person they have recently worked with; then employ them. After all, the new director you are seeking probably won't have done quite what you are asking them to do previously, anyway.

This time I asked many people, but it was Charlotte Black, talent development manager at Channel 4 (a highly under-rated job, as it is knowing who is best, and even more important upcoming, that probably matters most), who came up trumps. She is a queen of talent and careers.

I made a career in the BBC often hiring impossible talent that no one else was willing to manage, rejects from other departments thrilled to be given another go and warped enough to have a strange take on

---

CHARLOTTE BLACK

Talent Executive, Channel 4, UK

I look for contemporary thinkers, really interested in television's form, with lots of life experience so they can add texture and an angle, and most important they need to be very emotionally intelligent, and to understand light and shade. I think there's a certain personality type that's really worth hiring because they compulsively take responsibility for things. Constantly, in productions, it's juggling balls in the air and who is going to catch them and you want the people who are going to go and try and catch as many balls in the air, rather than let them drop and make excuses as to why they didn't, or blame someone else. People who are prepared to do anything for you.

life. Dominique Walker was none of these: on first meeting she seemed sane, driven, smart and very organised, and understood just what the problems of the series were. In fact she asked just the questions that were nagging me – in employing, my key question is do people understand the downsides, and the potential ways round them, because it is only through working through the downsides that you begin to understand how a film will work. And her referees were great. Only after employing her as *School Dinners* series producer, on the highest recommendations from different people – she had worked for Ruth Pitt, who used to run *Everyman*, the religious documentary strand, whom I particularly admire – did I find that she was hungry, charming, keen and lucky, and after a fine and lively chat with her, I finally got round to seeing some of her films. I might have been too scared to employ her if I had seen them sooner, as they were very good, but so different to what I wanted for *School Dinners*, but anyway it was too late. She turned out to be excellent, so it was lucky I hadn't. But that is just the point. Television is about teams – I could find madness or strong visual skills elsewhere. On some of my past series at the BBC the team chemistry had not been perfect. This time I was determined it would be. And although it was stretching her, the relative inexperience might help – I hoped she would be keen to learn, and work with my story-structure. If you want to tell your own story, again and again, it helps to have relatively inexperienced hungry talent, who will use the old structure but make it fresh themselves.

While some of my fellow executive producers continued to fight to hire the most experienced and safest film-makers, I always wanted to bring in the hungry, charming, keen and lucky new talent, which is partly why I prospered. I remembered the first time I went up on the BAFTA stage, for my first film; frankly I did not have a clue what I was doing. The second time, for *Blood on the Carpet*, the episode that I think did it for me was *Ice Cream Wars* (featuring Ben and Jerry *vs* Haagen Dazs), which was Simon Dickson's first big film of this sort. The third Academy Award was for *Back to the Floor*, the brilliant idea coming from a driven and persuasive assistant producer, Hugh Dehn, who co-made the first film in the series, and later became its series producer. And the *Back to the Floor* that was shown at the RTS awards, getting the ball rolling, was yet again the first observational film from another hungry new director, Adam Wishart. I had found him like many others by asking the editor of *Tomorrow's World*, each year, who their best young talent was. *A Class Apart* followed the headmistress of the famous girls' public school Benenden, as she became a supply teacher in a tough inner-city comprehensive. But it nearly never began, as he was so nervous he remembered everything but to fill the car with petrol. So, on the way to the first shoot, with a nervous headmistress in his car, the vehicle stumbled to a halt in the middle of nowhere on a small country lane. Scenes were lost but it was real! The headmistress warmed to his vulnerability and adored him. Magic was born in the lane, and it turned out to be a magical film. RTS judge Elizabeth Murdoch, who had helped make it win, even came up after the award to say how moving it was. One more triumph for hungry inexperience.

Another new young director who broke through was Patrick Collerton, whose documentary *The Boy Whose Skin Fell Off* was eventually commissioned by Simon Dickson (by then a commissioner at Channel 4), and also won many awards.

PATRICK COLLERTON

Director, *The Boy Whose Skin Fell Off*

In broadcasting it is helpful if you have patrons. I was at lunch with Charlotte Black, who does talent at Channel 4. Simon Dickson was next to us in the canteen queue and I started telling him about it, and he saw me with Charlotte and he said don't pitch at lunchtime, but he had actually seen me with Charlotte so I got to see him later. At the time Simon wanted to break out of his mould at Channel 4 and do something radical, and this was a radical story. But you have to be very lucky for all that to happen.

THE IMPORTANCE OF LUCK

So how do you put yourself in that lucky position so that, when employers like me want the best raw young talent, they alight on you? In my experience, to get on, you need, in reverse order, cleverness, charm, hunger and luck.

Cleverness, and the focus and analytic skills that are taught at university, may be important, but are less so than other qualities. In fact many people are employed because of the cleverness shown in their degrees, but it is surprising how, later on, it is not necessarily those with the best degrees who rise highest. As I was first struggling up, a high proportion of the BBC trainees came from Oxford or Cambridge, yet twenty years later hardly any of the top people did, neither the then Director General Greg Dyke, nor most of his channel controllers, nor many of his TV bosses or department heads.

Charm, and the social and persuasive skills that go with it, can matter even more than cleverness, and help you in persuading people, which is vital in most jobs. Much of the TV 'job' is essentially selling, both to bosses within and contributors without. Most important, you need to have, or to develop, the emotional sensitivity to know what you need, and the ability to charm people into doing it.

But even if you are clever, and have developed the charm, both these attributes are of little use unless you are determined to do something with them. Hunger is the all-important motivator: work is hard graft, and television is a craft that requires practical skills, and the passion and energy that go with hunger. Continual hunger leads to an attention to detail, and trying harder hour after hour. Often the people I employed were the ones who just kept on at me. They sent an email, then a month later another, rang up – even got as far as seeing me and being rejected, but coming back later with a reason I should employ them. It is those terrier-like, passionate qualities that will make you succeed out there. In business the single common attribute of almost all the successful bosses I have met is this hunger to get on.

It is only if you have this hunger and passion, as well as cleverness and charm, that you are likely to come across the most important ingredient of all: luck. But although hunger makes it more likely that you will chance on the luck you need, you will have to spot it when it passes by. After all, although I was so lucky to get Sir John Harvey-Jones, it was only after others had rejected him. Never underestimate the importance of luck, particularly when you 'post-hoc' rationalise how much better than everyone else you were to get to wherever you now are.

However, remember that luck needs not only hunger and the ability to spot it, but putting yourself in a position where you might come across it.

I was highly lucky to have created the format for *Back to the Floor* at the right time to make it a hit, winning a big audience and many awards (including the first BAFTA for formats). But when I tried to sell it to the big US networks they were not ready. Stephen Lambert picked up the idea five years later, dusted it down, added the twists which we are coming to, and tried it again in the UK, but could only get two companies to take part in the first series and it was transmitted without great noise. But then he sold it in the US and pushed it with American production values. He also gave it a brilliant title: *Undercover Boss*. Such business formats felt new to America, and the recession meant that it was just the right timing. The first episode, transmitted after the Super Bowl on CBS, got an unprecedented 38 million viewers.

STEPHEN LAMBERT

Chief Executive, Studio Lambert,
Executive Producer *Undercover Boss*

Luck is, for me, primarily about timing. You can have an idea that is great, but it's the wrong time for that idea – and then at a different time it is just the thing that will happen. It's the timing of what the buyer wants and it's the timing of what the viewers want: the moment of getting a big network to buy it, and then like it enough to go with it.

CBS wanted the boss to have an encounter with more characters than in Britain. Fortunately, Americans are all given media genes at birth, so a lot of the success was due to the fact that we were working with Americans as opposed to more reserved Brits.

In the US everything has to be more intense and everything has to be more clearly delineated, so you know exactly what you're meant to be getting out of every scene. There's much greater use of music, and that is telling you all the time what emotion you should be feeling. It has to be bigger and faster and more intense and more dramatic and more emotional.

Clearly the economic crisis hit just after we started . . . and it's a classic fairy tale. The prince goes out of his castle, disguised, among the paupers. I think fairy tales are a good way of looking for ideas. Fairy tales that are going to lead to this idea of conflict.

That's all very well about having to sell the shows (and remember Stephen Lambert then executes them brilliantly). But if you are a TV novice, wanting to get a lucky break, how best to put yourself in a position to get it, where you can demonstrate charm and hunger? Looking up, it can seem daunting to get through the eye of the needle and almost impossible to make the leap to directing primetime films. So before we get to becoming a director, series producer, show runner or executive, how to get going? One of the best ways is to start in the 'ranks' of technical jobs, something I did for years. Then you will be an experienced TV virgin, having at least done a lot of watching others when you eventually get your turn. There are quite a few ranks before you try move on to become an 'officer', directing films. In fact it is horribly like the army:

Officers

Field Marshal	MD/CEO/Director General, television broadcasters
General (various)	Top bureaucrats (various) in broadcasters and production companies
Brigadier	Executive Producer
Colonel	Series Producer/Show Runner
Major	Producer/Director
Captain	Assistant Producer/Associate Producer
Lieutenant	Researcher

Ranks

Sergeant	Cameraman/Sound Mixer/Editor/Production Manager
Corporal	Asst Cameraman/Edit Asst/Production Asst
Private	Runner/Secretary/Reception

You will pick up far more than you imagine if you start in the ranks as the equivalent of a private or corporal. I started pushing trolleys of film around in a film despatch, and becoming even a researcher seemed almost unattainable. I used to look up at assistant film editors as the absolute height of my ambition. If you had told me I could one day direct, let alone be an executive producer, and then employ directors, I would have thought you mad. So I spent my twenties thinking about making television, and desperately wanting to do so, but never quite getting there. I picked up more and more, from working in the tape library to sound mixing, and became hungrier and hungrier till when, after many years, I got the opportunity to research I was a coiled spring and totally went for it.

Becoming a researcher was the toughest – making the jump from the ranks to being a junior officer. Few people were even willing to give me an interview. Finally I managed to get one, but I was summarily rejected. They said I seemed so scared of talking that they couldn't employ me – how could I persuade someone to take part in a film, for example, if I was too scared to even talk on the phone? Now this is strange, as those who know me will testify – I am usually accused of being just about the most talkative person in television. And a year later, when I had finally become a researcher, I was happily bossing around Robert Maxwell, boss of the *Daily Mirror*, who scared his entire staff. But nothing is as scary as being interviewed. Having failed and failed again, and already being over thirty, I still needed something more to make the jump.

BRANDING YOURSELF

It helps hugely if you can brand yourself. A director such as Adam Curtis is branded as King of Archive, and even more specifically modern historical archive with wild theses. Series like *Power of Nightmares* and *Century of Self* build one on another: even the titles are branded. Pat Llewellyn, creator of *Naked Chef* and *Kitchen Nightmares*, was branded and remains a Queen of Cookery. And Thom Beers is the King of Dangerous Jobs, after *Deadliest Catch*, *Ice Road Truckers* and *Black Gold*.

Conversely, when many directors come to me for advice, having found it hard to get jobs, often it is because they are not known for being good at anything in particular. Back at the start I realised that my only way in was if I could create an identity, a speciality. I needed to persuade someone that they couldn't *not* employ me, because they needed my special expertise so much. For this purpose I needed to find something that I liked doing, but hopefully not too many other people did – something a bit unusual but useful. And *this unusual something* needed not only to be out of the box, but preferably out of everyone else's box too. Business turned out to be just it. For me, it was something

I had always been interested in and could develop. It might get my foot in the door.

How can you decide on this? I found that it helped to watch loads of TV, and in doing so to research and keep honing the area in which you would like to work, while also identifying the people (ideally the executive producers) on whose programmes you wanted a job. Narrow the number down, and then try to find out about everything they have made. Look at DVDs of their programmes, or find them online. Try to structure what, in your view, has worked best and what has worked less well. Find out what these executive producers might do next – even research a couple of ideas. Become knowledgeable.

Then be persistent in trying to get an interview. Treat interviews just like a job – do the research, and then structure them. Write and rewrite an application, show it to friends, ask advice. Read it and reread it, making sure there is a coherent argument structured like a programme, with a beginning, a middle and an end. Ensure that it is tailored to the audience for which it is intended. Keep it short and punchy, and most of all check the spelling (particularly of the recipient's programmes!) and check the grammar too. You would be amazed how many people came for jobs in my department without spelling their applications correctly, or even knowing what programmes we had made.

CHARLOTTE BLACK

Talent Executive, Channel 4 UK

Recently I saw this absolutely wonderful guy, and the only reason I saw him was that his email was really really good: 'Here I am, this is what I'm doing, this is what I've done, this is what I want to be, this is why I think I can do it.' It concluded: 'Yes I'm young and ambitious, but not in a smarmy and unrealistic way,' which says 'I know I sound like a tosser but actually I'm not.' Authenticity of personality, recognition of the game.

Explain why you have the cleverness, charm and persistence to deal with their problems, and what is special and different about you – most of all your persistence, reliability, doggedness and sheer tenacity. Show an intelligent interest in their output, and how you would persuade contributors in difficult circumstances, be ready with examples of how you have done so and how you have surmounted other problems (because we all hit them) – and how you want to do all this for them. You are really demonstrating your charm, wit and persuasive powers.

On *Jamie's School Dinners* my prospective series producer had done exactly that: she simply persuaded me of her powers. We then needed the rest of the team. We wanted to keep it small, without lots of layers, something I strongly advise on series that have four or six one-hour slots. So the series producer would not only run the series, but direct and edit two films. We would employ one other director to make and edit the other two films, and then just two assistant producers. And we would stagger arrivals. Remember we wanted to keep as much money as possible over for editing, and time to let the story evolve.

First we spent a long time finding the second director. I needed to persuade the series producer of the advantages of employing an opposite – she was brilliant at formats, he was very poetic. We both wanted the very best, so we interviewed twice or thrice. I even rang Guy Gilbert's previous presenter, Louis Theroux, who was glowing in his recommendation. Guy Gilbert was a brilliant maverick, the grit in the oyster who turned out to be vital in helping make the series what it was. Meantime my series producer found another top AP in Lana Salah, and this time it was me who had to be persuaded. Even with assistant producers, I like to meet them and ask the questions that worry me about the series and see how they answer. Lana was grilled in an interview she will always remember, and survived brilliantly. Finally the whole team had persuaded me, and the series producer, and Jamie's TV MD and executive producer Andrew Conrad was happy too. I had my perfect team in place.

CECILE FROT–COUTAZ

CEO, Fremantle Media, North America

Staffing is the hardest thing ever. I always say if you could mix American development ethos with British execution you'd be on top of the world. This company's very good at developing high concepts, thinking about big stakes, loud concepts, but where it really falls apart in the US is the execution. The execution is just not good enough. It's attention to detail, also it's vision and having the conviction and being able to stand by that conviction.

Assembling or joining the right team is so important, as the right team will find the right characters, the right story and plenty of conflict if asked to do so. My advice to any executive producer is simple: postpone production as long as you are able, until you have the best team. The same applies down the line.

RESEARCHING

Once you have the right team, the next pillar on which the whole endeavour stands or falls is the research. I call this the underpinnings of the film. It is just like the underpinnings of a house. Without them a small wind will blow the house over, and without strong underpinnings to your film the audience will see right through what you are doing.

So as well as having an ambitious idea, 'high-concept' TV programmes need to be well founded on a bedrock of good research if they are not to fall over. So many aren't, and give all of us a bad name. At a recent Edinburgh TV festival session, old TV hands were asked what advice they would give to someone starting out in the business: The first said, 'Get knives for teeth, a leather hide for skin, drink seven pints of syrup a day and line your larynx with velvet to aid in your skills of persuasion. Stand your ground even when sinking. If sinking, take as many with you – that way you'll escape unnoticed.' The next: 'If you would kill your own grandmother for the right storyline then you are perfect.' The third: 'It's who you know more than what you know that will help you progress.' And the next: 'Do it. Lots of women and drugs.'

It's a sad view of the industry. One is increasingly attacked with it by strangers at dinner parties, and tabloid press writers. Perhaps pursuing conflict has gone too far, with more and more failing reality programmes seeking to bolster it artificially. This may often be the case now, but I think it's unnecessary, and due to a misunderstanding of the importance of authentic conflict in drama. And overall it is not a view I share. For if you find an ambitious story and give it strong *authentic* underpinnings and meaning, it can really break through; in fact many of the hits of the last few years, that have fully succeeded, have done this: In *The Boy Whose Skin Fell Off*, Jonny Kennedy, the hero, attempted to win a promise from Tony Blair to come up with money for research that would end for everyone the existence of the disease that was killing him. He died as soon as he had done so. It was so real it won an Emmy. In *When Big Chef Met Little Chef* Heston Blumenthal tried to save a whole chain of restaurants. Both programmes were ambitious, both were real, both mattered. Both gained nearly 20 per cent audience share on Channel 4, which is a good hit.

UNDERPINNINGS

So often in the cutting room a film feels wet and floppy; and what makes it feel so thin is that, almost always when I interrogate the production team, they do not know what underpins their story. I worked in the cutting room on a *Cutting Edge* with a talented young director, many of whose films lacked the edge that his talent seemed to promise. This one was about a person who needed mental help. The director didn't know whether the key character, who was trying to help the protagonist right through the programme, was a psychiatrist, a psychologist, a psychoanalyst or something completely else – and this in a film that depended on a professional cure.

Another talented team I worked with in America was making a film about a German free-love community, but even having filmed there, when I met them in the cutting room they didn't know some of the most basic things about the community, such as its history or what the kids thought. My most useful tool has become Wikipedia, which often tells me more in thirty seconds than that team seemed to have found in six months, though of course it is only a start and what it says has to be checked. To be successful at research – and it is the key part of film-making, without which none of the rest will work – is to be like the little child forever asking why. Unless you genuinely want to know the answer to every little 'why', your research may well remain incomplete.

The other vital part of research is to do it without prejudging. Don't get the facts to try to fit your story. Find the facts first and then create the story. Even more important, don't make decisions about characters before you know them; they will sense whether you are open to them or prejudging them. When I researched the two films about Robert Maxwell, the newspaper magnate renowned for his outbursts, I tried not to judge him while researching, though he appeared to many as an ogre as he bawled out his subordinates in front of me. I just wanted to find out about him. He sensed this lack of prejudice and so opened up.

My small Jamie Oliver team were all top researchers so they set off to do proper research in an open way, thinking out of the box. First the team identified schools that still provided their own school dinners in London and around, visiting many. If you remember, we were spending more and more money, and badly needed to make a start. Haringey was good enough for me to visit with them, but not good enough. It is worth reiterating that we set ourselves a high bar, and how with a schedule demanding that filming start, the weary team still spent a little more time. We needed an even stronger character to have a chance of a hit. And it paid off in spades when they found Nora Sands. The extra persistence was to prove well worth it. But then there was the next peak as we had to persuade Greenwich Council to agree to their schools being in the first programme, and research the area's schools in detail. For the short time you are making a programme, you should be the expert on the subject, and not need to rely on anyone else.

LANA SALAH

Assistant Producer on *Jamie's School Dinners*,
now a director, who found Nora

I must have seen 120 schools to find her. I think it really pays off to be diligent. When I first went to see her, the PR and the council person who came with me were mortified, because she speaks her mind, and she was basically telling me to eff-off. Who was I to be asking her questions? Go away! She was hysterical, and she was the person for me.

I don't think you ever find people sitting behind a desk – you have to get out there. People rely on hiding behind the telephone and the internet, but I think the best way is to get out there knocking on doors.

For the second film in the series we researched Essex, and found Jamie's old primary school, which had just got rid of its caterers. But I was keen we get more characters from around Britain. It makes for a livelier and more representative series. Right from my very first series, *Troubleshooter*, I had a wall chart of the entire British Isles, and tried to find stories from all over, and this applies just as well in any country.

I hoped to avoid the south east of England as far as possible, because there is so much of it on TV, and more importantly it is harder to find great characters. There are always exceptions; often they are immigrants to London, with the gift of the gab – like Nora.

So we researched further north for more schools suitable to film in, and came up with Peterlee in County Durham, one of Britain's most deprived areas (the word 'most' is always very useful in narration), and the team came upon Eden primary school. Together with the schools in Greenwich, Jamie certainly now had enough kids with whom to contend.

Thinking out of the box and being open-minded is vital for this research process. So when you begin proper research for any film or series, I suggest you first throw away the proposal; the commissioning editors will never remember what they asked for – they only care if the completed programme is good or bad! Your job is to make great programmes – to take the *essence* of the proposal but not to take it too literally. So your research must be open-minded at the start, if you are to make the leap of imagination to the new idea that will make the film work. You then need to remain open right through the research process, so that you can keep forging new links between the pieces of information, keep rethinking what your story might be.

I liken it to an internal Socratic dialogue, in which you are continually arguing why the film will and won't work as you come to terms with each new bit of information, and are forced to rethink all the earlier ideas. It is absolutely crucial to go on researching and researching, discarding nothing until your head is over-full and you've temporarily become a real expert on the subject. Only towards the end of this process will it be time to sit down to write that dramatic story arc, the outline script. But before that moment you'll need to find the very essence of the story, for the truth of the film is in the research.

The more detailed the research the better the film. Often of course you don't have time, so it can help, especially as a director, to research one film while finishing another so you can spread out the time. In this way I was able to spend three months discussing the *Troubleshooter* series with Sir John Harvey-Jones, and working out what to do, while I was still working on *Tomorrow's World*. When I eventually set off to research the first film, I was given one invaluable piece of advice by the Head of Science at the BBC, who then appeared to ignore the project: to spend a fortnight at the factory before starting to shoot. This might seem a huge luxury, but as a result we shot a multi-award-winning film using less than ten hours of film overall, and it had been so fully researched that its winning heart was shot in a single day.

The day started at 9.30 a.m. and Sir John had to leave at 4.00 p.m., so it was a short day at that! I didn't realise that films take longer to shoot. After that we needed only a few odd hours between his other engagements on the three further days that Sir John could give me before jetting off. His itinerary included seeing Gorbachev and ex-President Ford, righting the wrongs of the world, setting strategy for companies like Burger King and Intercontinental Hotels (of which he was Deputy Chairman), and chairing a host of institutions, among them *The Economist*, the Wildfowl Trust and Bradford University, of which he was Chancellor. He didn't have much time for me, but I didn't mind. I didn't know presenters were supposed to give you far more. And I lucked out because the film was so well researched that it really could be shot far more quickly than usual.

FINDING HOW TO TELL YOUR STORY

Here is a final tip on how to put over your story compellingly, and how to tell when your research is beginning to work and which way it should be going. When you write your script, how do you work out what the film is about, and the most difficult bit – how to get into it? Every time you go to a party, or the pub, and you are stuck talking to someone, try talking to him or her about your story. If their eyes glaze over, which at your first attempt they invariably will, you haven't got it right. Keep experimenting with the poor dinner guests you are sitting next to, or at dreary functions, to see how quickly you begin to bore them. You will eventually find the best way of telling your story.

At first I just couldn't work out what my very first *Troubleshooter* was about or why anyone should care. I tried telling people it was about the history of a toy company, and they were bored. Then I began to work out another way of telling this story. A 'city man' had bought into the company and would be in conflict with the owner. Still my listeners were bored – though a bit less so. Then one Friday evening, around a pool table in Stiffkey village hall in deepest Norfolk, far from London, and after a long hard week, I started telling the story of a man who had bought the world's biggest toy company, and had changed its name by adding to it his daughter's. I mentioned that she was a wonderful Manchester Jewish 'princess', and that she had become sales director, responsible for selling the toys. But people weren't buying them, and so the business her father had spent a lifetime building, with her name outside, was about to be lost to the city, if something didn't change. I described her make-up, her relationship with her dad. I now had a human story, and I had my film. I had a tragic hero and a tragic heroine.

I had no assistant producer or researcher – 'assistant producer' was my own job title – and I was trying to save money to be able to research as long as possible. It was only after about a week of research that the staff became used to me – so used to me that, in the pub one evening after work, the middle managers finally trusted me enough to begin to tell me the truth about the factory. They claimed it was badly run, and it was a mess, and it became apparent whose fault they thought it was.

FINDING THE SUBTEXT

Discovering the big truth, the important subtext of your story, as you research can be the most interesting part of film-making. Staying on the *Ark Royal*, on active service off Bosnia, it turned out that the everyday boredom of war was shown in the recompense and central role of endless dressing-up and meals. After much lunch and tea, I was given not only a list of who would be at my dinner and where they were sitting, but found a copy left on my bunk. Finally, on arrival on the poop deck, we were presented with a model of the table with each of us in position around it, complete with uniform and decorations, as the captain chopped a cork off a bottle of champagne with his sword!

Researching in India, I was guest in his palace of the Maharana of Udaipur, a man proud to be the leader of the world's oldest monarchy. He decided to take me on a trip round Rajasthan in a fleet of cars, with imperial guards in uniform escorting us in a pair of open jeeps at front and back. He ensured we left hours late, a bit like a pop star, but hordes of people were still lining the route and cheering as we drove through towns and villages. When we arrived at our destination we were carried in a palanquin through ancient streets only a couple of metres wide, with overhanging wooden balconies packed with onlookers.

Finally we reached the huge, decaying palace of the local squire, where we ate a meal with all the assembled nobles, lit only by candles.

Then came the moment when the Maharana, who had remained aloof for days, had to go on to the balcony to address a crowd of thousands outside. 'How long will this last?' he asked me, meaning how long will I be the star? 'Till TV comes,' I replied, 'along with popular culture and international celebrities, which will be very soon.' We began discussing the fast-changing India and world, and this became the subtext of *Troubleshooter Returns to India*. Sir John now knew just what to ask, and I could mould a script and scenes into a story.

Such time spent in research may seem impossibly indulgent, but it means that once you start the really expensive bit, shooting, you can work fast, for you will have the story and logistics already. Remember television is 90 per cent craft and 10 per cent art. This was particularly the case in that first episode of *Troubleshooter*, featuring the toymaker Tri-ang, where we not only spent the time researching but thinking through the pre-shooting script, from how we would set up our story of a hero combating a giant, Sir John and the factory.

So, to conclude, time spent researching is the cheapest. Good, solid, detailed, obsessive research saves on both filming and editing days, which are much more expensive, when you have to pay for editors, film crew, other professionals, equipment, cutting rooms and location expenses – and of course the presenter or host, if you have one. Because we were focused – a direct result of the detailed research – both the filming and editing were quicker, so we were actually saving money. When I am now called in to mend films it is invariably because they didn't have the right team in place and did not spend enough time researching to find the right characters and the right, true story to tell. So they ended up not knowing what to cover, which can often lead to an expensive muddle in the editing room.

THE IMPORTANCE OF SCRIPTS

Which brings us finally to the difficult thing we have been postponing and postponing, the script. I only ever write scripts on Sundays – the only time I can muster the energy. Then usually, when I come to do it I decide it needs to bubble a bit more in my head, and postpone to a Sunday ahead. Because scriptwriting is really tough: it means running a non-existent television programme in your head, and then writing it down.

Filming was now imminent on *Jamie's School Dinners*. The director and team had done brilliant research, found the school and dinner lady, persuaded the headmistress, council and all who had to give permission; time had run out, the first filming date was fixed and the team were desperately sorting yet more permissions and contracts. They didn't have a moment to spare and were somewhat bemused when I asked them where the detailed shooting script was. But at least we had an outline. Many directors are puzzled, since they assume that if you are following a story in which you do not know what is going to happen, a script or even an outline would be pretty pointless. Especially with time running out, it is not top of their priorities and the brief initial treatment will do.

SIMON DICKSON

Deputy Head of Documentaries, Channel 4

I'm pro-sincerity in documentary. Documentaries are extraordinary things – an art form, a political vehicle, an entertainment product, all rolled into one.

You've got a responsibility to approach that territory not just with openness and transparency but with imagination – crucially with imagination. And that means not simply turning up with a camera and filming what happens, and then thinking about how to cut it after the fact, it's about having some big creative, upfront thoughts about how to do right by the territory, so that the audience, when they come to it, feel that you have thought hard about making that subject accessible to them and come away feeling inspired and enlightened by having gone on that journey.

The script provides the all-important framework which makes you think through what each sequence will do, and from which you can then depart, and begin to think out of the box as you film and the story changes, just because you have one. You will hopefully depart from the script in interesting ways, at least knowing how and why you are making your decisions. Often, in my experience, it can be very hard to get directors to write scripts, and to consider what their film is about – to have a box outside which to think. And then it becomes even harder to change direction when things go wrong. But, with the less experienced anyway, it can be easier to convince them to write scripts. They haven't yet learnt not to.

So now we needed that structure and detailed script. Although the series producer had at first been slightly surprised by this notion of a detailed script, she was open to the idea and took it up with gusto. As we structured and wrote, we iterated and reiterated what the series was about, we thought and we argued. Best of all, in the very process of writing, she had had to think it through, and the huge benefit for me was that I could now run the programme in my head from the paper she had written, see what it felt like, and argue intelligently about it.

DETAIL

Michael Jackson, former Controller of BBC2 and Chief Executive of Channel 4, gave me one piece of advice I never forget and often repeat. He said successful TV is all in the detail. The detail convinces you, and makes you feel that you are right inside the story. Director Nick Mirsky

---

NICK MIRSKY

Series Producer, *Blood on the Carpet*,
now Documentary Executive, BBC

In the film about the battle for control of Interflora there was a line how fate, in the form of a cold quiche buffet, conspired to play a decisive role. There were a thousand Interflora delegates, and with the whole meeting poised, somebody claimed the board of management were even ripping off the delegates over the price of these lunches. And suddenly this cold quiche buffet, for which they'd paid over the odds, became symptomatic of the board that some of them were trying to get rid of, and they used that lunch to whip up the fury of all the delegates.

In the Radio One film it was pasta bows. Then when you did the fact-checking [of the detail] you'd sometimes get very depressed because you'd find Dave Lee Travis didn't live on a ranch in Iver Heath or wherever it was.

---

drove this point home when he made the first *Blood on the Carpet* about Gerry Robinson's battle to take over a hotel empire from Rocco Forte. His films ended up full of lines like 'It was over a spaghetti carbonara washed down with a bottle of . . .'

Only by writing it down do we really think through deeper layers of detail to find the all-important pieces that will bring our film alive, what motivates each scene, and if that motivation is enough. But often directors will argue that they just don't have time, and will do anything to avoid this tough moment of truth. Then I just say, 'Start shooting your film later,' because, unless it is an event that lasts a brief time and is about to be over, I believe you can never start a film too late.

Happily, the series producer on *Jamie* was pleased to create a detailed pre-filming script, and taking the time which she didn't have. It is vital to focus you (who are doing the writing), and to make you think what the film is really about, before preparing to jump out of the box. On *Jamie's School Dinners* we had postponed filming and we had waited while we found the right school and dinner lady, and we had come up with scripts for the series.

FIRST OUTLINE AND SEQUENCE HEADINGS

The script is a route map – a clear idea of where you are going. The first step is to create an outline, a structure with headlines and single sentences that provide a motivation for each scene. This structure needs to be precise, brief and thought out, rather than a stream of consciousness. It should ideally have one headline, and one sentence, for each scene. This, for instance, is the pre-shooting outline for the third episode of *Jamie's School Dinners* and for each episode there was something similar. It already contains a pre-title sequence – the reason for the film. Then it has around a dozen sequences – events we intend to film. We will continue to work on this script and refine it, and because things often turn out differently we will think out of the box when filming and amend it further; but at least the bones are there.

Over the page is an early version (before it has moved to columns) of the sequences in a typical episode – and, most important for the outline, an entire programme in two pages.

JAMIE'S SCHOOL DINNERS, FRESH ONE FOR CHANNEL 4, SCENE LIST EPISODE 3

PRE-TITLE SEQUENCE

JO is trying to revolutionise school dinners. He's been working for the last three months in individual schools and it's not been easy.

But now he faces an even bigger challenge: to take over school dinners across the London borough of Greenwich – 20,000 kids, 71 schools.

Can JO change the eating habits of Britain's children?

TITLE

PART ONE

KIDBROOKE SCENE???

It's the new school year and Kidbrooke school has been part of a school dinners experiment for the last three months. Today Jamie's come to meet head cook Nora to . . . ???

JAMIE MEETS HIS TEAM AND PANICS

But while the experiment continues at Kidbrooke the borough takeover looms nearer. And Jamie's not sure if he's ready. His team don't think they can do it. But JO decides to forge ahead anyway.

NORA'S PROMOTION

Its an enormous project and he can't do it alone. He invites Nora to dinner to offer her a job. She doesn't want to leave the kids but a night of debate and fine dining and she finally agrees.

MEETING WITH COUNCIL AT TOWN HALL

Jamie goes to Greenwich Town Hall for his first meeting with the council to lay down his/their terms for the takeover.

Leaving home, saying bye to Jules and kids and prep for meeting with team in the car.

NORA JOINS JAMIE'S TEAM

A very excited Nora arrives at Fifteen offices for first day at her new job. JO calls his staff around and bigs up Nora.

PART TWO

JAMIE SETS UP 'TO-GO' TABLE AT SCHOOL GATES

Before he takes over the borough he needs to crack how to get more kids into the canteen. At the moment only half the school eat Jamie's food. This plan will work for the day but for the long term he needs to make the canteen cool.

KIDS' TRIP AWAY

8 kids on houseboat help JO come up with a superbrand. Nora and JO each head a team on a city 'treasure hunt' to gather cool ideas. Through the night they come up with a brand name, packaging and canteen design ideas. 10 a.m. next morning head teacher arrives and on the deck of the boat they pitch their ideas. Will she agree?

MAKEOVER CANTEEN

But over the next week, do the numbers and takings go up?

PART THREE

GREENWICH HEADTEACHER DINNER AT KIDBROOKE

Jamie invites the headteacher from every school in the borough. Can he persuade them all to join his crusade?

NORA'S AUDIT

Nora visits kitchens/cooks of schools that have signed up, reports back to Jamie and his team. She discovers that many of them won't be able to mimic the Kidbrooke model.

OVERNIGHT CENTRAL KITCHEN TRIAL AT KIDBROOKE

To ensure quality across the borough, JO decides that a centralised kitchen may be the answer. Through the night Jamie and Nora take over Kidbrooke kitchen to make batches of five basic sauces that form the heart of the school dinner menu.

NORA TRAINS ONE PRIMARY SCHOOL COOK

Can Nora get Georgina, a new-style primary school cook who's never done much more than reheat packaged food, to cook Jamie-style using the new products?

PART FOUR

DINNER LADY CAMP

In three days, can Jamie and Nora whip 100 dinner ladies into shape? In a week's time they'll have to be cooking school dinners the Jamie Oliver way.

THE TWO-COLUMN SCRIPT

Most of these ideas, as it turned out, were filmed, and this is usually the case – the director thought out of the box when things turned out differently. Only when you have your first outline, so that you know what the film might be about, is it worth going back and beginning to fill in this outline with a full two–column script.

The first thing in this proper script is to articulate the beginning, and get the big question right. I always want two columns – on the left I have pictures and short descriptions of what is going on; in the right-hand column a commentary and what the protagonists might say. As you progress through the film, much of the dialogue will come from your research notes – what your characters said to you on first meeting. In filming you will be trying to get back to that raw first encounter and your first impressions.

As we go through the film, inevitably the script will contain less and less detail. But it will have a strong beginning, a reasonable middle, and an end for which you are at least aiming. This is from the first episode:

JAMIE'S SCHOOL DINNERS, FRESH ONE FOR CHANNEL 4
PROGRAMME ONE EARLY TWO-COLUMN SCRIPT

GENERAL NOTES

1) Need to convey the busy-ness and frenetic pace of Jamie's life – Fifteen, Sainsbury's Tefal, JO merchandise, book writing, wife and kids etc.

2) Early in Episode 1 do we need to see Jamie meeting with catering managers of the LEA to put scale of challenge into context, not simply relying on commentary to do so? If so need to select LEA soon.

3) Danger of endless scenes in kit-chens – be it school, Fifteen, his test kitchen – so let's keep on think-ing about ways of taking JO out of the kitchen wherever possible.

PRE-TITLE TEASE

Shots chips, baked beans, turkey twizzlers.	VOICE-OVER: Jamie Oliver is convinced school food is muck off a truck – food is crap.
	JO: *'I wouldn't give my dog the kind of muck that we feed our kids.'*
	Jamie Oliver is planning his biggest challenge yet – a huge experiment to change the way our kids eat.
	Jamie Oliver is leaving the world of fancy restaurants and £50 bills.
Shots JO in school kitchen uniform washing up/frying chips.	And taking on British school dinners.
	He is going to have to cook meals for just 37p.
	Upsound sync.
	And persuade the kids to eat them.
	'Where's my chips?'
	If he gets it wrong, the money'll run out, he'll have to spend his own, and the kids who are free to go out will vote with their feet.
	If he can pull it off in one school, Greenwich Council have agreed he will have to take over the cooking for 30,000 school kids in just one term, competing with some of the biggest catering companies in Britain. Can Jamie Oliver change Kidbrooke School and the way kids across Britain eat?
	TITLES
Jamie making kids' lunch and chat.	*'I care desperately. Can do it at home but what will my kids eat at school?'*
Intercut ghastly trays?	Half the price of prisons, lowest of the low. We shouldn't be feeding our kids this muck.

Jamie's shopping for lunch and feeding kids.

Kidbrooke School, meet cook, who says she thinks the food's OK.

Across London in Greenwich, Nora – Kidbrooke School's cook – is cooking a very different kind of lunch. She's been making school dinners for thirty years. She's agreed to let Jamie take over her kitchen – to see if he can come up with a formula for a new gourmet kind of school dinner.

And see shit lunches, interviews head.

'Jamie will get the shock of his life. We've tried everything to get them to eat healthily, not sure it can be done.'

Back to JO and kid chaos. Jules returns, relief, off to the ease of cooking posh food for the nobs in Fifteen.

Cut to posh food at Fifteen.

Chat with students about school dinners. Nerves about starting work in a school kitchen.

DAY 1

Monday 6.30 a.m.

Today is JO's first day in Kidbrooke School.

JO at home getting dressed and kids getting up.

'I feel sick . . . nervous . . .'

Nora opening up kitchen.

He's going to work under head cook Nora.

'I'm nervous . . . he'd better do what he's told . . . or I'll sort him out.'

Jamie leaves Hampstead in Maserati and drives to Greenwich – getting lost and late on the way.

It's Monday morning 7.00 a.m.

JO arrives at school gates flustered as he's late for his meeting with the Headmistress.

Before Jamie gets started on revolutionising school dinners for the kids at Kidbrooke School, he's going to work as a kitchen assistant under head cook Nora – who's been serving up school dinners for almost thirty years.

Asks couple of kids the way to the Head's office. Finds it and nervously knocks on the door. He tells us he feels like he's a little boy who's about to get in trouble!

But before Jamie has the chance to meet any of the kids he'll be feeding, the Headmistress has called him to her office.

Trisha lectures JO on swearing and school rules, and that it's Nora's kitchen not his and he must do as he's told. Then she breaks to him that she's going to introduce him to school in assembly and she expects him to say a few words.

JO nervous look to cam – he's not been expecting this.

JO in assembly being introduced to school and fumbling thro a speech.

Couple of kids lead him to school kitchen where he meets his new boss Nora, gets his uniform (and hairnet) and is put on traying-up duty placing greasy sausage rolls in the ovens and taking out the rubbish. Jamie gives us first impressions of the food. Gets screamed at by Nora for washing his hands in the wrong sink. Etc.

NB: Lana to stop Nora doing all the work before JO starts. And make sure he has nasty hairnet to put on.

Chaos as lunch service is running late and Nora blames Jamie for being slow. Jamie wonders how he's going to pull off any changes if it's a struggle to get the food out on time when it's business as usual.

Lunchtime bell rings. Kids charging out of classrooms and down corridors towards dining room.

JO (still in uniform) dishing out pizza and chips. Dining hall is in chaos and queue out of control. Nora shouts at him to get a move on and serve quicker.

Intercut with lots of kids pointing and making comments about Jamie.

Trisha chatting to a couple of kids about what's going on.

Cleaning up the kitchen, mopping and scrubbing. Gives us his initial impressions.

Leftover food laid out and staff (inc. Jamie) tuck in to leftover burgers and spaghetti hoops.

End of the day. Everyone in smoking room – fags and tea. Dinner ladies in normal clothes now and ask him what he thinks of the food. Then general dinner lady chitter-chatter. They ask about Jules and the kids, how much money he earns etc.

Say their goodbyes and Jamie speeds off in his Maserati.

Reaction from Nora (and the other dinner ladies?)

Jamie goes back to his office to report to his team. How hard the dinner ladies work, how rubbish the food is and what a task he's set himself up for. Dying for beer, and to talk food, so he takes his exec chef Arthur out for a drink.

SCRIPT CONTINUES WITH PROGRESSIVELY LESS DETAIL.

Twice as many kids as normal have turned up for dinner to see Jamie Oliver. And he's not helping matters by chatting with the kids in the queue.

'Isn't he gorgeous?'

'No he's not, he's fatter than he looks on the telly!'

'You seen his car . . .?'

Etc.

'He's very slow . . . Don't know how he's going to manage next week when he's doing his own menu. I know it's early days, but not very impressed.'

Then as you film you can fill in the script further. Eventually you will have something ideal for the cutting room! And in the meantime something for your executive producer to be able to help you with. This email shortly after filming began sums it up.

Dear Dominique,

Good to talk today. I am very excited about how Kidbrooke is going. I think that what would help me hugely now is if you could try to add to, and subtract from, the script, to reflect what we have shot so far and what we are intending to in Programme 1, particularly emphasising what Jamie is up against, and who he is up against — the plot points that turn the story — getting progressively bigger for, as I know you say to me, these are the key, but it is well worth mapping them, so we can control and create them . . . The success of the series, as I know you know, is to do with real drama and conflict, and really not knowing how Jamie will do at particular moments, or plot points that change the drama, which are a real challenge to him, and involves people battling with him, in an increasing way. This could well include especially kids, but also teachers, heads, shopkeepers, suppliers such as Scholarest as well as cooks, family, colleagues, Fifteen, and anything else you can think of.

I think Nora is inspired, especially if she keeps battling, but does the unexpected. However I think you need other stuff in Jamie's life that is revealing to cut against if it is possible.

Thank you so much for working like such a maniac on this. I am sure it is worth it because series with energy and passion and real drama, conflict and transformation are the greatest success, much thanks as ever,

Robert

Of course as you continue filming it doesn't quite happen like you expect! For instance, after editing we cut Jamie driving down to the school for the first time, in his Maserati, from the film because it didn't look right, driven by a Jamie flustered at being late. Driving such a car not only made Jamie seem rich and aloof, but worse, as he fought with the satnav and became lost en route, he began to appear a lightweight 'cheeky chappy' – just the image we needed to escape from – it stopped the audience caring. We replaced the Maserati with another more serious interview, a timeless piece which could go anywhere, in which Jamie was not only driving inside a more ordinary and unidentifiable car, but talking with passion about school dinners, and how they had got this way, rather than about himself, and being late and getting lost, which we will come to later.

NICK STRINGER

Marketeer for *Jamie's School Dinners*, now at ad agency BBH

When I saw first the edit of him sitting high in his big Maserati it was a bit in-your-face without him knowingly doing it, it was just wear out. It just felt that once again he was taking on another quest and it was him on his giant steed riding in to save the day and it just felt like that's really going to jar with the way everyone is feeling about it. Moving to David against Goliath was a much better way of approaching it.

Jamie never sped back to his restaurant in his Maserati either, and when he got there he didn't go out for a cheery beer with his executive chef Arthur, as the pre-filming script suggested. Instead he arrived back in his restaurant shattered, hungry and desperate for some proper food. Nora didn't react quite as expected either – luckily for us in some ways she was even better. But nonetheless, the very well researched direction was right, and when it went differently at least the director had something to work from, and understood the characters' motivations that had led us into this project.

Scriptwriting is dealt with in more detail later, but the importance of well thought out plans and scripts in creating a framework for being able to think out of the box cannot be overestimated.

For me this is even more important because, as we have discussed, many of the best films come from giving hungry but inexperienced people big breaks. And that makes it vital that they have really clear scripts before beginning, especially when following a story when you don't know what is going to happen.

However, if your research has been thorough, you should be able to properly understand your characters' motivations, and what is true to their essence, so you can write a pre-shooting script that guesses the drama and plot points of what your character might do with surprising veracity. For if you do this well you may be surprised how often, after wrestling with a film through the cutting room, it reverts closely to this original storyline. And you end up where you thought you were going – but by a slightly different route.

I have emphasised the importance of anal, obsessive and detailed research and pre-shooting scripts; but once you get filming remember just the opposite is needed. You need to have the courage entirely to ignore what you have written when things turn out differently, despite your research. And they always will. Although this is counter-intuitive, if you have no script, or route map, it can actually be harder to be as fluid and open as you need. At the inevitable obstructions, without a script you'll almost certainly end up like a rabbit in the headlights, especially if inexperienced. Then it can be very hard to make decisions about which way to turn – to find a new route that will work for you. And being open when you hit obstructions, and recognising them as such, is vital – because often they *are* the film! Which brings us to my most counter-intuitive but useful film-making tip, quoted back at me more than any other by the many directors whom I have mentored. When film-making remember that often *when it seems wrong it is right*.

WHEN IT IS WRONG IT IS RIGHT

Once I had a director who was making a film about a big new transport project. It required huge investment and international co-operation, a recipe for disaster. Two of the senior managers disagreed about it. One of them was at a big trade show in the UK, so we had arranged to interview him there, on his stand. We set up and lit the interview very nicely, with a backcloth of large pictures of the project.

Just as we were ready to start filming, his rival turned up, un-announced, and they started screaming at each other off in a corner. My film director carried on setting up his perfect interview scene, and waited. There was nothing in his script about his protagonists having a fight today. I told him that his film was happening right before his eyes, the very conflict that would bring the dreary project alive by making it human and a battle. He thought for a second and immediately told me that I was right. Then he walked quietly over to the protagonists, and asked if they would mind moving, and having their fight in front of his camera. The consequence? Predictably, all the energy went from their fight that he had neither expected nor filmed. He had gone to film one thing, and was incapable of thinking out of the box.

Another friend was setting off to make a film about a group of well-known Danish women, including a Member of Parliament, riding horses across Iceland. But politicians are even more competitive, and

---

THOMAS HEURLIN

Managing Director, Koncern TV, and Executive Producer

If you wanted control you'd do it in the studio, but we wanted to see a real under-pressure situation. So we decided to create this pressure by sending them out on horseback. It meant they'd be in a situation with much more pressure and you'd see them in situations that were exciting and new. It is an adventure where you don't know what is going to happen.

Everything in that production went wrong. The day before they were to leave for Iceland the original director got a bad back, so we had to get another director in twenty-four hours who had almost no time to get into the story.

We were also so late getting the series commissioned and casting in place that it was becoming dangerous to ride the horses because the weather in Iceland was getting too bad. It got so bad that the whole group couldn't move from the hotel, and that was where a lot of the drama began happening. Everything went wrong: all the things that we had planned did not go as anticipated, but it was not being shot, just because it was not happening as we expected. Instead you should say that you have another film, what are the possibilities that these circum-stances raise? It could have been an even more beautiful film because of all these unexpected things. It is always easy afterwards to say we should have done that and that, but it was difficult for people on the spot.

One of the main directors was so frustrated that he also left. It was the most chaotic production I'd ever been involved in.

sensitive, than TV producers, and the Member of Parliament was worried from the outset, particularly as she was filmed saying she was giving up smoking for the trip but then carried on doing so. One of them went off to hospital and others went to join her. They all fought about how it should work, the MP stormed off and back home, and disappeared for a week. This all before they even got on horseback. Everything went wrong.

'What a brilliant film,' I said to Thomas Heurlin, the executive producer. 'No,' he replied wistfully. 'Sadly they didn't shoot it, they were so worried about the riding film not happening.' It would have been a far better film – about people and politics rather than about people and horses – but once again this was a director who sadly did not think out of the box at the crucial moment.

After *Jamie's School Dinners*, Jamie wanted to get back to his roots in cooking, and in particular he wanted to discover more at first hand about the Italian cooking that had always been such an influence on him. This would be his next series, *Jamie's Great Italian Escape*. At first it wasn't easy, developing the right storyline, the motivation and the big question, for the new series. As I sought a motivation for the Italian trip Jamie was intent on making, I thought back to the five weeks that I had spent at America's top business school a few years earlier.

The BBC had invested a small fortune sending me on the 'Advanced Management Programme' at Wharton Business School in Philadelphia. But, surrounded by top managers from large corporations around the world, the thing that surprised me most was not globalisation, international finance or business strategy. It was when we were asked questions about our lives, and then sorted into groups, according to the answers we gave. Some of us were from softer professions, advertising and the media, others were real macho men and proud of it, bosses from General Motors, Caterpillar and big oil. I had expected to be grouped with people who were softer, more liberal, predominantly female, coming from businesses like mine – media, advertising and the service industries. I had not expected to find myself in a group of extremely macho men. But surprisingly, to me at least, in answering philosophical questions about our big worries in life, we ended up grouped almost entirely by age.

It is remarkable how much we have in common because of our ages, rather than our politics or interests. Nearly all the men in the business school had followed the recognised pattern like me – setting a dream in their early twenties and then, at the end of that decade, going through a big 'age-thirty crisis', questioning it all; then sailing off into their thirties, before the 'mid-life crisis' hit as they turned forty. Now, as I wrestled with the script of *Jamie's Great Italian Escape*, I thought back to when I had first met Jamie Oliver, right at the beginning, before *School Dinners*.

I was told then, by people who knew him well and cared for him, that he was a bit lost and needed looking after. Just past twenty-eight, he was beginning his own 'age-thirty crisis', about which we talked more and more during the filming of the series. Exhausted and under the enormous stress of *School Dinners*, which had become a real campaign as well as a TV show, he now needed a break. Of course it was just that doubt, sometimes lack of confidence about bringing off the huge project and not being a big-head, that had made *School Dinners* so good.

Jamie would say things like, 'Mentally life is really tough right now because I have nothing but fear for the future of dinner ladies because I am genuinely scared and quite out of my depth.' Seeing what a tough time he was having and looking at the whites of his eyes, we would believe him. Our doubts about the project were genuine. At one point, worried, I even asked the Head of Programmes at Channel 4 what would happen if Jamie didn't succeed, because at times we really thought he wouldn't. He answered, 'Follow what happens and show if he fails, at least he tried,' which was a relief at least to me.

Unlike his friends Jamie had never had a gap year. He had never really travelled, except for work, and then usually in some style. He had been with Jules since they met in their teens, and had been working ever since. He never stopped. Sometimes he sped so fast – almost as though not to think – that he seemed to be suffering from attention deficit disorder. But Jamie is also a man of soul, and it seemed to be worth a shot at trying to explore this. At first I wanted to take him off to India, but that would have meant being a very long way from Jules and the children for weeks on end. So we settled on Italy, where he really wanted to go, as its food had inspired him in the first place.

I joined late, after the team had been chosen, researched round Italy, and come back to write a script. I tried to give it some more structure, starting with our motivation – Jamie getting away from it all, something that was true to his character. Best of all, his thirtieth birthday would take place in the final week of filming. So we made this the culmination of the script, and the series – a big family birthday party in Italy. Jules and the kids would come over to Italy to celebrate the big day, and – Jamie having rediscovered himself and come to terms with his thirties – the happy family would sail off into his next happy decade, reunited, visually and in fact. A universal coming-of-age theme with a happy ending.

But it didn't turn out that way. Towards the end of the filming of this outline script I got a desperate call from the director saying that Jules couldn't come to Italy. Could I please do something to try to persuade her? The answer was that, knowing Jules, it wouldn't be easy. She is fantastically natural on TV but that also means she usually does what she wants. So how should we react? It seemed to me that if this was indeed the truth, and what Jules really wanted, then maybe, maybe – although it seemed wrong, it was right. Go with the truth, think outside the box and follow what is happening, even if it is the opposite of the script. So instead of a family party we filmed a wistful Jamie on a hillside with just a couple of old friends pondering the future, which was far stronger, because it was real.

ALAN HAYLING

Commissioning Editor for Michael Moore, Channel 4

In the middle of making Bowling for Columbine *9 / 11 happened, and Michael completely lost confidence in the film, because he couldn't see why it was relevant any more. There was this huge thing that happened, and suddenly it felt like this film was about a relatively little incident. After 9 / 11 the truth is the film completely lost its way because Michael just lost confidence that it was relevant. But then instead of following his script Michael picked himself up and began to interrogate the general role of America in the world. Then he found that, near Columbine, there was a huge arms factory, and one of the kids' fathers worked there. So the film became much richer through interrogating links with the main story. It was three months of a very difficult period in the cutting room, but it made the film much stronger in the end. If you centre a film, you can hang other things off it; it was a question of being able to try to hang even 9 / 11 on it.*

JAN TOMALIN

Former Controller, Legal and Compliance, Channel 4,
MD, Media Law Consultancy

Don't ever sacrifice the truth for your format. Seeing the hero fail can be just as dramatic as seeing them succeed. Don't cheat the audience by faking an outcome to fit the format — I have seen that damage not only the broadcaster's reputation but the producer's and the talent's reputations too.

When it is wrong it is right really is a tip I bang on about, because it can be one of the hardest to believe, especially when you feel your film is falling apart, which can happen at any time. In the final editing of *Jamie's School Dinners* update, we received news that a pub which was pioneering cooking kitchenless Lincolnshire school dinners, and on which Jamie had pinned his hopes, was pulling out. But despite the director's worry it was no disaster, it just needed a bit of re-editing of the film to get this story going. It may be sad, but it is something happening, and it is real. So people who work for me really remember *when it is wrong it is right*, and so should you.

OUT-OF-THE-BOX SUCCESS STORIES

Thinking out of the box is not only important when researching, script-writing and filming, but almost anywhere in television, or in any line of creative or innovative business. For instance it is hardly surprising that many of the most successful, and award-winning, films come from 'the wrong place' – areas where people don't quite know how to do it, and so are forced into lateral thinking.

The BAFTA for a Science Programme didn't come from the BBC's Science Department. It went in 1993 to *Pandora's Box*. This was a brilliantly iconoclastic and challenging view of technological advance made by a strange film-maker in the Documentary Department – a department that never 'did' science. And when the Science Department did manage to win its BAFTA a couple of years earlier, it was not for science! The seldom-awarded BAFTA for Originality was given for

Troubleshooter, which was really a current affairs series about business, starring Sir John Harvey-Jones, a series that I had made in my innocence from my base in the Science Department. And a couple of years later the arts series *The House* won the BAFTA. This challenged the Royal Opera House in a way I don't think an arts producer would have thought of – it was made in the Documentary Department. Different genres banging into each other force people to think out of the box.

And what about presenters (or hosts)? Who would have thought that a fat, dishevelled, Sir Toby Belch-like businessman like Sir John Harvey-Jones would be a hit on television? Luckily for me, not the Documentary Department or anyone else. Or a nun presenting a show on paintings? Sister Wendy had been living a secluded life in a nunnery, and sounded a most unlikely arts presenter, but she became one of the most successful. A friend of mine bumped into a flamboyant black New York art collector in the Photographer's Gallery and got talking. My friend thought out of the box, sensing a star, and made Alvin Hall into the money expert who fronted *Your Money or Your Life* and a host of other shows, becoming Britain's leading personal finance presenter.

STEPHEN LAMBERT

Chief Executive, Studio Lambert, makers of *Undercover Boss*

When we had Gordon Ramsay as a mentor on Faking It, *little did I realise what an amazing property he could be turned into. I've never ended up with a property like that – shows that one has built around the most famous television chefs, for instance, or other onscreen talent. Other people think in different ways.*

The director who thought in different ways to spot Gordon Ramsay also thought out of the box when, in the background of a shoot she was doing in the River Café restaurant, she spotted a young assistant who seemed more like a barrow boy than a chef. TV chefs had been established chefs or cooks before, but Jamie Oliver was lively, good-looking, very young and, best of all, unlikely.

Had she been lucky, or had she 'spotted' the luck passing her nose that others would have missed? Given that she went on to spot many

JON ROWLANDS

Former Head of Development, BBC Factual,
Creative Director, Renegade

I passed on Graham Norton. I liked him and thought he was great but I could never see how he would translate – what he could do beyond his waspish stand-up. I just saw rude and brusque and very very edgy, and I didn't make the leap. Now I am much more open-minded about looking at playing talent out of position. Don't be bound by convention. Don't think just because they do this, they couldn't do that.

You've really got to keep your eyes open for new talent. People completely forget about radio, but they get through far more guests than TV, and the quality of the guests is stunning, plus they haven't got an agent and haven't thought about TV, and maybe you can find the new new thing.

other out-of-the-box presenters, the latter is more likely. Mary Queen of Shops, who troubleshoots failing shops – again a title that sums up the character – looked equally unlikely to me to be a business expert, yet she is another success.

All these out-of-the-box presenters are not only counter-intuitive, but passionate about what they do. Television is driven by energy and passion. I am forever being sent tapes of potential presenters, just like potential producers, who are interested in doing anything – but they are passionate about nothing but fame. I'm not looking for them; I *am* looking for someone who has a passion about a subject, someone who will bring something extra to it, someone who will take the subject out of the box.

So, in conclusion, it's simple but surprisingly hard. It's all about having a box in the first place, and then thinking out of it. If you set out to film a love scene in a corn field with soft evening sun and beautiful running in slow motion as the lovers approach each other, and it pours with rain and they fight, well, don't stop till the weather changes. It *could* be far more romantic to film love in the pouring rain, and far more dramatic to see the argument. TV directors are control freaks, but occasionally to make a great film they have to let go. Television, like so much in life, is full of paradoxes, and to succeed you should try to embrace the opposites to succeed.

So before you begin filming, find great characters, do the research, think OUT OF THE BOX, and remember, it is not only about having a really clear script, and then diverting from it, but also trying at all times to be open and think laterally what your film is about, who the presenter is, or the characters are, and how you're making it. And it's a great advantage to be working in a new area or a wrong area – that makes you really think OUT OF THE BOX!

Three

NARRATIVE DRIVE

AND FILMING

SETTING OFF TO FILM

So you have found your characters, worked out how to turn them into heroes and come up with a script from which you are willing to be diverted. Now you have to go and make the film. Which is scary, because on location you have to think on five planes at once. It is like being a surfer, and to stay on top of the enormous, winning wave you have to concentrate simultaneously on organising all the logistics, making your film visually interesting and persuading contributors, while motivating your team and journalistically telling the story.

And telling the story is the toughest of all. For it means that you have to store everything you have shot in your head, fitting it to your script and then, when the story changes and (for instance) another character comes to the fore, you have to think back through everything you've shot, edit that in your head into a new script, and thus work out exactly what to shoot next – all while filming and in seconds . . . Phew! It is all shatteringly tiring, one reason I hardly direct any more, wonderful though it is.

THE STORY ARC OF THE FILM

First there is one fixed rock, and finding this rock is hugely important, although it is often half-submerged and not that obvious. It is the big question of the film – the quest. In a way it is the reason for writing the script in the first place, for it helps you to find that rock.

This chapter is all about that big question, which leads to a big answer: the NARRATIVE DRIVE – the arc of the film, which needs continuous honing not only while creating the script, but also while filming and again while editing. Then we will come to creating sequences each of which needs a smaller question leading to a smaller answer, all of which should contribute to the answer of the film.

Most successful documentary or factual films are stories, and stories need this story arc if we are to be moved by their NARRATIVE DRIVE. We all tell and retell our own stories to ourselves, and then to others to suit us, giving structure to our stories and thus meaning to our lives. Telling our own stories is a defining characteristic of humans. On to the mass of chaotic material that makes up our lives we try to superimpose cause, effect and narrative. I often wonder if some of the stories I tell and retell myself about my youth have anything to do with reality at all – for instance, the quest to become a BBC sound trainee.

As I tell this story to myself, I spent years pushing trolleys of film, and working in the library, interspersed with unemployment, until I finally won the job as sound trainee at the second go. The evening before I was due at the BBC in London, for my first day as a trainee, I was getting on a train in Avignon, in the south of France, in a fit of indecision over whether to go back to the BBC at all. But did it happen that way, or is this just my 'in the beginning'? Did I leave my car, a convertible Karmann Ghia, in Avignon, to continue to Greece without me? Had it really cost £70? Had I really made the front wing myself out of fibreglass, so that it looked a bit like wedding-cake icing? And had I even driven it happily through London with no footbrake at all but only a handbrake?

Was I shoved on the train from Avignon having just been beaten up and armed with a bottle of brandy by a love I was now leaving for the BBC? Did I really arrive at the BBC straight from the overnight train in a bloodied T-shirt and hungover, to find all the other new trainees wearing suits? Remember this was the seventies, I had hair below my shoulders and thought such people only existed in old films. I have told these and many other stories to myself and others over and over again, embroidered and adapted, and all my stories make me what I am. Though how much they have changed over time and in the telling I can never be sure.

As humans we have a deep need to read, hear or view stories that help us create our own tales and meaning – the archetypal stories that enable us to make sense of our own lives. Which is why traditional storylines work so well.

In the traditional story, the one I use in TV, in which we follow the hero through the ups and downs of various trials to see if they win out in the end (my TV career story – anyway in the way I tell it to myself – as well as my films), the hero first needs a quest with which we can empathise.

ASKING THE BIG QUESTION

In fact the key to the success of any film is finding the big question to which we are made to want to know the answer, and clearly understanding the quest before embarking on any shooting. The word 'question' comes from *quaerere*, to ask or seek, and 'quest', the act of seeking, has of course the self-same derivation. It took on the romantic sense of an 'adventure undertaken by a knight' in the Middle Ages. In finding the question, you are articulating this *quest*. Later we will look at how you rephrase the question in the light of what you've shot, but for now, before you go shooting, what is the question you are trying to answer as you film?

A typical example of the process of finding the question is the series *When Big Chef Met Little Chef*, about the makeover of a once-popular roadside restaurant chain – a format about to be copied in the US and elsewhere. The Little Chef chain of roadside and service-area restaurants was old-fashioned, and had been having a tough time under the on-slaught of the likes of McDonald's and Burger King. An initial idea was for Jamie Oliver to buy the chain and try to transform it – what challenge and jeopardy, what a film. Even better, Jamie, with his Essex pub background and down-to-earth ways, seemed ideal for it. However, instead of being bought by Jamie, it was snapped up by a private equity group, though they too were interested in having a celebrity chef help them. However, rather than Jamie, the improbable star for this project was Channel 4's latest signing, chef Heston Blumenthal. He seemed the unlikeliest man to take on the challenge. In his one small restaurant in the Home Counties, the Fat Duck, he serves a set menu that costs £540 for two (inclusive of service and wine) and encompasses such culinary oxymorons as bacon-and-egg ice cream, salmon poached in liquorice and lashings of smoke and mirrors. Little Chef needed ordinary on a budget.

I was very worried about doing the programme with Heston, but remember that important maxim 'when it's wrong it's right'. The key was to make as much as possible of Heston being a fish out of water, the wrong man, so that it would now be a meeting of opposites with as much conflict as possible. We spend a great deal of time trying accurately to phrase the quest. In the end effort spent on this will save you lots of time later, as it is working out what your film is really about. And it has to be a quest that is continually leading somewhere, with doubt about whether you'll reach that destination so the audience is hooked.

One Easter, led by executive producer Juliette Rice and series producer Helen Richardson, we set out to articulate the question in *When Big Chef Met Little Chef*. This was the first stab at the story; the 'restaurant' is the Little Chef where Heston would trial his new food.

**WHEN BIG CHEF MET LITTLE CHEF,
TWO FOUR FOR CHANNEL 4
FIRST OUTLINE PROGRAMME 1**

First meeting between Heston and Little Chef.

Heston gets to know restaurant.

Stunt 1 – what do people think of Little Chef food?

First solutions – as extreme as possible.

Stunt 2 – the trial (back at Heston's Fat Duck).

Intro of Heston's new food to restaurant.

Stunt 3 – Little Chef management come to try.

Problems at restaurant.

New approach fails – Heston has to go back to drawing board – why did I take this on?

It is absolutely right to block out the sequences first, to be open before you come to write a more detailed script and articulate a question.

The next iteration three weeks later took the outline to script. This first version now contained far too much, particularly in the pre-title. This again is absolutely right – a necessary second step, unless you are a genius, and can get straight to the end. This is the whole pre-title at this stage, complete with a first stab at the question at the end.

**WHEN BIG CHEF MET LITTLE CHEF
TWO FOUR FOR CHANNEL 4
PROGRAMME 1 DRAFT PRE-TITLE**

VOICE-OVER
Heston Blumenthal is the world's most famous culinary wizard. At his restaurant, the Fat Duck, he's conjured up dishes that shocked us all: snail porridge and bacon-and-egg ice cream are just some of the wild and extravagant concoctions he's created. But taste is only the starting point for Heston.

HESTON

Food is the only experience which uses all our senses, so as a chef I can play with taste, sound, sight, feel when I create a dish. But I'm also getting into the subconscious – food evokes memories, and creates new experiences. Amazing!

VOICE-OVER

And he's taking the world by storm: three Michelin stars; his restaurant judged as being second-best in the world; diners prepared to wait months to get a table. Nobody can get enough of Heston's particular brand of magic – molecular gastronomy.

HESTON

Molecular gastronomy means that I approach ingredients scientifically – what is a potato, how do potato molecules react when they're heated? It's like a scientific mission, where the aim is to come back with the perfect essence of potato.

VOICE-OVER

But someone else is after Heston's magic touch – and they're going to take him a long way from the fat wallets and success of the Fat Duck.

Little Chef has over one hundred and eighty restaurants . . .

[SECTION ON LITTLE CHEF'S PROBLEMS.]

IAN PEGLAR (*Managing Director, Little Chef*)

Little Chef can't be allowed to die, it's been with us too long, we're a British institution – and people used to love us. We're the home of the breakfast, generations of people remember coming to Little Chef and loving it, but we're in a different world now. We need someone to reinvent us, and I think Heston can do it.

HESTON

I loved Little Chef as a child – have clear memories of eating there – I loved the breakfasts and free lollies, it can't die. But suppose I fail? I've only ever run two restaurants – nothing like this, never done food on anything like this scale. And the most difficult thing is to rescue something that's already gone wrong.

VOICE-OVER

And will the magic that's won Heston a worldwide reputation help him save a chain of roadside cafés? Or has Heston bitten off more than he can chew?

The question is that very last piece of voice-over.

A fortnight later we have reduced the pre-title but are rearticulating the big question at the end of the draft below:

WHEN BIG CHEF MET LITTLE CHEF
TWO FOUR FOR CHANNEL 4: DRAFT PRE-TITLE

In a last-ditch attempt to save the other 185 restaurants, Little Chef's management has called in Britain's top chef, Heston Blumenthal.

But will Heston be able to come up with the right food at the right price that'll put Little Chef back on the map, and bring customers flocking back? Will he be able to convince staff and managers that he's doing the right thing?

Can a Big Chef save the nation's Little Chef?

And a couple of days later we begin to refine it, tightening the quest while building the challenges en route, the sub-questions. I have indicated these elements in the left-hand column.

WHEN BIG CHEF MET LITTLE CHEF
TWO FOUR FOR CHANNEL 4: DRAFT PRE-TITLE (VOICE-OVER)

The Quest	(V/O) In a last-ditch attempt to save the ~~other 185 restaurants,~~ chain Little Chef~~'s management~~ has called in Britain's top chef, Heston Blumenthal.
The Challenges/ Hurdles en route	But will Heston be able to transform the menu?
	Get customers back in?
	Create a brand-new Little Chef?
	And come up with the right food at the right price that'll put Little Chef back on the map, and bring customers flocking back? Will he be able to convince staff and managers that he's doing the right thing?
The Big Question	Can a Big Chef save the nation's Little Chef?

And finally, six months later, after filming and editing the end of the pre-title, the question is not so different, just a little simpler, because it was worked out first. There are of course some of the best bits of synch between each of the commentary lines.

WHEN BIG CHEF MET LITTLE CHEF
TWO FOUR FOR CHANNEL 4: END OF PRE-TITLE AS TRANSMITTED

(V/O) To succeed Heston will have to transform the food.

Reinvent the Little Chef brand for the twenty-first century.

And persuade the Little Chef boss to put his money where his mouth is.

It's a huge clash of cultures. How on earth will a chef famous for culinary perfection turn out meals for under a tenner?

CREATING SEQUENCES

Once you have identified the film's *big question*, everything you film has to be contributing to its answer. Just like fractal theory, every scene in the film needs to be structured like the whole film, but in miniature. Each scene needs to start with a small question, just like the big question of the film, leading to a smaller pregnant answer, which in turn leads to a further question. The absolute test for every scene is whether its own smaller questions and smaller answers contribute to the big question of the film. Only if they do should they be there. Narrative drive, the arc of the film, is small questions and small answers which all contribute to the big question and big answer. I throw out, or change, so many scenes because there is no question. Without a question (which can be implicit as well as explicit) there is no reason to watch the scene, and without relevant and coherent questions no reason to watch the movie. For we have to embark on a scene with the expectation that it will take us somewhere different at the end than where it began.

Coming up with the big question of the film, and sequence sub-questions, for *Jamie's School Dinners* was a similar process. Four months after I had received the initial call asking me to work on the Jamie film, we had found a great character to play alongside him, we had a brilliant team in place and were all ready to film. Now, with the script, we had finally found the big question, and articulated it as ever in fairy-tale terms. An evil giant – big bad food – was rampaging round the land, leading to illness in children and even eventually to their early death. The government didn't seem to know what to do about it. So the big fairy-tale question became: could plucky Jamie slay the monster of big bad food, and show the wicked king – i.e. the government – that it could be done better, across a whole London borough? Remember, fairy tales help when articulating your quest.

FORMATTING

Now filming was about to begin, and Jamie might want to charge straight in and answer the big question immediately. The obvious thing would be to cook school food his way, straight away, to slay everything in sight at once. But this would barely last one film, let alone a series. I remembered the original miserable recce in the heat-exchanger factory all those years ago, for the pilot of the first *Troubleshooter* business-makeover series.

Sir John Harvey-Jones had been responsible for many hundreds of companies around the world, when he ran ICI, and had honed his forensic skills to be able to visit any of them for half an hour. In fact he thought he could tell pretty much the state of any company and what was wrong with them by looking through their accounts on paper, and then come up with a solution. That took him about ten minutes! If you remember, that initial visit to Herefordshire lasted a mere half-hour. Not only was it a very boring company with a very boring product, but within twenty minutes of walking in Sir John was saying that he knew exactly what was right and wrong with the company.

But, as I explained to him, if I filmed this reality, not only would it be boring, I would be making a forty-minute film out of a thirty-minute visit, and most of it, in fact the key part, involved him looking at pieces of paper. No one would want to watch this. We needed instead a story which would illustrate what he did in his head, show what the paper was telling him, and how much it mattered to him – and, even more important, how much it mattered to the workforce.

So we divided the film into sections, each one of which would contribute something new to our understanding of what was right and wrong with the company. First we would introduce the company with its problems and Sir John in anticipation at home. Then in each section we might meet a different person or persons and come up with a new part of the answer to the puzzle. Sir John would meet the boss, but only to get an initial view of the questions. Then he would arrive on the shop floor accompanied only by a middle manager, express shock, and tear his hair out as my able PA Jane Ashford propelled assembly workers into the hapless manager's path, and we would make sure it was workers who would really say what was wrong. Then, like a TV detective, he would investigate deeper for clues, visiting the marketing person to discover what was wrong with the product, and so on with the salesmen, the advertisers, the drivers etc. Each time people would bring out the problems and there would be drama. Then he would go off to investigate further before the big conclusion.

NARRATIVE AND FORMATS

These sections or sequences became the same each week – the format points. However, there turned out to be another problem. Sir John's solutions for the failing companies tended to be very similar, coming apparently from a very small selection of three: reduce the costs; put up the price by differentiating the product and making it look fancier, probably with nicer packaging or a bit of design; and finally send the managers away to a hotel to talk about the problem. If the problem was worse he would add one more: fire the middle management and/or boss. And if it was entirely intractable he would say sell the company. Using all these solutions each week would make the format just too similar, particularly when the series was recommissioned over many seasons – after all, the programmes were supposed to follow a format, not be repeats, and for that we needed different endings!

So again we had to divide out the solutions that came to the fore week by week while of course remaining true to what Sir John actually thought. As it turned out, with the first series of six films, in two the boss went following Sir John's visit; in two the part of the company they were best known for was sold; in one a fancier design was adopted – and in the last, Morgan cars, defying all, they didn't want his changes, including putting up the price, despite long waiting lists (good to have one in a series that disagrees, and doesn't work out as expected!).

While *Troubleshooter* might have been the precursor of makeover shows, and was loosely formatted, one of the parents of the true formats, from *Faking It* to *Wife Swap* and *Kitchen Nightmares*, was *Back to the Floor* (which of course, when given a makeover, became the winner of them all in the US, *Undercover Boss*). For each episode we would establish a problem, a reason for the boss to go back to his own shop floor. We would then film the boss leaving his palatial home and changing into work clothes at the factory. Ideally we wanted him not to be recognised, even right through to the end of filming, though we seldom found this possible. Then the boss would have a different task each day as a worker in the business, interacting with customers who had no idea who he or she was, before returning to the penthouse suite and managers to give them the news of what he or she had found, and what needed to change as a result. And all this would take place in five days. It was a true fairy tale of the prince going among the paupers, as a fish out of water, to discover the truth about the kingdom.

The challenge of formatting was just the same with *Jamie's School Dinners*. For our narrative to engage the viewers, and have them identify

---

STEPHEN LAMBERT

Creator of *Faking It*, *Wife Swap* and *Undercover Boss*

Fairy tales are a good way of looking for ideas – fairy tales that are going to lead to this idea of conflict.

Most of the projects that I've been successful with have been fish-out-of-water ideas. So the faker in Faking It *is immersed in a world they know nothing about – which is why it was always crucial that the faker wasn't interested already in that world, because they would then know too much about it.*

When we made Faking It *in America, for TLC, they kept wanting us to find fakers who had always wanted to be whatever it was! And that killed it, because it was the fact that the person knew nothing about it that made the show, as with the cellist who knew nothing about being a DJ being immersed in that world of contemporary music. It was the quality of fish out of water.* Wife Swap *is a classic example. They each immerse themselves in a world of completely different values.*

and care for the *quest*, we needed those authentic scenes with small questions and small answers, rather than Jamie just charging in and doing it all straight off.

We had already decided on a structure of four one-hour programmes. The one-hour made obvious sense: it is what Channel 4 plays in prime-time, and anyway half an hour is too short to allow a rich and multi-layered drama to fully unfold (once you subtract commercials, the hour on Channel 4 is around 48 minutes, and a half-hour only 24 minutes). And to have made them longer would make it harder to keep the audience engrossed. Four episodes was a somewhat random choice, but it seemed the minimum to make a proper series which could be marketed and make an impact. We also worried that, given the limits of Jamie's time, and the subject matter itself, we would be able to find material for only four good hours. Less is almost always more when it comes to how ruthless you are at cutting down your material.

Now that we had decided this structure, each programme would have to have its own question and answer, and then itself need to be divided into sub-questions and answers.

So even before we came up with outlines for the programmes, we needed to break down our hero's big quest into smaller tasks, each with jeopardy and a question of its own, the answer to which would lead us on to the next one, and contribute to the main quest. The big question was: could Jamie cook healthy food for 37p and get kids to eat it? This would be against the background of the question: would the government listen? So together with Jamie we worked out the following sub-structure for the big question. Through it all he would be up against Nora, who would transform into his helper.

1. First he would cook as an assistant in Nora's kitchen, cooking her junk food to her instruction. He would soon find out the problems, which wasn't easy for him. But how would he cope and what would he discover?

2. Then he would tentatively set forth to battle, trying to come up with his own healthier recipes for 37p. Could a chef used to fancy ingredients do this?

3. He would then cook his new recipes going head to head against Nora, who would continue to cook her usual fare. The kids would be able to choose which they wanted. How would his food do?

4. If they mostly chose Nora's familiar junk at the end of Programme 1, as seemed likely, it would show the size of the problem. So Jamie would head up north, to younger children in one of the most deprived parts of Britain, to try to discover why they chose junk from an early age, and to see if he could conquer them by taking over one class. This would be Programme 2.

5. Then we expected he would return to London, having discovered that the only thing that would persuade children to try the new and unfamiliar is removing choice. Nora's junk food would now be banned and she would have to cook only his. But would the kids choose to eat it or prefer to make other choices – from no dinner at all to going out, if allowed?

6. With children hard to convert, despite no choice, Jamie would try new tactics, like showing them how chicken nuggets are made, mixing the nastiest parts of a chicken in a blender. Would this convert them?

7. Then he would address the question of how to roll out his new school dinners across many schools throughout a borough. This would mean teaching hundreds of dinner ladies to cook differently. Would this be possible?

8. Rather than teach them all in their individual school kitchens – not easy – he would take them all to dinner lady camp. But would this succeed?

9. Then the roll-out across the borough would begin, with five schools cooking and serving Jamie's dinners exclusively. How would the dinner ladies, with only a small amount of training, cope? Would the kids eat anything?

10. With the dinner ladies finally cooking, and the kids eating, could he now persuade the politicians to support it round the country, and even Tony Blair to back it?

The End!

You have to be clear about the point of each of these sequences, its question, before you make your film, and then make the question clear in the script. In the US the audience is even less forgiving if you fail on this.

JANE ROOT

Former President, Discovery Networks, and Controller BBC2, now CEO, Nutopia

Storytelling is different in the US: it is much more upfront – you have to tell people what is going to happen. Lateral, meandering storytelling doesn't work, people lose interest much quicker, they have shorter attention spans. They want to know why something is a big deal. Networks are complete masters in the art of understanding an audience, so you have to know their audience really, really well and you have to get inside their heads.

VICTORIA DUMMER

Senior Vice President, ABC Alternative Series, Specials and Late Night, USA

In America, if you don't hook people right at the top they've changed the channel, and if you don't give them very clear signposting on 'How am I supposed to feel here? How am I supposed to feel there?' it's very difficult to engage them in the rest of the programme. Very clear signposting is needed. Where are we going, how is this story informing the next beat?

So you have constructed a narrative drive with small questions and small answers leading to big questions and big answers, and have made these clear. Now you have to film it. I often think of filming like farming. The script is a recipe, but the director has to go out in all weathers and fight the elements to grow the ingredients that will cut into the film, to give the strongest narrative drive. En route the director may find that although some ingredients have grown in abundance, others may not have grown at all – but there will almost certainly be some surprising ones you didn't expect! The cutting room, the kitchen of film-making, is like *Ready Steady Cook*. You have to make the best with what ingredients you have.

Not knowing what will happen in filming is particularly scary for American network television – one reason the *Back to the Floor* idea struggled to get on to an American network, despite it being so successful when it did. When another network finally took on *Jamie's School Dinners* it combined it with another series, *Jamie's Ministry of Food*, which was Jamie's attempt to change how the whole town of Rotherham ate, to create *Jamie's Food Revolution*, but even then they found it worrying.

VICTORIA DUMMER

Senior Vice President, ABC Alternative Series, Specials and Late Night, USA

We haven't done a lot of shows like Jamie's Food Revolution, *because it's not a formatted show. It is really as close to a documentary as we have ever done and that is scary for us. It's much better for us if we know what beat we need to hit. We need to do this, then we need to do that, then we need to do this, and then we have a happy ending.*

Or in the case of an arc show [the opposite of closed episodes, in which the action continues over many episodes] *we need another problem, or issue, that has got to be resolved in the next programme. We're much happier and feel much safer with at least a format. We can have deviations from the road, but at least we have a road.*

For modern hits, content that can be appreciated internationally and a slight feeling of unpredictability help, hence the unexpected success in the USA of *Undercover Boss* and the achievement of getting near-documentary to network TV as *Jamie's Food Revolution*, with a bigger audience than *Ramsay's Kitchen Nightmares*, even combining two different ideas so it's more diffuse than the original. But seeing the audience lap up these shows, the networks are coming round to the British model of brave and unpredictable single stories, at least sometimes.

THE FIVE DIMENSIONS OF FILM-MAKING

When you don't know quite what is going to happen everything depends on tending and gathering the right raw material, the filming.

Now we know that a strong script is vital, and then, equally important, thinking out of the box minute by minute while filming, so that

CHARLES WACHTER

Co-Executive Producer, *Jamie's Food Revolution*

School Dinners *alone is not enough for network TV. Hollywood wants this plus this,* Extreme Makeover *meets* Survivor. *You need to be broad, to hit all the demographics – dads, mums, families, kids. The second you go niche you have to go to cable. That's why campaign TV is new to American audiences.* Jamie's Food Revolution *is a unique series for primetime because it is not a constructed format that is guaranteed to deliver on the premise. We don't ultimately have control of the ending, because the ending is the real world.* Jamie's School Dinners *meets* Ministry of Food *is difficult because it's an unprovable premise. At the same time the power of television to change the real world is huge, as we've seen in the UK, so it is possible.*

as ingredients change you are thinking how they might go together. This can be very hard, because it means doing a lot of things at once, and few people are strong in every one of the elements that I call the five dimensions of film-making on location.

Filming on location is one of the toughest jobs there is. It is a process like five-dimensional chess, in which you have to work in all five dimensions simultaneously. All have to contribute to the thing that matters: gathering material that will tell the story. It can be very hard and very tiring, if not impossible, to continually think in all five dimensions at once, because not only are you concentrating on spinning five plates simultaneously but each of the plates is probably going off in its own direction.

FIRST DIMENSION: VISUAL FLAIR

You need to develop the ability to tell a story not only in words but in pictures. This means creating and spotting the pictures and mood that tell the story – for the visual extra dimension can really make a film. As a researcher on my very first recce, I was sent a day ahead of the director to the KitKat chocolate factory in York. One of my tasks was to work out how next day we should tell our cameraman to shoot the chocolate. I got there and nearly tore my hair out. I just didn't understand how to answer the question. The next day the director turned up and instantly identified three grammatical necessities: we needed some wide establishing shots, some interesting big close-up shots seeing pouring molten chocolate as we never usuually did, and an interesting point-of-view that we also wouldn't normally see, moving the camera, not just by panning or walking with it, but by putting it on the conveyor belt – to give a Malteser's-eye view.

It was a new language for me and I began to think about the simple basics. I learnt from this harsh lesson that as long as I shot some wide establishing shots, some big close-ups and an interesting, unexpected point-of-view, I would at least have the bones. The very tight shots can take time to film – focus and lighting can be tough – but they are worthwhile. In fact, well set up, complicated shots, sometimes even lit, are so important that although you may not have time to achieve them when filming actuality, it is well worth giving up one day of obser-vational filming towards the end of the shoot to go back and do them. By then you will know what you need to shoot – maybe just five or six shots that will change the film visually, and give it an identity.

First off this is likely to include big, wide establishers from interesting locations. As a documentary doctor, I often see sequences where I don't have a clue where I am. And so many films are shot with everything in midshot. When in doubt on location, as well as the usual midshots I have a basic 'rule of T.W.O.': *tight, wide* and *on the move* (and remember moving means not only the subject but the camera too).

For the *Troubleshooter* featuring Copella fruit juice I decided to have Sir John en route in a train. I wanted an important visual sequence bet-ween lots of talk, so I surveyed eighteen bridges and vantage points between Colchester and Ipswich to find the best. I then spent half a day shooting these wide shots and also some very tight, weird, almost abstract train wheels and carriages whizzing by. Then, in order to complete my fulfilment of this rule, I shot some point-of-views out of the train – including the overhead wires. Basic stuff, but then I don't have enough visual flair to avoid following ny own simple rules. The train became a visual motif for the film.

When filming a conversation berween two people with one camera, do some of it at ninety degrees to your participants so you can just gently pan between them, remembering to get some good tight shots of each as well as midshots. Also take two shots of both of them together, and move your camera right back to get a very wide which will show where you are and could be useful for any words. Most important, be brave and film over the shoulder of one, seeing the back of their head and the face of the other person full on. Do not worry that you are not getting both parts of the dialogue on camera, because you will get some great full-on talking and some great listening shots too. Which is important. Because it's also essential, if you only have one camera, to remember to shoot enough cutaways (just people listening to enable you to cut), and you may not get a chance to get these at the end. I know this seems obvious, but it is surprising how often establishing shots and cutaways just aren't there when you get to the cutting room.

Try to storyboard at least the beginning of the film; it is a great discipline to try to write the front of your film in pictures as well as words. For directors who come from advertising or music videos this is standard practice – hence they have an advantage at least in this respect!

To all this, add mystery and surprise – shoot the unusual we don't usually see. I learnt my craft on *Tomorrow's World*, that popular live presenter-fronted magazine series about new inventions. Directing the short five-minute insert films was even more useful than the studio as a learning tool; short films are a great place to try out your craft. But we didn't just have to write scripts for these films. We were also made to draw a storyboard, to tell the opening of the story with pictures alone. That means a sheet of paper with half-a-dozen TV-shaped boxes in which you actually draw pictures of what the audience will see shot by shot. Try it out at least on your next opening.

On *Tomorrow's World* there was a team of around a dozen people all competing to find the next best story, but there weren't enough stories around. So I became an avid reader of trade magazines from *Rubber Week* to *Lloyd's List* (my first full-length BAFTA winner came from the British Toy and Hobby Federation; even today I still find trade magazines the source for the occasional inspired story), just as now I continue to scour the press and internet.

Not long after I had begun, I found a story about a new kind of explosive. It came in a reel and was to be wrapped around the legs of oil rigs to demolish them when they had outlived their usefulness – an improvement on previous techniques, the inventor believed. It was very worthy but not, in truth, very exciting. But I remembered seeing an old submarine gently sinking in a scrapyard on the way in to Portsmouth. So I created a storyboard in which my presenter Peter McCann was in a strange corridor with a torch, looking lost and trapped in some diabolical place. Then a beam of his torch lights up what looks like an internal ship's door, but the door is jammed. So from the storyboard sketches Peter appears to be trapped deep inside a naval ship that is probably sinking, as he seems desperate to get out. Then, still with no words, he remembers something, and pulls a strong material that looks like thick white plastic tape from his bag, bends it and sticks it on to the submarine corridor wall in the shape of a door. But we still do not know quite where he is.

Then, still no words, the next scene cuts outside to the tight exterior hull of a submarine. There's a huge bang and a chunk of the hull, shaped like a full-size door, flies off the side. Before we shoot the bang, Peter (out of vision) happily gets well out of the way as this huge, massively heavy door-shaped lump of steel shoots out of the submarine, leaving a gaping hole, through which his head can then appear. Finally we reveal that it was a submarine rotting in Portsmouth harbour, and with the audience surprised and hooked Peter clambers on to a scrap destroyer's deck and explains how it worked.

So that was the storyboard. But how to make it happen in reality? It took a lot of persuasion to be allowed to cut a large chunk out of a submarine, albeit a scrap one, at no cost, and convincing BBC safety experts. Worse, despite having safety officers in attendance, the one-ton piece of metal flew off so high and fast we never did find it. A week later I received a letter from Portsmouth Council asking me never to film in Portsmouth again.

Beyond storyboarding, try to come up with a visual style of your own for the film. But this style needs to flow out of the story. For example, when I was filming a day in the life of the foreign currency markets my visual motif was endless tight smoking, burning cigarettes in ashtrays – because they all smoked back then, and it helped demonstrate the tension of their day. But it could be shooting from a particular angle, or always shooting close with a wide lens. In *Blood on the Carpet* the highly imaginative series producer, Nick Mirsky, had the idea of shooting the historical scenes, with the original protagonists from business battles, in Super-8 domestic film, frequently black-and-white, which gave the series its own feel.

NICK MIRSKY

Series Producer, *Blood on the Carpet*,
now BBC Documentary Executive

I'd never liked reconstruction with actors. The worst thing about reconstruction is often sound and hammy actors, so it takes away the two things that feel hunkiest and puts in something that feels quite other, and often the people themselves didn't quite know what they are reconstructing. There is something so forgiving about Super-8 that it can take you back; it feels like you are in a past-tense world.

However good or bad you might be at directing visually, there is one thing that can help if you can afford it – and often even on DV shoots there is a little in the budget for extra camera days, so, if you can afford it, employ the very best cameraperson you can, even if for a day or two. So make sure you know who *are* the very best – there is little more valuable information. It is easy to forget that the best, like presenters, need courting too. So court them; persuade them; ring them up yourself; tell them how much your film matters and why, with their help, it is going to be such a success. But you will still need to direct them. Often they tell me something is impossible – too hard or too dark to film – but I have insisted we try, and sometimes it works and is just what I want. The very best cameramen react badly if you appear not to know what you want, so give some decisive directions even if you don't have a clue. Then they will tell you how it can be done better, and happily take over and do it.

Visual skills are enough for a whole other book, but for now just be on the lookout for anything visual that might help the story, and try to give your viewer unusual views of everyday things, whether a hand or a skyscraper. But visual skills are not enough. I have seen many fantastic advertising and pop promo directors fail at documentary because despite coming from a hugely visual background they are not using the visuals to tell the story, and more important they are forgetting the people. They have failed because they have not persuaded their characters to fully participate, or have done so forgetting the importance of *people skills*. You need the ability to sell your idea continually to both contributors and your team, if they are to do what you need.

BO TENGBERG

Cameraman, winner of the World Union of Cinematographers
Most Inventive Cinematographer award

*Memory for images, as for music and smell, is much stronger than words.
When you see an image you relate to it, like when you hear that special
music which makes you think of a wonderful holiday. If you can touch
people with an image emotionally, you touch them very, very deeply.*

*Sit down and think about the essence of the story and how you could
contain the essence in pictures. What is the scene really about, what is
the emotional agenda? Maybe you have two people who appear to be
talking about normal life, but they are a married couple who are really
saying they will separate. Making images is about discovering the agenda
beneath the words and finding the images for that. If you can tell the
subtext of the scene in the images you'll hit people's emotions, the
subconscious, and they will understand totally what the scene is about,
even if the dialogue is saying something else, and these images will pull
you into an emotional state that is really hard to create with words.*

*A Killer Bargain, a film about globalisation and its flip side, won
the Prix Italia. They filmed an Indian man as he pours bleaching liquid
into a big basin for making cloth white. He's standing in it, and the
liquid is bubbling. And that's the image everyone remembers, they see
the image and they say: that's the programme. You could relate to a story
by seeing this one image*

*It is very easy to make nice, beautiful well-lit images, but finding images
that enhance the story is hard. I tend to look at painters and see how they
interpret emotion.*

SECOND DIMENSION: PEOPLE SKILLS

While thinking of your visual story it is vital to think of people too.
There are lots of different constituencies to keep happy, all in different
ways – no one said it was easy. You need to keep on board first your
contributors or presenters, then officials, PRs and bosses who you rely
on for permissions, and finally, but not least, your hired-in camera crew,
if you have one, and any of your own production team. And you have

to do all this while directing, which means you are probably being a rather intense and demanding person in order to get your film made, so it may not be easy.

We talked earlier about getting contributors on board initially, but you want to keep them on board when filming too! You need both to persuade your contributors to go in at the deep end and push themselves, while also comforting them and giving them trust. In a series like *Back to the Floor*, which relies almost entirely on one contributor and one used to getting his or her own way – the boss who is going to become a worker – this can be particularly challenging. The bosses would be risking their reputation as we filmed. As the cameras rolled we persuaded Sainsbury's supermarket supremo, Dino Adriano, to try some of the tasks that his workforce do routinely – such as pushing lines of trolleys through a car park, somewhat unsuccessfully – to see what it was like. We filmed the boss of Unijet, a package holiday company, working as one of his own holiday reps, having told the other reps that this was part of a new scheme to employ older people so that they didn't realise that their new rep was the boss of their company till he revealed it at the end. As customers abused him for late planes and dirty rooms it was hard work keeping him happy.

In another of the *Back to the Floor* series, *A Class Apart*, we sent the headmistress of Benenden, not to teach in her own posh public school, which was not far from her everyday life, but to a much tougher inner-city comprehensive, where we might get a stronger emotional journey. She was keen to know which school it would be, but we didn't tell her – we wanted it to be really new for her as she arrived on camera, so that her surprise was genuine as she approached the school for the first time. She even got lost going in, and we let the audience see this. Her first meeting with the head, despite his protestations, was also on camera from the first second – there wasn't a handshake before – to keep it real. Meeting for the first time for real is something on which I try to insist; and even if they have met some time before, I want to film this meeting from the first second – as I did when Jamie Oliver met Tony Blair. It is important that it feels genuine for the audience.

When the Benenden headmistress descended from the headmaster to the classroom she found the pupils more difficult than she had ever imagined. When, at the end of the day after filming, she burst into tears, we didn't leave her. We had been with her all the time, seeking only the reality, and she understood this as, crucially, we were tender afterwards. Most important, the Benenden headmistress, Gillian duCharme, really trusted the production team.

As a result of this TLC the experience ended up for her as life-changing and improving, but only because we were brave enough to make it real. Above all you need to convince your contributors to trust you, reminding them that if they look good you will look good too, and you will do everything to make this happen honestly. Sometimes I fail, as when Jamie was going to meet Tony Blair in the *School Dinners* update film, a year after the original series, to see what he had done. I discovered Jamie was having a pre-meet with the Prime Minister days before our filming, and it was too late to film it or stop it! But I don't let that happen often, as I love the rawness of reality.

Avoid going through PRs if you possibly can, as they can look clever by saying they saved their boss or company from your show and the risk for them is in taking part. And if you do have to go through them, do it as charmingly and quickly as possible. In a case like dinner lady Nora we had to go through the PR and head, as she was not empowered to give permission to film in a school herself.

DOMINIQUE WALKER

Series Producer, *Jamie's School Dinners*,
Commissioning Editor, Channel 4

Before you visit PRs, write a list of every reason that your contributor shouldn't do it, and if you were the PR adviser what you would tell them about why they shouldn't do it, and then think of all your counter-reasons. Then you go in, and before they've even said what their problem is you've reassured them, and then you've sort of built the trust.

You may also need to continue to keep officials or PRs happy as you film. If at all possible, keep them off location. If you have to have them, find a member of the production team who can be with them at all times, and engage them in conversation whenever you want to shoot something that might worry them, so hopefully they won't pay too much attention to it. And finally try to bore them in the initial shooting into disappearing, which is just what our team did when making a *Trouble at the Top* following Wandsworth Prison over a period of months.

MICHELE KURLAND

Executive Producer, *The Apprentice*,
former Series Producer, *Trouble at the Top*

The governor was taking lots of new initiatives, the PR people were very nervous and they wanted to show everything in a good light. PR people look at it with different antennae, and they often do their subjects in, in a way. Because what you need to do is show people coping under pressure. The biggest problem with PR people is they don't understand that everyone can cope with the wind behind them on a good day and they often only want contributors to cope with no pressure — that's not honest and the viewer knows it. However, when the viewers see contributors coping under pressure, they understand, for that's what happens in their own lives even if what they are trying to do doesn't succeed. If the contributors are shown trying, and doing everything they can, and giving one hundred per cent, then the viewer is with them and that is what PR people get wrong time and time again. In Wandsworth Prison we bored the PRs in the end so much they stopped coming.

Finally with all this going on you also need to keep the film crew happy too, which may not be easy because in actuality, unlike in drama, confusion helps contributors to be honest. You want your contributors to speak without worrying, to act naturally. I find it helps if you start and stop so much that contributors have no idea if you are filming or not, so they get too worn out to put on an act, and become real. But of course you have to explain you will be filming them. I always try to create a flurry of muddle and energy, to storm the contributors into saying what they think without time to reflect and then obfuscate.

But in keeping demanding and difficult contributors on side it can be easy to forget the team. So brief your team beforehand. Explain how you work, that you expect them to start filming as you are setting up, to slide into shooting, perhaps with only a small hand signal. Explain, also in advance, that you may appear offhand with them on occasion in order to appear to side with your contributor. It can help sometimes to appear to criticise the 'pushy' crew, asking 'Do you really need to film this?' (hopefully having arranged with the crew earlier that they will say yes!). But all this can be upsetting to a crew, so you need to talk with them beforehand about the importance of seeking truth, and how with powerful people, particularly guarded politicians, it can often be tough to disarm them.

And don't, at all costs, ignore the sound recordist, if you are lucky enough to have one, and don't forget that only the sound recordist may be hearing what is actually being said, especially if the contributors are on radio mikes far away, and you are shooting on a long lens. Sound is absolutely vital in documentary; in fact the audience can get far more upset about bad sound, not understanding what is wrong, but knowing something is, than bad pictures which they can immediately see are wrong. Conversely good sound can make a film. So even if you are self-shooting, always try to take along a second person who is good at recording sound, even if they're not a professional recordist. Record wild tracks – sound when no one is speaking – which will be vital for the editing, and especially any lovely noises like creaking doors that will help make the film in the dub.

THIRD DIMENSION: ORGANISATION

Your film will come to nothing unless you actually get to the right places with the right permissions. I often think that organising a film is a large part of the creative battle, because you are working out how to make it as you work it out logistically. As a director I always did as much of the arranging myself as possible, even down to hotels and getting deals on them, as I thought where crew and contributors would best want to be, and whether I wanted them together or separate, all at the cheapest cost to me, so more could go on the screen.

It is surprising how even a simple decision like having Jamie live in a house with the production team in Huntington, West Virginia, in *Jamie's Food Revolution*, can affect the team's relationships and the feel of the film. Every detail has an effect and needs to be thought through, from the order of shooting to where to have lunch and how to get from A to B. Doing this efficiently and meticulously should contribute to your film by making it run well, and by giving both crew and contributors confidence that you know what you are doing, and that you are considerate of their needs.

However, it is not just the crew and contributors. In *Jamie's School Dinners* there was an endless succession of people to be kept happy, from councillors to school heads. Leave anyone out, and just like *Space Invaders*, when it is the unexpected that kills you, that could be the one to wreck the whole film. When filming abroad it can be even tougher. You may well need a fixer. I was asked to make a BBC *Horizon/* WGBH *Nova* co-production, and knowing little about science I chose a story full of conflict about a battle to save the Javan rhino, once the most common in Asia, of which only around fifty survive. It was called *Playing at Noah* for *Horizon*, *Sex and the Single Rhino* for *Nova* (which says something) and followed the most aptly named American zoologist, Ulysses Seal, who wanted to capture them, put them in zoos and try to breed them there, to save the species, battling against conservationists who thought that would be the last thing to save them. But despite being about nature it was hard to know how to get filming permission in Indonesia. Who might be upset; who might allow us in? Who would need convincing? It seemed certain that we would need support from an Indonesian cabinet minister. The only answer was to find one central fixer with the right contacts who knew who to persuade and how.

When, shortly after the fall of communism, I made a film advising Poles how to embrace caring capitalism, and Lech Wałęsa how to run Poland (I think he wisely didn't listen!), I again found a brilliant local fixer, who even won us that access to the President. He appeared able to achieve anything: to help us around he persuaded a plane-maker to lend me an elderly Antonov and pilot, who appeared to plot his route by road, as he seemed to navigate by following the streets below. He travelled somewhat more slowly than the traffic that seemed just a few feet beneath us, so it took a long time, and we were all violently sick. The only thing he balked at was when I found a minibus company myself that turned out to be Jewish owned. I was shocked. We used them.

Permissions even in your own country can be very hard and take a long time. You will need persistence and every ounce of charm. Just as in persuading contributors (or attracting new lovers) try not to ask them to agree to a long-term relationship immediately. Court them for as much time as you have, and with every ounce of charm you can muster. Faint heart never won fair contributor.

Another important organisational skill is to draw up a schedule listing times and breaks, and then sticking to it. Work out logistically how to get as many sequences into a day as possible, but not so many that you don't give them enough time to evolve. Try to build in a couple of breaks – everyone will love you for thinking of it – and have sandwiches laid on for when you inevitably end up overrunning and miss them. If you are filming away, spend time on the recce, choosing hotels and restaurants. These do not need to be fancy, but quick and efficient, and should help to get everyone bonding away from the filming. In fact, a German country inn, complete with beer garden, at twenty-five euros a night, has been one of my most popular finds. If you do it yourself you can usually knock down prices to get better hotels – and by 'better' I mean more tranquil, not just fancier. When filming the South Yorkshire police in Sheffield, I survived a month staying in a de-luxe ex-stately home on the moors for the same price as a nasty Sheffield B&B. And my crew were particularly happy to stay with the Maharana of Udaipur, as guests in his palace, after yet another long day and flight! All a result of careful organisation.

When it comes to flying, television companies rarely pay for business-class seats, so try to get your team an upgrade, if you can. If you are the terrier who can win access in difficult situations when filming, you should be able to succeed at this much of the time. You can have four goes at trying to get an upgrade. First, you can ring ahead to the airline. Then there is a second opportunity on arrival at the check-in counter (always tell airport check-in staff, particularly when abroad, what you are filming – what hard work it is, and you might mention how it will show their country on TV, all of which is true). If you have tried these two, and you are abroad, you should be up to a 50 per cent chance by now, as long as you have also smiled and complimented the airline and country. If you have failed, try again at the gate – which often works best in Britain. There is a final chance as you actually get on board the aircraft, though this is the toughest.

I wouldn't go quite as far as the two celebrated TV producers who always used Virgin Atlantic to fly to America, who, in the story I was told, would get to the check-in counter, remember the name-tag of the person on the check-in, then retreat to a hidden corner and ring them – asking for them by name – and say: 'This is Richard Branson. I have two friends, X and Y, travelling today. Please treat them well.' The surprised check-in staff were only too happy to do their charismatic boss's bidding, and X and Y were always upgraded to upper class. Eventually they were approached by Virgin Security at Kennedy airport, told they had been discovered and warned that it was a serious federal offence. But they had the presence of mind to bluff: 'We knew nothing, our assistants just try too hard to please us, and they got carried away.' They were allowed to go on their way. Shortly thereafter they sold their company for millions, so can now afford full fare. However, that is definitely a step too far, for it is important always to be honest, and never lie, if you are to maintain your integrity, which is the most important thing you have as a factual programme-maker.

If it looks like you are going to fail on an upgrade you can also ask the check-in staff, if the aircraft is not too full, to block you out a wide centre row in economy. If this fails too, ask to look at the seating plan as you get into the boarding area, when everyone will be checked in, in case empty rows have become free. If you fail completely, remember rows towards the back are always emptier, especially at the very back, so you are likelier at least to end up with an empty seat beside you.

Apply this level of detail to every part of the logistics, from finding the very best train bridges from which to shoot, to where the crew will eat lunch and how, to how long each sequence will really take to film, and how you will get between them. Filming for *Tomorrow's World* in Germany, I had ten short films to shoot in ten days the entire length of the country. This meant tiring travelling every night, even though there might be another beer garden and inn beckoning. So as well as finding the inns I blagged upgrades from small cars to BMWs and Mercedes. A cared-for contributor, and cared-for crew, make a happy film. And if you get the logistics right you can film fast, and furious!

FOURTH DIMENSION: STORYTELLING

Storytelling is just as important on location, as beforehand when writing the script and afterwards in the cutting room. Storytelling is not just about writing a pre-shooting script with a strong narrative drive, but about the toughest dimension of film-making of all, keeping that storytelling going, as things change on location. You need to be able to re-edit your entire film in your head, and really think out of the box while filming when the unexpected starts happening. Each scene is like an index card, and one must lead to the next. It is also like a huge jigsaw puzzle: each time you pick up a new piece of the jigsaw you may have to rearrange all the others you have already laid down to fit it in, as it reveals a different picture. Worse, if you've shot on film, it is a jigsaw with about ten times as many pieces shot as you will use, and if you're working on tape or hard drive, maybe sadly fifty times too many.

With each new and surprising event on location changing the storyline, you will need to redecide what you now have to throw away because it doesn't inform the new storyline. So when that something new or surprising happens, don't ignore it, but instead instantly re-edit in your head what you have shot so far, to see how it can fit and what it means you have to ask or shoot next. That is one main reason why I find filming so utterly shattering. The other is listening intently. Working like a maniac to keep the show on the road with little sleep is easy in comparison.

So to sum up, as you film you have to decide almost instantly which earlier sequences, or even short phrases of interview, may contribute to the new action, so that you know what to ask next, or film next, and also how to follow up the new action. And that means you have to hold in your head everything you have filmed so far.

The very first *Trouble at the Top*, which was called *Nightmare at Canary Wharf*, didn't turn out at all as expected. In fact that wasn't what it was called at first because when we began filming we had not imagined the eventual outcome. We set out to make a story following Janet Street-Porter through the ups and downs of creating one of Britain's first cable TV stations with our heroine winning out in the end. Set up by the *Mirror* newspaper group L!ve TV was to be live twenty-four hours a day. It was only part way through filming that it became apparent that someone else, who had only been in the background of a few shots, thought he was in charge of the station too – ex-*Sun* editor Kelvin MacKenzie. Street-Porter and MacKenzie appeared to hate each other. Suddenly I needed to remember back to every small shot of Kelvin I had, and any reference to the battle between them. The story of the film had turned.

Clearly this is difficult to do on the hoof, so it is also very helpful after each day's filming to spend some time adjusting your original script in the light of what has just happened. For me, storytelling is having a strong narrative but adjusting it in the light of reality. So it is a continually changing strong narrative, but it is always answering your big question, which doesn't often change.

Of course, once you get filming you *try* to capture the material the audience will care about, using strong narrative drive and big questions and answers, as we have outlined above. But what about when nothing happens? After all, what we are looking for are our heroes learning, and changing as they come under pressure. If nothing much happens at the beginning, don't lose your nerve, hang on in there ... After all, you chose your question for a reason, that something eventually would happen! And with time on location, something almost always does.

Often much of the early material you shoot will be thrown away anyway in the cutting room as you get to know your characters better, and work out your story, so don't be too disheartened. In fact, with most films shot sequentially over time to follow developing action, so much early footage will be thrown away that it will be surprising if the first half of what you have shot lasts even a quarter of the film.

The speed of editing is often dependent on how ruthlessly you follow this process. The firmer you are about throwing away the early stuff the better your film will be. So hang on and stay cool. If you have chosen a story with strong characters and potential conflict, given time something will change and the drama will get progressively more exciting, particularly as your characters open up. And the timeframe doesn't need to be long. If the strongest material is shot in the final week of a six-week shoot, it simply doesn't matter. A *Back to the Floor* in which all the action happens in a week, can be just as effective as a *Troubleshooter* shot over a year. But invariably, in both, the footage should improve through the filming.

FIFTH DIMENSION: PERSUASIVE SKILLS

Much successful documentary-making involves an element of hard journalism, even investigation, and ensuring that the story is right, truthful, adheres to guidelines, and is legal. A period in current affairs is immensely useful preparation for this but, when in doubt, refer up, and always consult executive producers and lawyers. Building a close relationship with the Legal Department and Editorial Policy at the broadcaster, and showing that you are reliable and sensible, will mean that you are more likely to get permission to take calculated but important risks for the story, like the doorstep interview or secret filming 'in the public interest'. If you do so without asking permission, you are unlikely to do so again. A lot of factual television is about pushing, and investigating hard, to get at the truth. The more scandalous this is, the harder you may be allowed to push.

Sir John Harvey-Jones used to call me Jekyll and Hyde. Usually I am a fearful and careful person, but once filming I suddenly (and perhaps unfortunately) became afraid of nothing and nobody. All at once I was happy running in front of traffic to stop it, taking on tyrants and asking any passer-by to do anything. But you must always be fair, and prejudge as little as possible.

One of the challenges is to show what you have seen in your long and painstaking research. When we first got to film at the Tri-ang toy factory it became a cat-and-mouse game in which I was very keen that the tired factory remained just as it was, right up to filming. Similarly one can nudge conversations in order to focus contributors on the subject you are filming, and to remind them of what they said on a recce visit. If they start discussing their summer holidays when you are trying to make a film about the perils of bridge building, it can be worth joining in to steer the conversation back on message. It can also be worth joining the conversation briefly to get it back towards what the contributors said to you before any filming began, not with direction that will interrupt, but just gently joining in and adding to it before quietly disappearing. Many people in our industry feel uncomfortable with this approach. But I'm trying to get people to say what they really think – it's up to you what you think is right. Being honest and truthful is extremely important, but it's for you to wrestle with how you get there while remaining fair. To some extent this depends on whom you are filming, and why for instance politicians and other powerful people deserve a firmer grilling than the simpler contributors who often get it. We will discuss this more in the chapter on interview technique.

Sometimes you will never be given permission to film by contributors, but there is no question that, journalistically, it is in the public interest. When I took over the long-running BBC business strand *The*

Money Programme from the Current Affairs Department, the production team were immensely keen on secret filming and doorstepping. In fact they loved nothing better because it was macho, though remember, when doing this, you will need to convince lawyers and Editorial Policy of the reason why, and have detailed internal discussion and permissions. And sometimes they were right – for example in *The Men Who Killed Marconi* they door-stepped Lord Simpson, who had helped bring the company down, when they were investigating the trade in rotten meat, condemned as only fit for animals, being passed off for human consumption, or a film on identity fraud. But you need to marry this tough journalism with all the other skills and rules I've outlined so far, otherwise you will have a dry and arid programme.

Unless you are an investigative journalist with a hidden camera or tough doorstepping methods, it is usually only by persuading contributors to take part and do what you need that you can make TV. And such *persuasion* needs to be carefully calculated, with good journalistic skills. You need to push hard enough without going too far. Slow persistence can help in this. I learnt this first, again, as a researcher. The owners of the mass-circulation tabloid *Daily Mirror* wanted to sell it, and they had brought in a new boss Clive Thornton, famed for transforming the huge mortgage lender Abbey National, to oversee a big public people's flotation (a mass IPO). But soon after Thornton arrived he began to feel something was wrong. He suspected the *Mirror* group of papers was being stalked by Robert Maxwell, the rich and controversial magnate desperate to own his own newspaper group, and that one of his own directors was secretly giving information to the predatory Maxwell that might enable him to pounce before the flotation went through. Only he did not know which director it was.

All alone in his large office, high up in the *Mirror*'s tower, he didn't know who to confide in. We did not have full access, but we wanted it. And we certainly couldn't justify hidden cameras or doorstepping: there was no crime or subterfuge that made it 'in the public interest'. So we hung around and we hung around, and eventually, as we were always there and not involved, Thornton began to trust us above everyone else, and to confide in us – who else could he trust? As a result the film became a journalistic and documentary success.

It's a wonderful moment when this happens. Many powerful people are lonely, so it can pay to be their fool, and in fact most people, unless

---

SIMON DICKSON

Deputy Head of Documentaries, Channel 4

Contributors might not quite know what to make of you at first, but by the end of the journey they're ringing you up and you have become part of their support network. You have become, in some cases, the only person who listens to them actively, because as a director, if you're any good, you practise a form of highly attuned, active listening. Whereas in normal day-to-day life we drift in and out of conversation, and we're distracted, and our phone rings, and we reach for our BlackBerry, when you're directing a documentary film, if you're not listening to what's being said to you, thinking about what that means to the person that's saying it to you, then you're never going to make a good film. And that's why when I see people doing it for me, the best directors are always knackered because they are unique among us – they have spent hours and hours of the preceding week listening really hard to what somebody has been saying to them. How many of us can say we honestly do that in our day-to-day lives?

---

they have a therapist, are desperate for someone to talk to. If it isn't a mistress it had better be you.

So we were intimate with Clive, but seeing the way the cookie was crumbling we were making overtures to the predator Maxwell too. We were just very careful not to tell the one what the other had said to us. When one day Robert Maxwell pounced and made his bid to buy the paper, and it was accepted, we were already so close to him that at nearly midnight that very evening we were able to drive into the *Mirror* building with him in his Rolls-Royce. We went straight to the private lift, which whisked us up to the boss's lair, above all the presses and journalists, the very room in which we had been so intimate with Clive Thornton just hours before.

I used to talk to close psychiatrist and psychologist friends about parallels between our jobs. For when giving therapy they would get very close to each patient, who would in transference consider they had an important relationship with their therapist. But at the end of the allotted hour the therapist would move to the next patient. And at the end of the day the therapist would come home and ask where the shopping was, or be complained at for not getting it. Similarly it pays to get very close to contributors, but also to remember they are just that, and not your friends; they should be more like your patients, and you must keep a perspective. Which is why sharing a house with your contributors on location can be difficult and tiring. For you always need to try to keep enough perspective while appearing charming, so that you can make a truthful film. The danger is 'going native'.

While you must remember all five dimensions of film-making on location, you should always, and through all of them, try to adhere to the larger truths you have researched. You need to use the five dimensions to tell a story people will watch, but you also need to make moral judgements, which is why this fifth dimension is the bedrock of filming. Filming on hospital watch in Liverpool I was given the task of shooting a kidney transplant between a young man and his brother. In the excitement of the surgeon removing the kidney I failed to film the key moment, as the kidney came out, quite right. So I asked him to put it back. Like many surgeons he was keen to be a TV star and he did. I had overstepped the line, even though it was a second of an arm moving up and down and made no difference to the patient.

CECILE FROT-COUTAZ

CEO, Fremantle Media, North America

People often ask me why Idol *is so successful. I always say it's because it's real. We want to find a star and kids really want to be that winner. It is not engineered by producers — it is a completely real show. I think that authenticity is really important, but is often lost in the shuffle.*

Idol *works because of the unpredictability. Shows fail because of the lack of authenticity and their predictability — this notion that we tell people what they should like is very patronising, or the show where someone was going to help struggling families, but it was not authentic.* Jamie's Kitchen *had real stakes, real jeopardy — it was his money, his career was at a low point, his wife seemed pissed off he was even doing it. That was part of the show, and the stakes were real.* Undercover Boss *works because of storytelling, authenticity, character and it's very relatable.*

I never asked anyone to put a live body organ back again. In filming, as in medicine, morality is as important as technique, and not only because it is right, but also because the audience will feel it. It imbues a film with authenticity, which will make the story itself feel right. You need to be able to make a good film without changing the essence of the story. Tenacity and knowing how far to go – the moral edge to this fifth dimension – can make it the most important of all, and one every film-maker must master.

So to sum up: to win in directing you really will need to be at least adequate in all the five dimensions, so you can work in them all simultaneously as you shoot, although it can be fearfully demanding and confusing, especially when so much extra effort is involved to master what you may be weakest at.

Often, for instance, people with a background in arts programming can be strong in visuals but not journalism. People in current affairs are mostly employed for journalism, not their aesthetic sense. At least you might expect people making science programmes, who are employed for their analytical skills, to be highly organised, but often they aren't. Very few people are strong in all areas, so it is worth trying to work in as many as possible on the way up. In fact many of the best people in documentaries have had early experience in current affairs, many of the best people in arts films have earlier documentary experience, and many of the best people in current affairs or news have worked on more visual films. When I was weak visually early on, I made films for *Tomorrow's World*, where there was a high visual demand, and that shot-by-shot storyboarding proved invaluable for me.

But in the end there will always be some areas you do not master as well as others. In fact I have seen many people fail by being just too inadequate in one of them. As hardly anyone is brilliant in all five dimensions of film-making, and you need them all, you can do one of two things – or even better, both. Try to learn the bits you are not so good at early on in your career, not only working in an area that may help develop some of your weaker skills, but also working for directors with varying skills on your way up. Try to choose who you work with, at all levels, so they have these different skills from you, and not only compensate for your weaker areas, but also maybe improve them. And then when you build or join a team, try to compensate by working with people who have the skills you don't (an area we will cover more fully in discussing team building).

With *Jamie's School Dinners* the excellent small team with very different skills had now come together so that, helping each other, they could really film in all five dimensions. Helping visual skills one of the team was an excellent self-shooter, which encouraged us all to try to think this way, and we had a great camera crew too. The whole team had people skills in spades, though some were more emotional and gentle, some more upfront. And for the third dimension our series producer was a superb organiser. From a small Highbury garage she timed a succession of complex almost military manoeuvres, from dinner-lady camp to the roll-out around different schools, right down to Jamie's impossible diary, and I was lucky she had very strong persuasive and journalistic skills too. The whole team knew they had to be thinking in all five dimensions, as far as they could, all the time they filmed. Using these, they succeeded in filming the complex narrative drive that gave Jamie his set of hurdles to clear, the small questions and answers, from Greenwich to County Durham to the dinner-lady camp at an Aldershot army base.

As well as adhering to the five dimensions of filming on location, there is one more thing you have to think of – especially if the editing, which comes next, is to be successful, fun and easy: not to film too much! If you return with reams of footage, some of which you will never even get a chance to see, you are going to have a much harder and longer time in the cutting room when you come to what should be the most satisfying part of film-making, where you are finally in control and can do what you want creatively as you edit. You only need a few magic moments from your characters in the cutting room to be able to construct the tastiest dish. If you succeed in filming in all five dimensions, you should get many.

Mastering all five dimensions on the hoof, and making sure you work with others who make up for your deficiencies, you have succeeded in shooting your film. You have shaped the big question, focused it in the script and made a narrative drive out of small questions and answers, amending them to circumstances as you go along. Now you come to what should be the best bit, if you've followed the rules so far. This is putting the material you have shot together in the cutting room. For a film is developed and created in the edit just as much as at its inception or filming. And here again you are going to have to think right out of the box.

Four

FRONT

AND EDITING

STORYTELLING IN THE CUTTING ROOM

You don't just have to work out what the film is about before you make it and while shooting. One of the keys to successful film-making is how you continue this in the cutting room. This chapter is about how you make the all-important 'front' that will make or break the film, get the story going fast, and deal with characters and storylines. All of which I had to learn how to do fast as a BBC creative director. I sometimes had three or four films transmitting each week, all of which I signed off in the cutting room. And much of my time was taken up with a diary of endless meetings with channel controllers, lawyers, editorial policy, fellow creative directors, initiatives with names like 'Making It Happen', creativity meetings and a lot more acronyms and jargon. In common with much of the public sector, the BBC was keen to make the organisation more businesslike. However, sometimes they confused efficiency for accountability and thought 'businesslike' meant endless performance reviews and five-year strategies which would never see the light of day, rather than just giving individuals clear and simple goals to meet, or be fired.

Once I was teamed with Laurence Rees, who made the brilliant *Nazis: A Warning from History*, and asked to envisage where the BBC should be in ten years' time, and given a selection of origami cut-outs to help us do so. When our turn came we said we hoped the BBC would be 'making brilliant programmes' loads of people watched and loved. This was not the required answer.

All of which navel-gazing and self-flagellation meant I would invariably arrive in the cutting room late from a meeting that overran. Sometimes, even worse, my hectic timetable of dreary meetings would mean, as the day wore on, that I was over an hour late, as more and more overran. It seemed that some BBC bosses ran on a time clock where they started a day just a few minutes after GMT and became progressively later and later so that 5 p.m. would often mean 7 p.m., making others later too. Just as patients feel horribly disempowered waiting in a doctor's consulting room hours past an appointment time they were given – even though it is not the doctor's fault – so if you arrive in a cutting room late to view a film, it makes the film-makers feel you are trying to put them down, and exert your power. I now try to avoid this any way I can, and strongly recommend you ring, if running as little as five minutes late, even if as a director just to your editor.

If you are a director and want an executive to arrive on time for your viewing, book them first thing in the morning – even before they have time to go to their office or start on the phone calls that will make them late. But if you want longer than the allotted time, book them at the end of the day and provide wine and nibbles.

So, with many meetings overrunning, I would often arrive in the cutting room not only late but with just seventy minutes to view an hour-long film, and then to comment on it and even help write it. Sadly this left little time for small talk or social niceties, as these would eat into the ten minutes I had at the end to change the film. But the lack of time didn't really matter, because even if I had half a day in the cutting room I almost always said the same two things. I could just as well have been a cardboard cut-out wheeled in. Maybe at times I was.

First, I could never say often enough: make a strong front with some of the strongest footage that tells you the reason for the film, the big question, and makes you care especially about the main characters. Put some of the best bits in the first two minutes, especially the best bits of the best characters who we will be following, and give us a route map of where we are going, the dangers our hero will face, and thus a reason for watching. Second, lose the endless explanation after the title, and start with one of your best story scenes. This hardly ever seems to happen in the cutting room without executive intervention, because directors get too close to their films to do it. Sometimes execs get too close too, and don't manage it either, but a film needs to get going immediately, rather than wallowing in background. It must have its own momentum.

CREATING THE FIRST TWO MINUTES

First of all to the pre-title, which is make-or-break time. Of course you have the opening of your original shooting script, assuming you had one, but in the light of all the things that happened *out of the box*, and how you have decided to cut the film, you are likely to need to redo this. It is a very good idea to start on this early in the editing process, as it will take a lot of honing. Moreover, when you have got it right, you will have worked out what your film is about, which will make it much easier to cut the body of it!

So I suggest that as soon as you are on your second assembly, maybe halfway through your editing schedule, you should have a first stab at the all-important front of the film that will set up who the heroes are and why you should care. As with the initial script, many people postpone this moment of truth, because it is hard. For the pre-title needs to do a highly complex job. In fact, it needs to do three things fast and grippingly.

First, it needs to set up what has happened – the problem that has made the hero embark on the adventure. And it needs to do this convincingly, with evidence, so that we are drawn in. This is the reason for the film.

Second, it is also the route map for the film, telling you what kind of journey you are embarking on, so you know how to view what comes next and can then follow the ensuing, narrative storyline with its small questions and answers in each scene, understanding how they build and where they are going, to lead to the answer to the big question articulated at the front.

And third, it introduces you to the hero or heroes so you know who they are, and most important why you should care about them and their quest.

We re-edited the front of *Jamie's School Dinners* a lot of times, trying desperately to get this right, and we didn't. I was a very hands-on exec and getting too close. Moreover we knew we had a battle to make the audience care. As you may remember, research showed some of the sceptical public had tired of Jamie immediately before *School Dinners* transmitted. Back then he wasn't mostly seen as 'Jamie who wants to improve the world', he was Jamie of the Sainsbury's ads, whose private life was always in the papers, which wanted to have a go at him. It's a very usual cycle in the life of a presenter from being lauded to attacked as the press want something new. Much of the public seemed to have forgotten *Jamie's Kitchen* and its needy students whose lives Jamie had transformed at considerable personal risk, though Jamie was still just the same, working like a maniac to try to improve something.

We wanted to film right up to transmission, so we began cutting while still filming and decided to have one editor cutting three of the four films so we could start the edit very early. This would take nearly six months, getting on for two months a film. And as we wanted to transmit as soon as we finished, it would mean beginning less than halfway through the shoot. This can be very useful in seeing what the material is saying and what is missing before you have finished shooting.

The directors got the first two programmes' bodies pretty well right, I honed them over many days, and the enigmatic Channel 4 commissioning editor, Peter Dale, had been to see them. He said, 'Make them more filmic,' and pushed us to make them more picture-, actuality- and mood-driven as I had, as usual, got a bit prosaic. For some reason I still was not happy. Although we had got the body of the first programme pretty right, we still hadn't cracked the first five minutes.

We paused the first episode of *Jamie's School Dinners* for over two months, while we began cutting later films in the series. And all the time that first programme and its failing front continued to niggle me, but not enough that I had thought of anything better by the time we had edited the second programme, so I was going to accept it.

TAPPING INTO OTHER PEOPLE'S TALENT

I have always been a robber in television; in fact I consider robbery a key part of television production. I recommend that you ask everyone, and anyone else what they think — you do not have to follow what they say, but it may stimulate you to think differently. And not just film people. I have had some of the most improving ideas from my cleaning lady, long-suffering friends or partners, made to look through a film at 3 a.m. – the *Great Italian Escape* was seriously affected by a clap doctor (off-duty!). I hauled a partner (non-TV) to the *Nightmare at Canary Wharf* cutting room at 4 a.m. Remember hunger!

So I strongly recommend showing your film to other bright people and using their ideas. If you are a director, you will look better to the executive producer when they come to see it, as hopefully others will have spotted the biggest mistakes. I show my films to as many people as I can; their answers may not be right, but they will point out where it doesn't work for them. Everybody, even including executive producers, can get too close to their films. So if you can listen to different ideas from different people, taking them on board or discarding them depending on their value, the film remains yours, just better. It is the creative process.

I was only finally shocked into a rethink of *Jamie's School Dinners* at the last moment, not in the cutting room, but on a small island off the southern Danish coast. I was giving some advice to TV2, Denmark's Channel 4, and persuaded a very clever Danish commissioning executive to invite me to his cottage on a Saturday evening. I brought some expensive alcohol with me. After offering him a bottle of fine champagne before dinner, and even lighting his fire for him, I persuaded him that the recompense was to spend his evening watching the first two assembled Jamie programmes. He told me what crap the first one was, based in the secondary school in Greenwich. But the second one became an emotional journey as Jamie engaged with a small class of primary kids in one of the poorest parts of Britain, County Durham. Jamie appeared truly shocked at what he saw.

It shook me because he was right. The emotion was in the second programme, which was a bit late. But although I knew something was wrong I had never noticed it was this bad. Even as an involved exec, you can take the film to a certain point, then you get tired and need someone to shake you, to say you have got to this peak but the real top of the mountain is over the next brow, and you have to summon the energy to get going again. And this is far more so for a director. The end of editing is like the end of a long run when you are exhausted and shattered. But the winners are the hungry obsessives who push that bit more.

I asked him what to do, and my commissioning friend, Thomas Breinholt, said, 'Simple, just reverse the order so Programme 2, the more emotional journey, is transmitted first.' The problem now was that I couldn't put Programme 2 first, because the action was sequential and many scenes not only built from, but referred to, the previous ones, or had even caused them. Remember that many of the best scenes answer a question that leads you to pose the next one, or even causes the next scene, so are not time immaterial and cannot be reversed. Moreover Programme 2 was also intercut with Jamie revisiting Nora in Greenwich to see what had happened while he was away, and that was integral to making it work, but happened *after* the action in Programme 1. I could unpick these, but then Programme 2 would fall apart. We had tried it, but the film needed parallel action.

So we were stuck with starting with Programme 1, about which we didn't care, mainly I thought because we just couldn't get the first few minutes right. It began like this, with pictures of Jamie at home, in his restaurant, etc., with commentary over, to be recorded by a narrator.

JAMIE'S SCHOOL DINNERS FRESH ONE FOR CHANNEL 4,
Early Commentary Script, Version 10, 24 Sept 2004
(five months before transmission)

At 28, Jamie Oliver's got a lot on his plate:

Two babies –

A new batch of unemployed teenagers to mould into chefs –

And a wife who barely sees him –

Despite it all, Jamie has a new passion. He's desperate to change school dinners.

In a massive experiment he wants to transform what 20,000 south London children eat at school.

He'll have to get the dinner ladies cooking Jamie-style.

Get the kids to eat his food.

And all for 37p a head.

Can Jamie Oliver change what Britain's kids eat at school?

The initial problem was that the first paragraph didn't make you care at all. It was all about Jamie and his problems, not the problems of Britain's kids. In fact what it really says to the audience is: 'At twenty-eight Jamie Oliver's got a lot on his plate, two babies, a new batch of unemployed teenagers to mould into chefs, a wife who barely sees him – and a contract with Channel 4, and they want him to do school dinners.' Which made the question seem: What the hell is Jamie going to do? Oh yeah, why not do school dinners? some mug suggested to him, so he sort of thought, Oh, all right I'll turn up and do school dinners.

Which was not only off-putting, but the opposite of the truth. Not only had Jamie conceived the idea, but he had spent a load of his own money beyond the TV series (hundreds of thousands of pounds) on the dinners campaign, because he cared more for the campaign than for the publicity. Though it was something unique, with life beyond a TV series, we were saying the exact opposite. Which was letting him down.

The difficulty was that our film started off about Jamie, Jamie, Jamie. It was from Jamie's point of view, which then actually made Jamie feel and look as if he was a rather pompous person going in, instead of the audience feeling the truth and believing Jamie had a passion and was desperate to change school food, which was a real problem.

Key to any film is the motivation, the 'oomph', the thing that gets the film going, the evidence of the problem that the hero reacts to. The difficulty with the first cut of *Jamie's School Dinners* remained that the series appeared to be about rather nice Jamie Oliver, who earns lots of money on the telly, who's got his business and everything, and is wondering what to do next, so concealing the wonderful truth of the real problem and its heroic solution. Although (or because) I was so close to the film, I didn't quite realise that at the time.

It took another week till the answer dawned. If Programme 2 is so much better because you see Jamie experiencing and truly shocked by small kids eating horrid food, filmed up at the primary in County Durham, but we need to show Programme 1 first, why not put a bit of 2 at the front of 1 in its tease? It won't actually turn up later on in that first film, so will be an unusual tease, and that is why I had not thought of it, but actually why should it matter?

SHOW NOT TELL

We tried just this, choosing a moving section with Jamie as he witnesses how Durham primary kids eat for the very first time. It was shocking, moving, real, and actuality – which is always more convincing than commentary. It showed the problem rather than telling it – always important in a visual medium – and one that cried out to be solved. Jamie was part way to being David. By changing the opening to the film we suddenly had a big bad giant, wicked food that was endangering sweet kids, a reason for Jamie to become heroic. We were showing evidence of the problem for our hero to react to, rather than our hero just setting out on a jaunt from the castle.

Once we had developed this front it became the same for each programme with minor variations. Directors often say won't the public mind repetition. But unlike directors, viewers love a format where they know the dramatic structure within which they are watching something. Look at *Weakest Link*, *Extreme Home Makeover*, *Wife Swap*, *Back to the Floor* or *Undercover Boss* – same narrative each week, different heroes. What follows is the front of Programme 1 as changed, together with my additions for this book in the left-hand column:

JAMIE'S SCHOOL DINNERS, FRESH ONE FOR CHANNEL 4
PRE-TITLE AS TRANSMITTED

The problem, complete with evidence.

[Jamie showing vegetable to kids, who shake their heads.]

JAMIE   Do you know what that is? Do you know what that is? Do you know what that is? How old are you? Do you know what that is? Jesus, I hold up a courgette and a stick of celery and you don't have a clue what it is.

[Jamie eating deep-fried shaped meat product for lunch with kids.]

JAMIE   What on earth is that?
KID   I think it's a fish or a chicken foot.
JAMIE   I honestly, honestly have no idea what is in that. Look at us – we are in a beautiful room surrounded by beautiful children, innocent, pure, their bodies and their bones are growing up, the most important time in their life, and you know they are being fed this. It's not right, it's not right, these kids deserve better.

[Up music.]

First narration. By now we should be beginning to care, so this commentary can reinforce what we have heard (rather than just tell us).

COMMENTARY   *School dinners are in a deepening crisis with a diet of fatty processed food threatening our children's health.*

JAMIE   I wouldn't feed that to my dog – I mean I would feed it to my dog, but I wouldn't feed it to my mate, certainly not my kids.

The quest (complete with ambition).

COMMENTARY   *The government doesn't seem to have the answers so Jamie Oliver wants to prove they can be better by transforming what kids eat at school.*

The route map: Challenge 1.

COMMENTARY   *First he'll have to get the dinner ladies cooking Jamie style –*

NORA   This isn't working out either.

Challenge 2.	COMMENTARY *Get the kids to eat his food –*
	KID I don't like it, it's nasty.
Challenge 3.	COMMENTARY *And all on a tiny budget.*
	JAMIE I've never banged my head against the wall so many times.
The Big Question.	COMMENTARY *Can Jamie Oliver change what Britain's kids eat at school?*
	JAMIE I'm doing this because I want the kids to eat better food. I want the kids to be healthier. I want them to grow up with better habits. I want us to have a f—ing better cooler cleverer healthier nation.

Now Jamie no longer erroneously looks as though he is showing off: it's about kids. Now he can seem heroic as he tries to save them. This front makes one care about kids – it says what the challenge is, it gives you the route map, it tells you who it's about and it tells you the big question, so you want to see if it is going to be answered.

And it is not afraid of showing you some of the best bits of the film. Remember the front of the film is also your trailer. This front is always difficult, often also because it can be hard to work out who your film is about.

WHO IS YOUR FILM ABOUT?

I recently helped on two American TV series, one about a fire station, one about a coastguard station. The fire station film featured firefighters near the front fighting the blaze – they were obviously the heroes. The coastguard film similarly featured the coastguards.

But when I was called in to look at the material for the first time, when it was already part way through editing, one thing jumped out at me – the emotional importance of the victims. Within the films there were people whose lives were being threatened in blazing houses with flames shooting out. If they stayed in their houses they'd die, and if they got out then they wouldn't. But for the firemen, although it might be a dangerous job, in the end it was just another fire. The coastguards film was similar. There was film of a sinking boat of amateur fishermen in a very rough sea off the Washington coast – in fact the sea was so dangerous that as the crew filmed from the helicopter, the winchman wondered how he would be able to get down, as the boat was actually sinking, and the terrified passengers about to jump off into the raging sea. So again who had the biggest stakes, who was it most worrying for? The coastguards who would be late for dinner, or the people about to die in the water unless something extraordinary was done very quickly?

Well, not the coastguards. Or the firemen. Because the front of the film needs to make you care, and people who are about to die unless something dramatic happens usually do that. There is nothing more motivating than a film in which the hero may die/get killed/murdered. Hence the idea of starting with the kids who may even die early because of junk school dinners – or the building on fire and coastguard victims.

Working out who the film is about can be even harder when you have a lot of possible main characters. We battled with the front of another series I worked on called *The House of Obsessive Compulsives*. It followed three sufferers from OCD through a revolutionary treatment. They were going to live in a house together, under the care of a team of doctors from Britain's leading psychiatric hospital, the Maudsley. The doctors would make them confront their illness, trying to help them together, and working with their partners as well. The pre-title when I first saw it included a lot of people – the three sufferers, the three partners and the team of doctors. So again who mattered most? We weren't sure who to care about.

**THE HOUSE OF OBSESSIVE COMPULSIVES,
MONKEY KINGDOM FOR CHANNEL 4, ROUGHCUT PRE-TITLE**

	These three people suffer from Obsessive Compulsive Disorder, a mental illness that has affected their and their family's lives for twenty years or more.
Character 1.	CHARACTER 1 The OCD has completely taken charge . . . of my life.

Character 2.	CHARACTER 2 Sometimes I feel at the end of my tether, that I really can't cope any more.
Character 3.	CHARACTER 3 OCD has been a serious issue with me in my life since my early twenties.
	They have tried everything from therapy to drugs. They've even considered a brain lobotomy to get rid of it. There appears to be no hope.
Character 4, Partner 1.	PARTNER 1 The worry for me is it will get worse rather than better.
Character 5, Partner 2.	PARTNER 2 It can be absolutely awful.
Characters 6, 7, 8. The doctor and his team.	*But now in a unique and unprecedented experiment a team of super therapists from London's Maudsley Hospital Institute of Psychiatry are going to attempt to cure them of this debilitating condition in just two weeks.*
	SYNCH CHARACTER 1 It's two weeks . . .
	SYNCH CHARACTER 2 Can't stay as I am now . . .
	SYNCH CHARACTER 3 It would be nice to be able to do things . . .
	Over the next fortnight all three sufferers have agreed to leave their families and move in together where they will undergo an intensive and harrowing therapy to overcome their greatest fears. All captured on camera.
	SYNCH DOCTOR There's a team of us and we are going to be working day and night.
	The sufferers are hoping for a miracle cure, but this has never been done before.
Big question is for Doctor – what it will be like being filmed.	SYNCH DOCTOR It does feel a huge challenge for two reasons. One is that we are trying something entirely new, and the other challenge is also being filmed – we might fail.
	For all three of them this is the last chance saloon. Welcome to the OCD house.

Not only were there too many characters here, but you didn't know which to follow. It's a bit like the coastguards and firefighters. Is it the doctor's problem or is it the OCD sufferers' problem? And do the sufferers include the partners? This pre-title concludes with a question: what will it be like for the doctor being filmed? If he fails, will his colleagues seen him in a worse light? But the people for whom it mattered most were not the doctors but the victims. So this was the wrong question, and the wrong person's question.

This is a mistake frequently made. So we tried starting the next version by making it about just one OCD sufferer. But this was *too* particular, and not a route map of what we were actually going to see. So we made a third version, which started following one character, who took us in to the other two characters. It also used extraordinarily strong bits of actuality we found within the film that director Andrew O'Connell, and executive producer Syeda Irtizaali, had managed to get as evidence of the problem which made the audience really care. The opening gave us strong evidence in actuality — something we could see, not just be told about. And at the end this version had a very answerable question. Finally it made a compelling front that drew people in, so that they watched quite differently. This is the right column of the final script.

THE HOUSE OF OBSESSIVE COMPULSIVES
A MONKEYKINGDOM PRODUCTION FOR CHANNEL 4
PRE-TITLE AS TRANSMITTED

CHARACTER 1   I can't touch anybody, can't sleep with my husband, I very rarely go out. I can't cook, I can't open the front door. I can't pick up the post. I can't have a shower. I never shop, I throw away clothes constantly . . .

v/o   *Wendy Johnson is one of two million people in Britain suffering from Obsessive Compulsive Disorder – OCD.*

CHARACTER 1   You've checked the front, you've checked the back, you've checked the sleeves, you've checked the cuffs, you've checked the collar – can I take it, is it safe? . . . And it's safe for me to put on later, promise . . .?

v/o   *Her irrational fear of coming into contact with shiny flecks of dirt, paint and glitter has prevented her touching her husband and their two children for three years.*

HUSBAND   It's difficult to have a sex life when you don't touch each other.

> CHARACTER 1   Yep, but we miss it, I do.
>
> v/o   *She has tried everything from drugs to therapy, and now in a last-ditch attempt to conquer her obsessions, Britain's leading expert on OCD has come up with a revolutionary idea . . .*
>
> v/o   *Wendy will move into a house with two other extreme sufferers and a team of top therapists. Together they will confront their nightmares and help each other to overcome their illness once and for all.*
>
> CHARACTER 2   I'll look on the soles of my shoes and step back and look at the floor . . .
>
> DOCTOR   Listen to that little voice that's saying do this do this and do exactly the opposite, so come on –
>
> CHARACTER 3   Oh –
>
> CHARACTER 1   Wow this is hard.
>
> v/o   *The OCD house will be their home until they're cured of their obsessions.*

Another series I worked on, *The Babyrace*, was even tougher. It followed thirty-five women of thirty-five, mostly without partners, as they tried to have babies in differing ways from donor insemination to adoption. The problem from the start is thirty-five is far too many characters to care for, so in the cutting room we reduced it to a few key characters for each programme.

A FILING SYSTEM

I often think of editing like filing – you can organise the papers on your desk by the date, by who wrote them, by the subject, by which are bills and which letters, by which are work and which personal, and so on. It doesn't really matter as long as you have an organising principle for the mash of information. The same applies to editing. Before you can really hone what your film is about there are the initial weeks of work to be done in the cutting room, amassing your material into an assembly, when it pays not to be too clever. We could have organised the baby race chronologically, but we decided to organise it round different methods of having a child. One programme would include the donor insemination stories, one the adoptions, one using a friend and so on. It doesn't matter how you organise the material, but whatever you have shot it has to be done.

In the eight-part Danish hit series *Skolen*, about the transformation of a Danish school using new teaching methods, we solved the problem by organising the material both ways with a single key character who would have a problem, such as not being good at maths, at the start and their attempt to transform by the end, as well as following the story chronologically through the school year, as the school attempted to climb right up the league table from near bottom to top.

Sometimes as well as different characters there are the different storylines they inhabit. As with heroes there is also a limit to how many storylines you can use, and the audience need to know which to concentrate on. Up to two storylines is relatively easy – you intercut. The only question is how long to stay on each story, and to find a motivation for swapping from one to another. When you have three it gets more difficult. In fact when we made a pilot for a series about village wars, we had an English couple, who had moved to France, fighting the village of Camembert as they set up a rival cheese shop to the Mayor; a couple setting up a pub and fighting a West Country village – and a third story that we dropped completely in the cutting room because it was one too many, even though it had been shot. We did the same in *Gerry's Big Decision*: we also had him visit two businesses rather than three, as in the initial treatment, though this time we made the decision from experience before filming, which saved a lot of tape, and also helped it (somewhat surprisingly to me at least) win the 2010 Best Documentary Format in the Los Angeles Factual Entertainment Awards.

Sometimes you end up in the cutting room with many storylines. Then I like to give each storyline a letter, and make sure they aren't treated equally. Invariably you will start story A, then story B, then back to A then back to B before going to C. Storylines D, E, F will probably only figure small and later, if at all, because we need to latch on to one or two big stories, and the others should be sub-stories.

Oprah's Big Give was an American network show in which people would be tested in charitable situations to see who was the biggest and best giver. Despite some great performances, with Oprah and Jamie as judges, there was a basic challenge to this concept in that each week someone would be fired for being the worst – hardly very true to the concept of charity. But there was a bigger problem as originally edited. First, contestants were introduced briefly in the cold open, then each with a call from Oprah and a piece about why they should win, so for many minutes we did not know who mattered most. Moreover the story had not yet got going. Then the characters were put into five pairs and each pair was given a task, which again we watched sequentially. In films we do not need to know all about everything, we want to latch on to a character or two, a storyline, and get the drama going. Only as we go on should you bring in other characters and subplots. The great danger of editing, as we keep trying to emphasise, is to think the audience need to know everything before the story begins. In fact it is quite the opposite.

Another series I helped, on teenagers, had such a difficult intercut and chronology, for the three teenagers it was following, that we started by separating out the three individual characters and cut them together as three separate stories to understand their chronology and their narrative drive. This is often the best solution when the intercut is so complex you cannot make head or tale of the story or even where it is happening. If in doubt, just try not to be too clever with your intercuts to start with, especially as you get more characters. Another trick, when it is all together, is just to write out a line with a letter for each character (as you did with stories) as they appear in the film: if it goes A B C D E F G A B C D E F G A B C D E F G and ends, you do not have a good film: it should look more like A B A B C B D A B C D A E F C D A, so you just have a couple of initial characters, who you know are the most important, then a third and a few minor ones – and I would drop G at least!

I recently worked on a documentary feature called *The Plan*, a follow-up to the award-winning *The Planet*, about the ecological dangers the earth faces, which was shown at film festivals around the world. The initial cut of *The Plan*, which showed individuals fighting back, had over forty characters, all separate and coming up one at a time. My first approach was to make a list dividing them into twenty-three characters who were actually doing something, and then another eighteen, from journalists to academics, who were talking about it. Then we chose just the few best to feature and introduce, and made clear they were the important ones to follow, and I ended up suggesting character A, then B, then back to A before bringing in C then back to B. There is no hard and fast rule other than to make sure you make clear who your few main characters are, and feature them strongly.

CHOOSING AND MOTIVATING EDITORS

I often think of the cutting room as the hot kitchen of film-making. You set out to grow the ingredients you need for your recipe, to film the ingredients you need, but when you get to the kitchen, the cutting room, at least a few will probably be missing and you will have brought home some new ones you didn't expect. The cutting room is like *Ready Steady Cook*, where you have to make the very best you can out of the ingredients you actually filmed successfully against the clock. The editor is your cook and the single most important person you employ. Above all you should trust them. Your editor may see a different film to the one you intended to make, or your cutting order suggests, because the rushes do tell their own story, and the editor is most likely to spot what those rushes are really trying to say. So unless you really have to do it yourself, I thoroughly recommend employing an editor, for seeing your rushes as they really are, without the benefit of hindsight. As Orson Welles said, 'To shoot is human, to edit divine.'

ALAN HAYLING

Former Head of BBC Documentaries, and
Documentary Commissioner, Channel 4, who looked after
Bowling for Columbine with Michael Moore

Michael Moore's films are really substantially made in the cutting room. He has a brilliant editor, Kurt Engfehr, with a really strong sense of narrative, very strong sense of the absurd, very strong sense of humour and brilliant sense of comic timing in the way he edits.

PETER MOORE

Former Head of Documentaries, Channel 4

People often choose editors and cameramen who don't question them, and that's what they like about them. However, I think that's how they lose track of the big picture. People just get too close to the material and can't see it in any other construction than the way they have filmed it.

So seek out the best editors, months in advance. Remember that they are prima donnas too, and will need to be courted and persuaded that working on your material will be interesting, and can make an original film. In TV you will often find production managers insisting that you work with a particular editor. If this favoured editor has already been contracted by the production you may have to use them. But if the editor who has been thrust upon you has not yet been booked, appeal to the executive producer. Everyone wants a better film if they can afford it. If you have attracted the best, and found a way to pay for it within your budget, you should hopefully be able to convince your bosses. You may not have control of the budget, but again try to know at least what it is, and make strong suggestions.

Whoever is editing, court this editor even before you begin the edit. Over time, if you are lucky, you will build relationships with a small handful. I suggest that you even speak to them before and while making every film, even if you are not going to edit with them as they so often put their finger on the real problem before and during filming. These should be wise editors who have a truly visceral understanding of film. Choose them, as other members of your team, by looking at what has been edited well, but mostly by recommendation, and meeting if possible.

Stefan Ronowicz has won many awards, partly because of his great talent (a Polish film-maker, he began teaching in the London Film School), but also because he chooses the right projects – another recommendation that applies to editors too. *Enemies of the People*, about the Cambodian Pol Pot regime, had been ten years in the making, when he began cutting it. It had taken journalist Thet Sambath, who co-produced it, five years just persuading the main protagonist to take part, until one day he told Sambath that he had observed him for many years and had realised he was honest. Talk about slow burners. A morass of material, but unique. The edited film won the World Cinema Special Jury Prize at Sundance 2010. Later the same year Stefan also went on the BAFTA stage with the winning *Terror in Mumbai*.

It is also helpful if the editors you choose are strong and opinionated, again like the rest of your team (if you are brave enough). Stefan is particularly so – the one editor who has physically thrown me out of the cutting room on to the street, because he thought I was too obsessively concerned about the commentary. I respect anyone who does that.

STEFAN RONOWICZ'S EDITING TIPS
NO. 1: THE COURTING

I never agree to do a film unless I meet the director. I have to visualise what I can do with it, I have to like it, because the job is so hard you have to get something else from it than just money – you have to be interested, you have to care. And it is important if it is going to take six to eight weeks that you get on. People like Pawel Pawlikowski [director of BAFTA-winning feature films *My Summer of Love* and *Last Resort*], *even when he made documentaries, would come before he shot the film to talk about the idea – we have pre-editing so you are both thinking about the subject. The good film-maker will come to the film editor long long before he shoots the film. Then he brings some rushes, as with* Dostoevsky's Travels [multi-award-winning film following Dostoevsky's great-grandson's tour of Europe to buy a used Mercedes]. *This guy speaks to me from the screen – we both look and agree I could spend an hour with this guy.*

Remember an editor lives and breathes the film just as you do. It becomes 'their' film, and if it is really working they will tell their friends excitedly how 'their' film is going. Just like contributors – give them ownership. Find extra money for the editing by scrimping on filming, graphics, music, anything.

LOGGING THE FILM

The first part of editing is to know what you have got. If you haven't shot too much, view it all and get it in your head. As you do so for the first time, note what is best and what it says, and highlight those best bits with whatever system you like, then it is those bits with loads of stars or lots of lines in the margin which will make the film. If you have shot too much you may use someone to view and log the material for you, but at least try to view and master what you can. Really interrogate the logger about what they think the story is, and what is great.

Then, either as you go along, or when you finish, create a cutting order, using sequences you have shot, with time-code, and in-points and out-points, filling these in back on your original script that you have been steadily amending in the light of filming.

Again you need to be open, and to do this in the light of what you actually shot rather than what you intended to shoot.

AXEL ARNO

Chairman, EBU Documentary Group, and Commissioning Editor SVT, investor in many international documentaries

It is vital to be able to write a structure or script before you go shooting, and more important before you get to the edit suite. I can't understand people who go into the editing suit with 150 hours of film and start editing without knowing where they are going.

When I get challenged by film-makers saying you have to be open to everything, my answer is you don't have to do everything on camera, you have to do research first, then start filming when you know the story.

I always tried not to shoot too much so I could view the material in advance, and again with the editor, as the more the editor sees at the start the better they will be able to cook the best film. So often I have been in cutting rooms, as a troubleshooter, when we have found a wonderful sequence that makes the film, but that the editor never even saw!

You can almost always get by with less material shot – in fact it speeds the editing process and, as we have said, what you don't have when you get to the cutting room doesn't matter, as your editor will make the film only out of what he or she can see in the rushes. So in an ideal world you will be able to spend the first couple of days of your edit (obviously less for a short film) viewing as much of the material as possible with the editor. If you haven't overshot you will be able to view a greater proportion or even all of it together.

Once you have done the viewing, the first thing to work out with the editor is: what is the big question coming out of the film, now that it is shot? Is it the same as in the pre-shooting script? And who are the heroes now, and why should you care about them? You need to decide from whose point of view you are telling the story.

STEFAN RONOWICZ'S EDITING TIPS
NO. 2: FIND WHICH CHARACTERS WORK

You need to find out who the strongest characters are. And for that you need to come to the cutting room, because on location you eat dinners with your characters, you talk to them off screen, you have a drink with them and get a completely false idea of what you have got in your rushes. What you have got on your rushes is not the people you met — it is only what your camera saw.

Finally you must work out an organising principle, the filing, which is going to create the story. And you must work all this out in the light of what you actually shot, not what you intended to shoot, which is where an editor can be so useful. This is almost like a precursor to what you will be doing on the pre-title in a couple of weeks.

Take the editor out to lunch or a drink and discuss what the film is about. Stefan Ronowicz once told me the best editing is done in the garden with a glass of wine. Perhaps as an editor he would! But what he means is that you need to take some time to sit back to discuss what the film is really about. This may only need hours, but it could save days if you know what you are trying to make. Then you get cutting.

STEFAN RONOWICZ'S EDITING TIPS
NO. 3: START WITH A CHUNKY SCENE

You don't start cutting a film by cutting the beginning, because that's crap. You will find out how it should start later, so you go first for a key scene. The good director should point you towards an area of the film that has one — there is always a key scene. That scene could be in the middle, or nearer the beginning, but you have to establish the power, you have to establish the credentials of the film. If it speaks with that sequence you have cut, you can expand both ways, backwards and forwards — you are building the narrative. Usually you only build the beginning once you know how it ends.

If you can bring yourself to do it, leave the editor alone to put it together for a few days, while you concentrate on your next film, or just take a break.

STEFAN RONOWICZ'S EDITING TIPS
NO. 4: LEAVE THE EDITOR ALONE

The amazing thing is that people always say editing makes the film, but that's nonsense because lots of good films get wrecked by bad editing. If you overload the film with information and you haven't decided what it is about, you ruin the film trying to tell people everything all the time, in a film which is about a specific subject. The wise director knows that to use an editor as the animal who hunts stories is a sensible thing. So leave your editor alone as much as possible to see what he or she thinks. Very often what you will find is there's a lot more, and a different, perhaps a better story than you initially thought.

Few directors do leave their editors alone enough in the early stages, but the best do. If you have shot so much that the editor can never get on top of it, and you feel that you have to sit right through the assembly with them, then at least give them a chance to be on their own once you have done so. Directors are mostly control freaks, but at this point it benefits hugely to let go a bit. For the editor may really see your material differently, and surprise you. And you will be able to see what they present more freshly. Even late on, as you get very involved, it is vital to give editors days alone if they are to show their craft. You can always change what they have cut back again, but you can never get there if you didn't give the editor the freedom.

However you do it, you need to edit quickly once you have viewed to create a skeleton of your film. Don't add music and pretty pictures, just whack it down to see what it tells you. The quicker you can get to an assembly that is only double or treble the length of your film the better. My advice is to try to do this in a third of the editing time, so you have two-thirds left to hone it. Don't try to cut too well, or add advertisement breaks at this stage, because your film will keep changing. Only add them late on when you know what the film is, and it is only five minutes or so over-length.

The first bit of the honing, which hopefully you are starting less than halfway through your edit, because you have concentrated on structure not detail, is to begin work on that pre-title or cold open we discussed, or at least its first version. The next thing is to remove the introduction you have added immediately after the title.

GET THE STORY GOING FAST

Once you have found your story, it is important to remember, in the edit, too, that films do not post-title need introductions, they need to get going. The opening of your film, not just the pre-title but the first few minutes, will determine how people care and how many watch.

This is one of the most important, but also one of the most difficult, rules to follow. Your viewers usually won't be sitting in a cinema for two hours, where, in a darkened theatre with no distractions, you could start slowly because the audience have heard about the film from friends and reviewers who have already seen it, invested in the trip and a ticket. If you are lucky enough to have inherited or attracted many viewers at the beginning of your TV film, you need to grab them fast, because TV audiences can switch channels, read the paper, play on the computer, or whatever they fancy. As their hands hover with their remotes they will decide within the first minute or two if it is the sort of film they want to watch, if it is gripping with strong characters and a quest they care about, if it is well made or not. This is the time you have to sell your programme. But even if you grab them at the top you are still on trial; after a fast opening, and the title or subtitle, you then need to hold your audience by getting straight into some of the best actuality, and a meaty scene that gets the story going.

I have seen so many films fail because the first few minutes are slow, or don't make one care. So many directors have said to me, 'Watch the first ten minutes, because it gets really good after that,' and they made it that way: why? Similarly many series fail because of their first episode. They may have a great concept, but they start with an introductory programme setting the scene, before the story gets going. So many series do this: why? Even though we may all need an outside view, we should at least try to get the opening of our film right.

The key point yet again is that you do not need a lot of background information before you get your story going. So you should only drop in information on a 'needs must' basis, and exposition should come out of action. The temptation in the initial cut of *Jamie's School Dinners*, for instance, might be to give all the information you think the audience needs to know after the title and before the story begins. For instance, many directors might have been tempted to let us know that Jamie is starting in Kidbrooke School, which is in Greenwich, which is south of the River Thames. The population is 220,000, of which 21 per cent are under fifteen, and 46 per cent are from socio-economic groups C2, D and E. There are 66 primary schools and 14 secondary schools, so-many-hundred school dinner ladies, of which such-and-such per cent are part-time, and this number of languages spoken . . . etc. By which time you have lost the will to live and turned over to another channel. It was a temptation we all resisted.

But if you think of Hollywood movies (and it often helps when making factual programmes) they rarely start with loads of information about Dodge City and the cowboy hero's background, his immigrant grandparents, how many siblings he has, where he was born etc., before the story begins. They start with action. Pace is even more important and faster in the US.

ANDREA WONG

Former Chief Executive, Lifetime Networks, and Executive Vice President of Alternative Programming, ABC

Studio-based shows from Europe generally translate almost exactly the way they are to the US so you don't have to change a lot. Reality shows require a different kind of pacing. Americans like a faster pace and much greater rollercoasters, meaning they need to be hit on the head and told how to feel at any point of time in the show. Americans don't like subtlety as much, they don't have as much desire to look for the subtlety and the emotion – they want to be told this is a happy moment or this is a sad moment or this is where you should feel anxious. They need editing, music, everything you can put into it to make them feel that way.

However, when working on your own movie, for some reason it is almost impossible not to feel the need to give too much information. I can't resist when I direct myself. Almost any roughcut will do this to a greater or lesser degree, but one that is typical is an average *Trouble at*

the Top I worked on during the series' many seasons. The film, made in
the early 2000s, was about a struggling private school called Rannoch,
based in a lonely Scottish castle, and whether it would survive. When
I first got to the cutting room the pre-title was again a mash of characters – schoolkids, a head, a bursar etc. There was no route map, and
rather than a question there was an answer. The pre-title was the closing
day, which gave away the answer (that it had failed), not the question.
So there was little reason to care. Of course, as I have said, when I direct
films myself it's the same for me, because it's really hard to focus on
what the film is about, why it matters and why you should care without
outside help, and again there were some gems hidden inside.

Jane Root, then boss of BBC2, and till recently of the Discovery
Channels, always has a buzzword. Back then it was 'trope', now it is 'in the
moment'. Both applied this time. 'Trope' was used to mean something
that defined the film and made it different. It could be lots of tight shots
of people smoking (back when people smoked in offices), as in *Billion
Dollar Day*, the film I directed about currency dealers; black-and-white
hi-8 footage for the history sequences in *Blood on the Carpet*; snippets of
couples saying what had gone wrong for them, *Harry Met Sally* fashion,
to up the jeopardy before the main scenes in *Living the Dream*, a series
following people leaving humdrum jobs to set up dream businesses like
a B&B. These were even framed in postcards to give them a stronger
identity. It could be a colour tint or a very wide lens – anything stylistic.

JANE ROOT

Former President, Discovery Networks, and Controller BBC2,
now CEO Nutopia

*A trope is like a device, a theme that's very memorable and sticks in
your mind, something that somebody does or a graphic look or something
that's the trademark. It's like a world that you conjure up, often without
people quite knowing. In* The Office *there's a wonderful title sequence
with the photocopier churning out pieces of paper that completely sums
up the mundanity and greyness of the world and its repetitive nature.
Office machinery grinding on was the trope of that one.* Deadliest
Catch *is about imminent waves smashing into you – there's always a
wave out there about to get you.*

Part way through the film, there was a scene with a train coming across Rannoch Moor. As soon as I saw the train, I thought of the Harry Potter film that had recently been released. There was also a lively actuality sequence, along the Harry Potter trope. And after all Rannoch looked like Hogwarts! So why couldn't Harry Potter be the trope right from the start? I suggested first, to the director, that we could start the film with the train coming over Rannoch Moor, with the kids on it, to the Harry Potter soundtrack. He had shot some original and highly visual scenes but was rightly worried that most kids arrived by car. It's good for directors to worry, but I replied that I was sure some of them come in the train because I had just seen a scene of this, in the middle of the film, so we agreed it was fine. I absolutely believe in the importance of the authentic in what we do. I even think that's often what differentiates good films from bad films. But I also think it makes little difference to the understanding of the story whether eight people come in a train or fifteen people come in a train or whether three more arrive in Volvos! This will be discussed in more detail later . . .

So we started with the train, with pupils on board whose future was in doubt. The heroic quest became whether an extraordinary new marketing director, charged with attracting more pupils, could do so.

And the big question was articulated: whether the school would survive or not.

START A TIMELINE

Immediately after the title, rather than lots of information about the school, we got the clock going with a simple line – 'Term is about to begin at Rannoch School' – and then soon after our hero set out on a journey. The lively actuality sequence that I had spotted for this was not time-specific. In it the new marketing director set out to attract more pupils, outside a cinema showing the first Harry Potter film. It had energy, and it displayed visually what she was trying to do all the time. The lightness needed to come sooner. Yet again the director had shot a wonderful sequence that was hidden further down the film, but would make it start off with lively and immediate action when pulled up. And again it was not affected by time, as long as it happened while she was still struggling to attract pupils. Here's the opening scene I liked, with my comments on the left.

TROUBLE AT THE TOP
THE HEADLESS SCHOOL OF RANNOCH MOOR, BBC TV

Time clock gets going.	COMMENTARY Term begins. All the school's hopes are pinned on its marketing director. Rannoch school is too remote to have any day pupils but some new boarders wouldn't go amiss.
	[Driving through forest.]
Actuality scene with energy.	COMMENTARY Helen sets off to Perth, a mere ninety-minute drive, where she is hoping to conjure up some new kids.
	Up sound Helen interview while driving.
	[Arrive at cinema.]
What a great idea – need to exploit it more in the film.	COMMENTARY She's not alone. Helen has taken her very own Harry Harrison from Rannoch's first form complete with cape and glasses.
	Up sound. Actuality outside cinema.

In a twist of art following reality, the producers of *Harry Potter and the Deathly Hallows* went to Rannoch Station, complete with Harry and the crowd, to film the Hogwarts Express arriving there for their final film!

So once you have made a pre-title, on the next pass at cutting get rid of the next ten minutes – or at least dramatically shorten the next ten minutes, and get going with some good action, straight into some of the best actuality. Get the story going in time and with motivation, and with a very brief commentary only if you need it. Above all get actuality going as quickly as possible. My pad at viewings is mostly covered with questions like these: 'What is it about?', 'What is happening?', 'When is it happening?' and 'I don't know where I am' – all continuously repeated as we go through the film! This is what needs saying, particularly at the front.

EXPOSITION ONLY OUT OF ACTION

In drama you learn the background out of the story as it goes along, and exposition comes from plot. Yet so many documentary-makers, despite trying to follow a dramatic structure, feel they need to tell you every background detail sometimes for ten minutes before the actual story begins, rather than making it clear where the story is going using plot.

Instead, this Rannoch actuality sequence has set up the conflict and jeopardy for the heroine, and her quest – whether she will be able to keep the school open – and we see it all in action, rather than tell it.

If the conflict is between a hero and anti-hero, another good way of starting post-title is with counterpointed actuality that sets this conflict up. In *Jamie's School Dinners*, for instance, after the title we went straight into an actuality scene of Jamie at home, cooking with his family, talking about how much it cost to feed his small daughter Poppy as he spoon-fed her. During the edit, however, we decided that this scene wasn't working well enough on its own. Jamie's filmed words were not quite right (they had been filmed a year before the edit so this was hardly surprising). They were a bit light and again weren't referring to the size of the problem he had to solve and its history, which was what we felt we now needed. And we didn't want more commentary.

So we went and shot a new scene to go here, a single piece to camera, in the same location, his kitchen at home. In this Jamie passionately outlined the historic problem with school dinners. Again, it was a timeless piece, the equivalent of an on-camera piece of narration, the stuff of American network factual TV.

Once we had successfully set up Jamie as knowledgeable, caring and reacting to a problem, we then intercut him at home with the school dinner lady Nora in the rough-and-tumble of the noisy Kidbrooke School canteen, to keep the motivation and energy up. And we asked her what she expected of Jamie.

This meant that we had both their expectations, and it increased the tension of what might happen when they met. We also honed down each piece of Jamie and Nora, the anticipation, so we got to the school quicker. But one thing was still wrong. Jamie's drive to his first day at school in that Maserati. It had been my stupid idea that he set off to meet Nora for the first time in his smartest car. It had even taken some time persuading him to do it. Yet it again only emphasised the Jamie that some people had grown to hate. Not only was it a smart car, but he spent his journey getting lost with his satnav and ending up late, which might seem funny, but certainly made it seem he didn't care. It was another reason the front wasn't working.

It is vital to admit to yourself when you are wrong, which happens frequently to me (and should to anyone in TV or they are not trying). It helps when your friend in Denmark has said the first film in your series is a pile of rubbish, about which the audience will never care.

It motivated us to find the very caring piece to camera from Jamie later in the film when driving in his Range Rover. Again it was a time-less piece about the state of our schools, so could fit anywhere. Replacing the flippant Maserati drive with it really helped to change Jamie from the cheeky chappy to someone who really cared about a real problem that was being ignored. Which again also helped the audience to care.

Editing sometimes feels like driving an old steam train with lots of levers to adjust, and moving just two or three can completely change the film. *School Dinners* was totally transformed by these three simple things:

- Putting kids suffering because of their dinners at the very front of the pre-title – so you cared.

- Having the newly shot piece of Jamie in the first actuality sequence, showing the magnitude of his challenge – so you cared.

- Dropping the Maserati on the drive down, and putting in a passionate piece – so you cared.

But it's not enough just getting the pre-title and the first few minutes right. Once you have the audience hooked, you need to keep them. Sequences with pregnancy will help, each with their small question and small answer, a continuing drama. It needs pace as well, like a symphony or stage play that has differently paced movements or acts. But despite your best efforts there will come a point where the film will sag, and the audience may flag too. It might happen sooner, but is highly likely two-thirds of the way through: in a forty-seven-minute film (a Channel 4 hour) it is often around thirty minutes in. Then you need a bit of drama at this point, and preferably a surprise, to give a twist or a turn. Moving a strong sequence here helps. In the first episode of *School Dinners* our twist two-thirds through was to get dinner lady Nora to go and work at Jamie's fancy restaurant Fifteen in a classic job swap.

TWIST AND SURPRISES

Even if you have begun with a strong pre-title, continued with strong actuality, and put a good twist in two-thirds of the way through, this still isn't enough. Just as there is a big question and a big answer, and then smaller ones in sequences, so also there is the big twist and smaller twists.

As you work at the scenes, and move them around or speed them up, you will be trying to give your film pace and surprise. You will try to pull on the levers of emotion to adjust the film, so the audience is not quite sure what is coming next, and wants to know. However, as you try to give your film drama and pace, you will discover one of the most miserable aspects of editing. As you try things out, often they won't work. Quite frequently they make the film worse. When this happens it is important to remember that the best editing should be two steps forward, one step back. The step back shouldn't bother you. It is because you are trying big changes.

This applies to commissioning too. Remember *Top Gear*. At the end of the nineties the car review show had been running for many years, going on as it was. It was hard to envisage the leap it needed, and it looked doomed. But when its lead presenter Jeremy Clarkson left it and went off to do other series, including a journey round Europe, and his own chat show, it was the step back that enabled two steps forwards, to create the radical super-hit we discussed earlier. It is just the same in editing, so be brave, and also listen to radical suggestions.

BE BRAVE AND MAKE BIG CHANGES

So it is most important to try outlandish things, especially in the edit. Only by seeing your film really differently will you be able to recognise the necessary incremental change, especially if it isn't working.

If you just try small changes you may never get there. In fact sometimes the film can and should go into complete reverse when you get to the cutting room, compared with what you intended. For it is vital to think *out of the box* again – though only about what you have filmed, not what you set out to film. In fact you now have to learn that it doesn't matter what you don't film, only what you do.

STEFAN RONOWICZ'S EDITING TIPS
NO. 5: WHEN IT GOES WRONG

Just as in life very often people become trapped, so characters in your film can get trapped in a circular situation, where they keep coming back to the same point. But a film has to move forward, so you have to break the circle and make it linear. If you can't find a story, if the film becomes circular – and a lot of films do – and you start at a certain point and halfway through realise you are back where you started, the nightmare of editing the circular narrative, you have to find a way out of it.

Narrative is building the bones of the film. Once you have got the bones you can start cutting, but you can't put decorations on a Christmas tree if you haven't got a tree. You've got to have trunk and branches to hang the goodies on.

It is also wise, as you shorten the film, not to salami-slice every scene but to throw some out in their entirety, along with some characters. You may be very wedded to them, but you must forget them once they have gone and move on. The audience will never know they were there and, however good, probably be relieved they aren't because they didn't help your story.

STEFAN RONOWICZ'S EDITING TIPS
NO. 6: THE DAY OF RAPE

With too many characters prune them. There is often the day of rape when you have to persuade the director, with the film over-length, to get rid of beloved scenes and characters. Pair some characters up and lose those who don't fit. There is always one strongest who emerges who becomes the person who is telling the story.

Moving sequences around can change the overall feeling. But dropping one completely, and replacing it with another, does this far more, especially as you set up the film in the first few minutes. With *Jamie's School Dinners* the whole feeling of the film was altered by removing those Jamie cheeky-chappy bits and replacing them with a couple of more serious ones, and the pre-title.

Sometimes, just like a puzzle, when you take one bit out you may want to put a bit back that you had discarded. Simon Dickson, Deputy Head of Documentaries at Channel 4, is a master in the cutting room. I have been with him in a viewing when he suggests doing something, then on seeing the change next day asks for it to be undone. Sometimes the director asks grumpily why he asked for it in the first place – to which Simon replies the film is now a different film. Indeed, every time you recut it is a different film, so maybe what didn't work in the previous cut is now exactly what you need. Conversely it pays to be big enough that when you try something that doesn't work, you admit it.

SIMON DICKSON

Deputy Head of Documentaries, Channel 4,
Commissioner, *The Family* and *One Born Every Minute*

A good editor will be a combination of sensitivity and brutality. Editing means throwing away, paring down, getting rid of stuff. We talked about the fidelity of the storytelling and how true is always better. But no documentary should contain everything. It should never distort or misrepresent what went on, but by heck it should never contain everything that happened just because you filmed it.

With The Family *or* One Born Every Minute *there are up to forty cameras each able to record twenty-four hours a day in three streams. But that doesn't mean you have to show it all. If you wanted to see everything that happened in a maternity hospital during a three-week period, you should go and sit in a maternity hospital for three weeks. Documentary is not a time-and-motion technique. Documentary is something much more than that. Even when you're using forty cameras, you're still showing an individual's interpretation of what happened in that space during that time. It's what he or she wants the audience to see, and what journey he or she wants the audience to go on.*

Of course those individuals who are staring at seventy-two hours of footage per calendar day of turning over time, from time to time lose the ability to see the wood from the trees. And somebody coming in and making an honest and sympathetic assessment of what's working, and what's not, is the most powerful and helpful thing that can happen to any good director during the editing process.

With all this, editing takes time. So try to save money elsewhere in the budget to win a longer edit schedule, or beg extra at the end. When scheduling, secretly pencil in an extra week if you can, but for emergencies, and then work as though it isn't there. You'll probably need it anyway. Or use subterfuge to get more time. After the success of the *Troubleshooter* series, the next film I directed was a *QED*, *The Family Game*. *QED* was a long-running strand of popular science documentaries, and I chose to follow the transformation of a very naughty child, a sort of one-off *Supernanny* precursor. When it came to the edit I had dramatic and touching material, but I knew the *QED* editing budget wouldn't be enough. I wanted a really big audience, so I would need more edit time. How to get more than the *QED* norm?

The film involved a multi-camera shoot, which I used as a justification for pioneering a new kind of editing so new to the BBC. Non-linear editing on computer is the way almost all films are cut now, but back then it was highly experimental. The computer had a single-gigabyte hard drive – at that time considered huge, and very expensive, but not enough to hold much film material, even at atrocious, fuzzy quality. When it came to saving this material, on what is now called a DVD, each disc cost hundreds of pounds, and was considered highly valuable! I persuaded the BBC to let me be the first factual programme-maker to try this newfangled kit. Then I claimed that it would take longer to edit on. And they believed me; I got an extra week.

It was actually just a week more to think and edit, since the computer was quicker, despite our muddled fingers and its many crashes. The film was a success, partly because of the extra editing time I had won, getting a 39 per cent share of viewers and its share of awards. (Funny, isn't it, how Avids were supposed to speed up editing, but schedules have returned to much what they were with film, partly because so much more is shot, and the edit is revised far more often. It's a bit like word-processing, that has ended up taking just as long or longer, certainly doing this!)

During the *Family Game* edit I attempted to be radical, following my own rule for, as I have stressed, unless you are willing to go off at tangents that may not work it is very difficult to come back to the film you had, but now with a few changes far better.

The executive producer on *QED* came to the cutting room one morning for a viewing, and arrived before I did. I had been in the middle of one of these changes, which she quickly looked at before I arrived, and didn't like. So she recut the film herself – the wonders of the computer. I told the editor to ignore it. It was not part of our iterative process. I am going to regret saying this, but keep executive producers in their place, especially when they are wrong.

STEFAN RONOWICZ'S EDITING TIPS
NO 7: HOW YOU KNOW IT IS WORKING

The moment you know you have got a successful film is the day the director is rude to you, because he or she is no longer frightened. Inevitably most directors one day will put you down, and you go, 'Aha, there is a good film there!' They are totally confident, they've got it, and they don't have to be nice to you any more.

To sum up, the best thing about the cutting room is it does not matter what you have missed – the editor doesn't know and the audience will never know. After all, you could never film everything. So try to remember to get to an assembly fast by working out what the film is about, then put on your first pre-title just a third of the way through your edit. Get rid of the next ten minutes and start instead with a lively scene, and above all work with what you shot and let it tell the story.

As long as you have a few magic moments you can have fun in the cutting room. Whatever you have, you should hopefully be able to construct a story as you edit. When I am called to the cutting room, often late in the day, to sort out films that aren't working, many people think I will suggest going out and shooting more. I hardly ever do. When I am called in early, with days left to shoot, I often say stop shooting for a bit, save money, and concentrate on editing. You can almost always have too much footage, but an edit can hardly ever be long enough. Think about it.

Five

LOVE

AND MANAGING YOUR STARS AND CAREER

MANAGING PRESENTERS

Scripting, shooting and editing are all very important, but equally vital is motivating people and managing them – from stars and contributors, to your team, or sometimes that most difficult one of all, your bosses' boss as you try to get on. We'll begin with presenters or hosts.

Most of the best films are about people, as are most stories. Just as in drama, dealing with actors and getting the best out of them is a vital part of the job, so, in factual television, is managing your presenter, or contributor. They can have very fragile egos, especially if they are continuously putting themselves on the line. So listen to them intently, and try to be interested and amused. After all, if you're not, who will be? (It helps a lot if you have a funny, bright and perceptive presenter like Sir John or Jamie, with the real gift of the gab.) Remember you are forming a relationship, and as in a love relationship, you need to be clear and consistent about how it will work from the outset. You are the solid, reliable, trustworthy craftsman, the rock on which presenters can perform their flighty pirouettes – which you will LOVE and admire and then gently cajole them into giving you what you actually need.

The better the presenter looks, the better you will look, so do not try to take the glory while filming. Then the presenters will trust you more. It may not be that nice when they tell the press that what you think were your ideas were theirs, but that is just a mark of your success. It can also be galling when members of the public compliment the presenter for merely implementing your instructions, but it does not matter because you are then more likely to have a better film, a better next film, and perhaps pick up some awards. I have seen so many directors, with fragile egos of their own, try to show off in front of presenters. Worse, if they fail at this they often resort to some very fancy show-off directing, which interrupts the naturalness of the show and in the end just annoys the presenter and results in a worse film.

You can have presenters like Sir John Harvey-Jones, or Jamie Oliver, who have miraculously not been corrupted by celebrity, and remain true, but how do you LOVE presenters who are difficult, impossible and arrogant, and make them feel good? The first thing is to remember

MICHELE KURLAND

Executive Producer, *The Apprentice*

I was the first person to film with Anne Robinson. Often people say she is a monster but she is not. Like Alan Sugar, she just doesn't suffer fools. They can do things much faster in the real world, so they don't have much time or patience with people who don't know what they're doing.

I think it is always worth explaining the process. Just because they are on the screen doesn't mean they understand the process — they aren't familiar with editing or all you need to make your story. Also I often see people create a bigger problem because they treat the person as a species apart and then wonder why they don't muck in when they're running late or they need that bit extra. If you only see the talent when you're filming, and it's raining, and a fuse has gone, it's not conducive. So go and have a coffee and a meal and a chat. You need a relationship to cope when things go wrong. They should feel part of the team.

that, just as directors run on the dual fuel of arrogance and insecurity, and if one much outweighs the other they explode, performers run on the same combustible mixture. But theirs is very high-octane, propelling them not just on screen but — if they are famous — resulting in their performing much of the time, as they put themselves out there to be judged, not just in the film but in their celebrity lives too. It is very easy to notice the arrogance in presenters, but sometimes hard to remember how difficult it is for them to put themselves out there all the time, how very fragile they are, and how many insecurities they have to conceal.

So it helps, too, to have a healthy love of your presenter when making the film, and to make them feel that they can rely on you utterly. Make them feel big and confident, and remember you can never compliment contributors or presenters enough — confidence is key, especially when they are out there bravely fighting the world. Never tell them what to do, but josh them along playfully as though it is a game you are playing together. They are surrounded by people telling them how wonderful they are, they are asserting this to themselves, while inside desperately worrying — even more than directors — that they will be found out. And the second thing to remember is, if a presenter is being particularly difficult, that you will have control of the edit – or should do. I remember one time when I disagreed with Jeremy Clarkson, who had come into the cutting room to write. He said, 'I don't agree with democracy in the cutting room.' I replied, 'Neither do I.' I explained that I was the storyteller and it was my job here to use the rules of television and my craft skills to make him look good, and he would have to trust me! I just about managed it, and we had a great time completing the series *Speed* about all sorts of fast vehicles. He learnt more about big questions and structure – and, ever the opportunist, once we started working together I tried to pick up a little of his wit.

WHEN TO USE PRESENTERS' IDEAS

It can be extremely useful to get presenters involved in script discussions. They can have great ideas even if, like Sir John, they may not completely understand TV or storytelling. So do try to incorporate them where you can. Many presenters do not understand the detail of how television is made, but they do have a deep intuitive understanding of the medium, which is why they are so successful in it. So they will often come up with original and clever ideas which may fit your story, or may be utterly inappropriate. So think carefully before discarding them and, even if you think they are unlikely, sometimes humour the presenter and film them anyway. You never know: you might be wrong and they might work. When you are sure an idea doesn't fit, humour the presenter again, and say you will think about it, while quietly forgetting it. When it comes to your ideas, be careful not to be too bossy. Your job is to make presenters look and feel good.

Often insecure directors want to prove the ideas are theirs, and tell the presenter bossily what to do, but the absolutely key thing with presenters is to tickle their insecurity and as you progress through filming to continue to make them think that your ideas are their ideas too. After all, they have got to own and present them. Even if you fail to get them to think the idea is theirs, still try to avoid telling them what to do in a bossy fashion.

MICHELE KURLAND

Executive Producer, *The Apprentice*

If you do get tantrums from a presenter it's because if they were bland and pushovers you wouldn't want them on the screen — they wouldn't be big characters. The flip side of an opinionated character, which is what you need to engage an audience, is they are opinionated off camera as well as on. If they get upset, listen to them. What's bothering them is that their face is on screen, they're the ones who will look foolish to the public if they visibly screw up or don't deliver. They are more needy so they need reassurance. They want the show to be better too, so if they're still throwing a wobbly it's because we haven't explained what we need and why we need it.

ZOË COLLINS

Executive Producer, Jamie Oliver

Remember sometimes to be nice.

LOOK BAD TO LOOK GOOD

Once on location you will need presenters (and contributors) to do things for you that they may not particularly want to, even though it is ultimately in their interest. For this you will need to have built a relationship beforehand so you can really love and play with them, be really close to them, joking and joshing them into doing what you want rather than bossing them. But not always! For at the same time you need to have loved them so much and made them feel so secure you can be brave and do what is really best for them. Here is one of the most important rules of television: you have to persuade presenters that you need to make them look bad to look good. This is particularly tough, but it is vitally necessary.

You may want to keep certain bits of the script a surprise even for a presenter, so they feel spontaneous and real. For you can only make presenters look good if they have to overcome challenges. So having won their trust you need then to convince them that to seem heroic they need to be seen to surmount obstacles, which means there must be some obstacles to surmount. You need to give them problems to solve or get around, but you need to call them challenges. Always ask 'What is your greatest challenge?' rather than 'What is your biggest problem?' – it is less threatening but works better and gets the same result.

It can be something tiny. For instance, if a Jamie Oliver storyline requires him to face the challenge of finding the right ingredients on camera in a street market, when in fact they aren't easy to find, then Jamie has assistants who he knows can come up with anything. If you tell him point blank that he can't use them to help him out, it will just wind him up, and if he does use them to do his work it might destroy the point of the sequence. So he has to be amusingly joshed into not having help, since the challenge is part of the sequence. Not 'No, you mustn't,' but, 'You silly man, you know you can do it without them!' In the end it comes down to building a relationship and trust, so make certain you appear to know just what you are doing

Like much to do with presenters, this also applies to contributors, although you are unlikely to show them the script at all unless they are verging on a presenting role. Persuading them they need to be seen to rise to challenges to seem heroic can be even harder, as TV is not their profession. Many bosses found it very hard to go *Back to the Floor*. In another fish-out-of-water storyline, Gillian duCharme, headmistress of Benenden, the posh public school, was reduced to tears by her first tough class of inner-city comprehensive kids; but because she was persuaded to continue and rise to further and bigger challenges, the audience respected her and fell in love with her – and in the process learnt something about British education. It was a memorable film; she was thrilled – and it changed her life, as she decided to leave her Benenden job. Sometimes things get tougher. Luke Johnson, then boss of Belgo, tore off his radio mike when confronted by a fellow worker in the kitchen on his own restaurant 'shop floor', shouting, 'I've had enough and you can shove your programme right up there!' The director called me out and together, in what seemed like a Belgo cupboard, we persuaded him to carry on, and I think he came out looking good.

Even Jamie would sometimes balk at the number of challenges he had to face. It isn't easy, and it's very tiring and stressful. But your job is to be brave and push the presenter or contributor in a loving, playful, cajoling way into the next challenge which will make him or her look better, because if they are not surmounting anything they are neither revealing their character under pressure nor looking heroic, so the audience will not fully appreciate them.

With presenters and contributors, then, you need the kind of tough love that is prepared to tell them what is best for them, but in a jocular fashion, while always listening because they *might* be more right than you. This can be hard for a new director, coming on to a show with presenters or contributors who are used to working with the previous director. In this case, bonding time, if you can get it, is even more important. When Jamie went on his *Italian Escape* with yet another new director, he felt he had had enough of challenges, for *Jamie's Kitchen* and *School Dinners* had been tough. It was a hard assignment for a new director, because Channel 4 (and I) believed Jamie still needed those challenges if there was to be a story and he was not to look like a Sainsbury's ad. It was an equally tough assignment for the director who moved into *Nightmare at Canary Wharf* that I had begun with Janet Street-Porter, or taking on Sir John Harvey-Jones.

When persuading the reluctant hero of the need to be challenged, the harder the challenge the more it helps if the director looks relaxed, so they can continue to play and josh the presenter into doing what they want while inside they are a bundle of nerves. When all is falling apart, and you think the film is a disaster, don't let the contributors know. If they are not doing well for you, don't say so or they will collapse. Say you are really pleased, *but* . . . Even this they will find devastating. Remember they are sensitive out there.

When it gets to the edit, I find it helpful if you can get on with it, and only show the presenter the cut towards the end, unless it is a specialist subject, or current affairs/news, in which case you may be producing it together. For instance, on *Tomorrow's World* the presenters often wrote the initial scripts and were very involved in the edit, as are many on-screen journalists. If they are also producers like David Attenborough or Michael Moore (who makes his films in the edit), I would expect them to be. But it can often be most satisfying for a director when you have busy and trusting presenters like Sir John, Heston Blumenthal or Jamie Oliver, who just let you get on with it, but will throw in an idea or some great lines at the end.

At the outset of *School Dinners* I persuaded Jamie that if I made the series he could not come to the cutting room at all till the films were almost done, just like Sir John Harvey-Jones, and if there was anything he didn't like it would ultimately be my call whether to change it, because I had the objectivity, even if he owned the company.

Jamie was invited to a formal viewing of the near-finished first *School Dinners*, with wine, to discuss questions of accuracy just like any contributor (we will come to the fraught question of viewings with contributors later). Luckily he liked them, and we convinced him the difficult bits looked good, which they did, because he is brave and understands TV. In fact he was trusting, the best thing a presenter can be, for it is very hard to judge your own performance. Later we just sent him the programmes on DVD.

On viewing, we never had a disagreement with either Sir John or Jamie, because they recognised the films as fair, accurate and heroic, and we made huge efforts to make them so. Jamie's worries, if he had any, would almost always be about food, Sir John's about business – both areas in which they were expert and passionate. In my view if the presenter owns the company, which is becoming more frequently the case, it is even more important that they don't get over-involved in an edit to which they may be too close, with the resulting loss of objectivity.

DEALING WITH CONTRIBUTORS

Contributors are a far more difficult version of presenters, as most are appearing for the first time, and usually you are making a film about them rather than with them. They understand far less what is going on, and you have to persuade them to take part, though there isn't the downside of having to deal with fame, or – usually – the dual fuels of arrogance and insecurity. When you first meet, getting close to contributors is even more important, so try to find something you share – you almost always can. It is worth spending as much time and charm as you have to win their trust and get them on board, then seize the luck that comes past your nose.

A few years ago I was spending Christmas in a very simple tree house – a mattress on a simple platform, suspended amid palm trees looking over the sea in southern India – a good antidote to executive producing. On Christmas Eve a strange uniformed bicyclist turned up, and said, 'Facksy message, sir.' I couldn't work out what he wanted till he stuffed a gnarled piece of paper in my hand. It turned out to be a

Christmas present from the Holy Land, a fax about about one of the world's very richest men. An enterprising producer in my team, Adam Wishart, had come across Sheldon Adelson while both were holidaying in Israel. Should he buy a suit and go to meet him? Self-made billionaire Sheldon (the world's third richest man as I began this book, after Bill Gates and Warren Buffett, worth over $20 billion on the Forbes Rich List) had apparently bought the Sands Hotel in the middle of Las Vegas, and blown it up. His plan was to spend two and a half billion dollars building a six-thousand-suite hotel set in a replica Venice, complete with St Mark's Square, the Rialto Bridge, Doge's Palace and Grand Canal, as that was where he had met his wife. It sounded heroic (and romantic), so I said, 'Yes, please, but forget the suit.' I received another facksy message back after the meeting. There was a potential story but the billionaire was wary. I needed to persuade him too.

Three months later, after much negotiating, I made a special trip to Passover in Israel, to chat Sheldon up and make him comfortable. It proved highly worthwhile. It usually does.

PETER MOORE

Former Executive Producer, *The Apprentice*

Try to convince them they'd be far better off appearing in the programme than watching it without themselves in it. They would regret not being in the film because they have something to say that is really valuable.

MICHELE KURLAND

Executive Producer, *The Apprentice*

You have to give them a reason for doing it; they're never going to do it because your programme is going to be better or it suits you. It could be anything: sharing a problem or their passion, something that matters to them that we want to follow. Every producer has to find their own reason for that person. You can't make someone do something they don't want to, and if they do, it will be boring television and you'll end up cutting them out of the film.

The care went on. Sheldon agreed to be in the film, and a month later I found myself at Marco Polo airport in Venice just as his private jet landed, to see what he and his designers might rebuild on the Las Vegas strip. It was the start of filming with just what you would expect of a billionaire – a typical high-maintenance prima donna, who had struggled to become a success from the bottom up. The director, Simon Dickson again, ever keen on his food, happened to mention some particularly fine roast onions he had once eaten in London. Soon after we were back from Italy I received a call. Sheldon Adelson wanted some. So we booked a table at the Bibendum restaurant in Fulham for the appointed night. When the (to me) pint-sized Danny DeVito lookalike arrived – late, not surprisingly – he was in a bit of a fury. It appeared that he hadn't been able to land his jet where he wanted, so had had to drive in from some inferior and more distant airport. He sat down, took one look at the menu, and demanded that his meal should be cooked differently. The restaurant – surprisingly unused to prima-donna billionaires – was not amused, but found something he was just about willing to eat, including the onions.

I was hugely relieved as the bill came and we paid. We had just about survived. I innocently asked reception if they could get us a taxi. They replied, 'No, it is perfectly easy to hail one yourself on the street.' Unfor-tunately there were other people outside, all I supposed waiting for taxis, so I walked to the corner to stand a better chance. Sheldon stayed behind. Finally I saw the first of the restaurant queue succeed in hailing a cab, only for Sheldon to try to get into it. I tore back to tell him he couldn't do that; even a billionaire had to wait his turn in the queue. Sheldon replied, 'Yes I can. The queue is mine.' They were his security guards and entourage, who had flown in to protect him and were 'waiting' outside the restaurant. They piled into vehicles of their own.

Surprisingly, the meal was a judged a success. We continued filming following the construction of The Venetian, including a quarter-mile indoor Grand Canal. Then Simon, our director, twisted his ankle. The singing gondoliers for the hotel's second-floor canal were to be audi-tioned in Los Angeles, and he could no longer make it. I had a trip to Australia planned, so I stopped off en route in Hollywood, and went straight off the plane to a sad little dance studio, where I filmed an even sadder endless succession of has-beens and never-beens as they played their fiddles, sang their songs in desperate versions of pop stars, till a few

hopefuls were selected to pole their way up the canal in their electric-
ally assisted gondolas, singing occasionally, almost like the real thing.

There was another reason I was filming – to keep Sheldon on board.
His tiny brand-new son was having his foreskin cut off in Las Vegas. The
call came – would I like to attend the ceremony? Now completely
shattered, I had to say yes to the honour, and next morning flew in. At
his house the morning guests were enjoying cocktails and canapés in
his large and glitzy sitting room. The baby was lying on pieces of
material, his penis apparently erect. A man looking like a fearsome
barber lifted what – to me, finding it very hard to look – appeared to
be a knife, and ceremoniously brought it down to a prehistoric scream.
Jet lag, failed gondoliers and bits of cut-off penis were enough for me.
I decided to miss the rest of Las Vegas, which I had never visited, raced
straight back to the airport, checked in, and went to the gate. I called
Simon back in London. I was so traumatised I didn't notice the rest of
the passengers get in the plane, or that it was taxiing away with my
luggage. All the other planes were full because of some huge conference, but finally I bought a new ticket and late at night finally landed
back at LAX with minutes to spare for my connection to Australia.
Finally I saw one very lonely piece of luggage going round, all by itself
on the carousel, in a big empty arrivals hall. It was mine. Another
contributor had been kept happy, and I really ended up enjoying working with Sheldon, though he had some very bad press.

Everything depends again on trust, and contributors can sense what
you are thinking and how you feel. So if you are to get on with them
you must try not to judge them, at least before the edit. First, they will
sense if you do; and second, in factual TV it is important not to prejudge the story or character – but it is not just in the research phase that
you should try to judge as little as possible, as you try to think out of the
box. It applies to the filming too. So wait till you have finished. Let the
rushes speak – the time to judge what the truth is, is in the cutting room.

KEEPING CONTRIBUTORS ON BOARD

When visiting India some people are so shocked by the poverty, dirt,
squalor and people's behaviour towards each other that they find it hard
to recover and see what is there. But others look, take it in, and do not
judge while there, which would just stop them seeing. They take it for

what it is, and then judge mercilessly afterwards on their return. Apply this to presenters, contributors and colleagues. After all, you will have plenty of time in the cutting room to judge.

When I arrived at the *Daily Mirror* at midnight with Robert Maxwell, the day he took over, I sympathised with the psychiatrist I then lived with. We both had our patients and now I was up on the top floor of the *Mirror* building with a brand-new one, Mr Maxwell. He was an appalling man who screamed uncontrollably at both his subordinates, revelling in putting them down in public, and even his children, whom he tried to employ. But as a new patient I had to suspend disbelief and not judge him till the cutting room. And I really enjoyed his company while filming. Sometimes you will film villains, even murderers, and the same applies. When Truman Capote wrote his famous *In Cold Blood*, following two men on Death Row found guilty of murdering an old couple in their farmhouse, as he researched and wrote the murderers thought they had found their real and only friend. He listened, he tried to understand, he really didn't judge as he visited the prison week after week. He tried to put himself into their heads. He was their friend. It was only when he started putting all his notes together, and writing his book, that his judgement came to the fore, surprising them. If it had done so earlier he would never have really understood, nor got the material.

As filming with Robert Maxwell continued, he reminded me of Orson Welles in *The Third Man*. Although Welles's character is killing little children with bogus penicillin the director, Carol Reed, actually gets the audience to sympathise with him, to admire his chutzpah and charm, as he metaphorically opens his great coat to offer you rows of stolen watches.

Ian Robert Maxwell was originally Jan Ludwik Hoch, a poor Ruthenian woodcutter's son from an orthodox Jewish family. As war swept across central Europe he escaped across the Continent, rapidly learning English, and persuaded the British he could be an instant posh British officer with a new name, Leslie du Maurier. After the war with another new name, Robert Maxwell, he got his own personal revenge as he used the Germans' scientific publishing industry as the foundation of his fortune. This was our 'other story', the subtext of the monster, and it had tragedy written all over it.

The day's filming leading to Maxwell's triumphant arrival at the *Mirror*, back in Maxwell's eponymous HQ, 'Maxwell House', had been fraught. It was only towards the evening that we knew Maxwell had won. We had got close enough to stick with him, and as midnight neared we managed to film the drive with him to the *Mirror* building in his gleaming maroon Rolls-Royce. And we travelled up to the top floor, with Maxwell itching to take control of the editorial staff for the next morning's edition! It was the culmination of a very long dream. Now, shortly after midnight, and without asking, our film crew followed him into what a few hours before had been the office of ousted boss Clive Thornton. It was full of Maxwell's henchmen and *Mirror* bosses, assembled for their first summit meeting with the new man on how to make the next day's paper happen. Then Maxwell looked at us and his voice boomed, 'What are you doing here? Get out!' Now the director I was working with was David Dugan, now boss of Windfall Films, from whom I had learnt a great deal. And he just scratched his head and appeared not to understand.

It was a technique I had seen him perfect in a shoot in the forests of Côte d'Ivoire. We had passed a grave site in the jungle and decided to film it. A group of locals who spoke no English began to assemble. They started waving machetes, looking more and more menacing. My director shrugged his shoulders, scratched his head, and appeared not to understand. One of the jobs of an assistant producer is to prevent himself and his foolhardy director getting killed. I had to manhandle him into the car very fast and drove down the dusty track at full speed.

David's secret was to appear to contributors to be well meaning but slightly silly. It was a top tip, which has worked brilliantly for me – I highly recommend it. On this film, at least Robert Maxwell and his henchmen had no machetes, and my director continued filming as the meeting began. After about five minutes Maxwell looked up, seemed to notice us again, and this time boomed, 'I thought I told you to f—k off.' And the director scratched his head, looked stupid, and carried on filming. I was full of admiration. Finally after a bit more filming Maxwell got up and started screaming and we had to leave. It is what I call the importance of understanding when 'f—k off' means f—k off. But half an hour later, as soon as the door opened, our director was back in again, to film Maxwell screaming at one of his subordinates, partly for our benefit. It is a game! Especially with manipulative people.

As the weeks went by Robert Maxwell would call his editor or managing director in, and abuse them in front of us, just for fun. He would even do it with his children. It was appalling behaviour in retro-spect, but at the time we just filmed and watched, and he knew that we were not judging him and so he gave us more. Contributors need to feel loved and respected if they are to give their best. The true time to judge the truth is, as ever, in the cutting room.

THOMAS BREINHOLT

Former Commissioning Editor Factual, TV2 Denmark.
Executive Producer, *Don't Tell the Bride*, Denmark

Keeping contributors and presenters in a programme has so much to do with the ability to empathise with them. With the Danish Don't Tell the Bride [the format in which the man organises the wedding while the bride stays away till the big day] *about one and a half weeks into filming, having spent all this money casting and filming, I get a phone call that the main character doesn't want to participate any more because he thinks his girlfriend is being badly handled.*

So I took the first train to Aarhus at the other end of the country, and just started schmoozing. I bought the girlfriend a big dinner, put her in a hotel, and let them make a phone call they weren't supposed to. I talked to him, told him how great he was, but he was fuming with rage. I spent Friday evening and Saturday getting him back on board and managed to do it.

It's all psychology at the end of the day – the ability to get them to like you. You're their friend, you understand all the troubles they have with the programme, you think the same, and you understand it, but . . .

PERSUADING CONTRIBUTORS WHAT TO DO

It doesn't matter if you go weeks without getting anything good, or miss great dramas, just as long as you get something. On *The Dome: Trouble at the Big Top*, the series we made following the Millennium Dome, it was very hard to get a master interview with the minister whose dream it was, Peter Mandelson. It became even tougher when he resigned because of a scandal about how his house purchase was financed, and he was no longer responsible for the Dome. I persevered, asking again and again. One day I met him, and chatted away generally, then just as he went off to the lavatory I mentioned the Dome, and said maybe it will be a success, but will anybody now remember your part in making it happen? He returned from the lavatory, having mulled this over, and said, 'Maybe you should interview me.' As a result, over a year after starting work on the series, I finally won that master interview with Peter Mandelson, at his behest (I always said contributors are like lovers and need to think it is their decision).

It was a single interview of an hour at his home (the place he was selling because of the scandal), an informal conversation. My first question was a quiet, 'Why did you take on the Dome?' 'Because I was told to,' he replied, and he continued in a surprisingly honest vein, remembering back to the early days of its construction when the press were on the warpath. It was enough to transform the entire series. Persistence and persuasion had paid off. Mandelson had decided to be honest because he trusted us with answers like this:

THE DOME: TROUBLE AT THE BIG TOP
BBC, EPISODE 1, AS TRANSMITTED

PETER MANDELSON   It certainly felt a bit lonely – there was nobody, none of my colleagues, nobody was speaking up for it, saying, look leave me alone. Even the Prime Minister was wondering, 'What is it doing to my government?' As we went into the New Year I felt my own career was slightly shaky – people were looking at me differently and wondering, 'What is going on – is this man going to survive?'

Sometimes you may not even know when you are shooting what may become the all-important magic sequence, so push for access to the unlikeliest moments with key contributors. But there is a limit. One day, while still minister responsible for the Dome, Mandelson seemed a bit out of sorts as he wandered round the building followed by a large entourage. He seemed obsessed by his pager, and then moved away to have a conversation on the mobile phone. Even though I was the executive producer I was jointly directing with series producer Adam Wishart – I wouldn't have missed filming someone as intriguing as Mandelson, and I hated being stuck in an office. Not knowing what was happening on the phone, we continued to film, but although we had sound from a distant radio mike, I didn't hear it till it was replayed later.

Soon we were at the tour's end and Mandelson charged into his car to return to No. 10 and the Prime Minister. I tried to get in too but he slammed the door, with me still remonstrating that he had to let me in. It was only as Adam, thinking that I was maybe going too far, told me in no uncertain terms that I had to move out of the way, that the car was able to speed off to the Prime Minister. I had been 'saved' like my producer David Dugan in Africa all those years ago. Later that evening the news reported that Mandelson had resigned. Looking the next day at what we had filmed, it turned out that we had the conversations leading up to this from the radio mike without knowing it. Luck again, but time and persistence certainly helped.

For many contributors the filming team is like a lover about whom they have mixed feelings. The thought of being with the crew drives them mad, the thought of being without it even madder. In the very first *Trouble at the Top*, *Nightmare at Canary Wharf*, there was a lot that we didn't film because of this. Years after following Robert Maxwell (he had drowned in strange circumstances) and the tower having been torn down, the *Mirror* group moved to a new building on Canary Wharf, under a new owner, David Montgomery, and decided to expand into television. I was back there now making a film with Janet Street-Porter about the setting up of one of Britain's first cable stations, L!ve TV.

But when Janet agreed to give us access to film the setting up of what she thought was her baby, I couldn't get round to starting. Again I was supposed to be an executive producer but wanted to direct such an amazing lady (when commissioning, my surest test of a pitch was if I desperately wanted to direct it myself, or would prefer to avoid it). But I prevaricated about making the film at all; it was to be the pilot for *Trouble at the Top*, which was the first business series I was being allowed to make since the original *Troubleshooter* – despite all *Troubleshooter*'s success, the BBC still didn't really trust programmes on business, and was doubtful about making many more.

I was so worried it wouldn't work that I was loath to commit and start filming this pilot, so Janet wrote to the boss of BBC2 asking where I was. I had yet to begin because following the success of *Troubleshooter* I found it hard to start filming anything else in case I got found out. So the success of this new pilot once more mattered very much to me.

Also I had become spoilt. Sir John Harvey-Jones, *Troubleshooter's* presenter, had been truly used to delegating in his business life, and completely trusted me, although I had just started with him as a first-time directing assistant producer. He was not fired by the combustible TV fuels of arrogance and insecurity, having been well recognised for his brilliance in business, and always jetting off to world leaders to discuss how they should run the world. Now at least I was wanted by another star contributor, but it was scary speculating what she would be like to work with. Against this, the combination of a new TV station, with Janet Street-Porter managing it, in the building of the macho *Daily Mirror*, sounded promising. It seemed like she would be great TV, and if her past was anything to go by she would fulminate honestly against anything she didn't like.

PETER MOORE

Executive Producer, *The Apprentice*

For the apprentices we wanted a mixture of people who would be outstanding businesspeople, who were characterful, and whose personality is written large, who more often than not say what they think without thinking what they say.

I had really admired Janet when at the BBC she had said just what she thought at the weekly programme review meeting, looking at the past week's programmes, when many department heads laced their views with what would be politically expedient – which would be death in a TV character. In fact, following the experience at Montgomery's *Mirror*, Janet was to make a tough speech at the Edinburgh Festival attacking the four 'M's of media – middle-class, middle-aged, mediocre, men. Funny that Montgomery and *Mirror* began with 'M's too.

So I took the plunge and began. Except many mornings, having checked I was coming with my office the evening before, as we arrived Janet's opening words were, quite understandably perhaps, 'What the f—k are you doing here?' There would ensue a cat-and-mouse game of whether I could film or not. One day she had an important summit meeting with tough Ulster protestant *Mirror* boss Montgomery, and when I turned up to film it she wouldn't let me. I wasn't fully aware of the huge pressure she was under, and that both she and Kelvin MacKenzie, the tough newspaper editor, appeared to think they were going to be in charge. Afterwards I made her feel so guilty she let me film her returning furious to her office. It was the best scene of the film. Always be prepared to give up something to get something better, and when forced to give up something make sure you do. Guilt is another motivator alongside charm and flattery.

As I was now also busy as an executive producer doing more and more, I found another director to take over. But it is very hard when you have courted a contributor, and done the foreplay, then to say sorry, I am not the person who will actually marry you, I was just warming you up, I'm leaving you with someone else instead. This is one reason why, when directing, I prefer to have a first meeting with contributors myself, and certainly be at many subsequent ones, rather than taking over from someone else who has made the relationship.

My director was quickly seen off – he couldn't take it, or vice versa. Then another brave director stepped in to help, young and inexperienced; he got some great moments but, finally, he was exasperated by all the things he couldn't film. The evening before yet another key meeting he wasn't being allowed to film, he rang Janet at home and threatened to call Montgomery and pull out, if she didn't agree to the filming. Janet was in the middle of a dinner party and not amused.

Brinksmanship in television is difficult, however tough the going, and if at all possible it is handy to leave yourself a let-out clause from which you can climb down. The ultimatum was brushed aside, Janet got her way, and I ended up finishing the film myself. I tried to explain to the whole team that Janet was having a tough time, she is a creative person, but put up with it – you do not need many magic moments and she is a star who is sure to give them.

Just like in any relationship, you need to choose what you want to fight over, what to be willing to give way over. Often you can give in on something that might even be quite boring, making a big fuss about it, and then use this loss as moral blackmail to film the very thing you do want. Confronting Janet head on was a mistake; but I adored her and respected her outbursts as she struggled in a very different den of newspapermen. She has passion, says what she thinks, and that's great TV!

THE IMPORTANCE OF FILMING AT HOME

So you have filmed your hero through challenges and supported them through difficult times, but there is still more you need to do to turn them into sympathetic human beings. It really helps if you film contributors and presenters at home and with their families. It is surprising how much visiting someone at home reveals. In a US psychological test, a panel was given descriptions of a group of students and shown photographs of their various rooms. Then they were asked to pair the photographs with descriptions. They did so with uncanny success. People's rooms, and how they relate to partners and children, can be highly revealing, especially when, in the cat-and-mouse game of documentary, they are often trying to hide their true selves.

The success of *School Dinners* was partly down to the vulnerability Jamie showed at home. It was tough for his wife Jules to put up with a film crew in the house, so we didn't film there often, but you don't need much and persistence wins out – as when Jamie arrived home after a shattering week in Durham only for his team to turn up just as we were filming and explain that the papers were threatening to carry another story about his 'marriage crisis', resulting in a very 'lively' family conversation in the kitchen and sitting room. The camera follows as Jamie explains to Jules that the latest story was that he'd 'shagged' some waitress in Amsterdam. Jules was upset as Jamie tried to explain it was all untrue, and walked out saying she couldn't take any more. She was fed up with the family and the kids being put through press hell because of his fame.

It was a very intimate moment and it showed the pressure Jamie was under from all directions as he fought to make better school meals. The sequence was, I believe, very important for the series. It showed Jamie as a vulnerable human being, thus helping the public actually to love him more, but it wasn't an easy one to cut and include. We debated among ourselves whether these bits were too intrusive. We put them in and removed them again. We shortened and lengthened them, and finally settled on the minimum that would make them work without feeling indulgent. You might think these bits are intrusive, but if you remove the sequences of Jamie at home as extraneous, you discover that they are absolutely integral to making people care. They make you worry much more about how Jamie is doing with the task in hand, the school dinners. Filming contributors at home makes so much difference as in this instance to our feeling for Jamie, because we need to care about our heroes and see what pressure they are under.

However, filming at home can be particularly hard. You have to thicken your skin to take many rejections, and still charmingly ask again. When we made *Trouble at the Big Top* there were two opposing characters – the minister, Peter Mandelson, who eventually gave that great interview at home; and the chief executive of the New Millennium Experience Company responsible for making it happen, Jennie Page. Those two certainly didn't see eye to eye. I succeeded in filming neither at home through most of the filming, nor did they seem human enough for an audience to care enough about or to seem heroic. It was only when Mandelson finally relented, as we saw, that he, perhaps surprisingly, was the one to become more human for the audience.

He also had the added emotional burden that his grandfather, Herbert Morrison, had been the minister responsible for the last great exhibition, the Festival of Britain in 1951. But he seemed an unlikely hero of the series, with such limited access, talking mostly like the politician he was, and then the unfortunate resignation from his job less than halfway through filming, when he pretty much disappeared from the series. So it was incredibly helpful in humanising him when I got that master interview at home. It was just what was needed to transform the series. We were able to spot it right through the four programmes, which were already in edit, transforming them into a personal odyssey. Because the interview took place at home it revealed far more, and even made him heroic. We never got into Jennie Page's house – I was told a designer, copper-clad house in the Midlands – so one sympathised with her less. After all, most fairy tales have a sequence at home. So filming at home is another area where terrier-like persistence – smiling, wagging your tail, but never letting go – can be well worth it. Often, as with Mandelson, you will win in the end, though it may take most of the filming period to get there.

Another film, also a *Trouble at the Top*, was made by a sequence at home, but in a different way. The film followed Gerald Ratner into his new health-club business. A few years earlier Ratner had been the proud head of his first family company, a jewellery empire which he had expanded from 130 stores into the world's largest chain of jewellers with 2,500 stores – a huge public company trading under many names from Ratner to H. Samuel and Ernest Jones. Until one day, addressing the Institute of Directors at what he thought was a private function, he told the truth. How could he sell a decanter, glasses and silver-plated tray set for less than a fiver? Because they were 'total crap', he said. He went on to remark that some of his earrings were cheaper than a Marks & Spencer prawn sandwich, but probably wouldn't last as long. It implied he was selling cheap tat with massive mark-ups. It hit the front pages, and what had been a brilliant business was wrecked almost overnight. The share price fell and Ratner left. Five years later we were following him as the wounded tycoon ventured back into business, setting up his new venture, a health club that was intended to be the first of a chain, near his home in Berkshire. But we needed the real Gerald to sympathise with, to make him a hero.

The director, Michele Kurland, managed to persuade Gerald that we could do a short interview at home. It could be very significant for the film, even transforming it. Reluctantly he agreed, and given its importance I went along with her. We arrived early and the family were having breakfast round their kitchen breakfast bar. I asked the crew to get ready as quickly as possible outside by the van, and when they came in to start filming quietly on my signal. I always like to be filming as fast as possible, so there is no time for discussion, or thought, on seeing the scary camera – it is just straight in.

As the crew prepared, Michele and I chatted to Ratner, his wife and daughter as they ate. Breakfast was still going on as the crew came in. 'What are they doing?' Gerald wanted to know. 'The interview is happening after breakfast.' 'This is how we do it,' I replied. 'Don't worry. We'll just do a bit of you together with your wife and daughter.' She was twelve, and, with a few initial questions from us within the conversation and encouraging smiles, a brilliant performer. It is important to remember how much a presenter needs positive feedback, especially silent, encouraging facial expressions. We continued chatting, the steamroller going, and I quietly removed myself from the field of vision, and shut up – something that isn't easy. The scene that followed transformed the film.

The health club would have a crèche so mothers could visit. Gerald's wife knew just when it should be open, but as in many families Gerald didn't want to listen, and used his manager to hide behind. It took his daughter to ask what we would all want to (with a bit of help from me off camera, which was left in). It happened so fast Gerald Ratner never had the chance to think or say no. Children, immediately before adolescence shuts them up, can ask the most brilliant and obvious questions that others wouldn't think of or dare. Use them when you have the opportunity.

TROUBLE AT THE TOP: RATNER'S RETURN, BBC TELEVISION

DAUGHTER   It might turn out like his last jewellery shop.

ME   What do you mean?

DAUGHTER   It didn't work out with his last jewellery shop.

ME   But the gym – are you excited about the gym?

DAUGHTER   But the gym might be successful because he's got partners –

GERALD RATNER'S WIFE   I assume that they'll pick a reasonable two hours, and the morning is always the best time.

GERALD RATNER   Yes, between eleven and one.

WIFE   Well, I should think that's probably the worst time to have a crèche open, Gerald, over lunchtime. I would have thought ten till twelve. Who did make this decision?

GERALD   Tony [*Gerald's General Manager*].

DAUGHTER   Did you agree with it? Did you?

GERALD   Ermm . . . yeah.

DAUGHTER   But you see, Daddy, the things that Mummy asked you, who made this decision? Let's say Tony made it, you still agreed with it. If you didn't agree with it, then it wouldn't happen, I mean.

WIFE   He's just trying to annoy me.

GERALD   I know, I know, but I still think it's right.

DAUGHTER   Then say to Mummy, then say to Mummy, Tony said it but I agreed with it cos I thought it was right. Don't go and said Tony thought of it.

GERALD   Tony said it, but I agreed with it cos I thought it was right.

Wife laughs loudly.

Afterwards we spent time and effort sweet-talking him. I cannot emphasise enough the huge importance of after care, which should continue till the film goes out. But you don't need to take on their every problem for life. As with a good therapist, there has to be an end point or you would end up with too many intense TV relationships.

MOTIVATING YOUR TEAM

Like presenters and contributors, the rest of your production team can also be fragile prima donnas. But it can be worse for them, since many never get praise and become disillusioned. They need a bit of tummy-tickling as well. And of course you are one of them, too, and none of us get our tummies tickled enough – I certainly don't.

So to be successful try to avoid becoming jaundiced. In fact the two most important attributes I have found in a film-making career, as in life, are first to avoid getting bitter and twisted, and second, loyalty. Loyalty is a rare quality in TV but therefore all the more valuable. People you work with, and for, will feel it. In fact you are likely to get on further just because your bosses don't feel threatened (remember they run on the same combustible fuel as presenters and, though appearing arrogant, will probably be insecure in equal, if not greater, measure). To make great films you also need to remain loyal to your ideas and beliefs, and to truth, in making your own story.

Not getting bitter and twisted is equally important if you are to survive and get on. Stuff happens. People die, you lose lovers, get fired, stars leave, films fail. Pick yourself up and try to make it a learning experience rather than getting bitter – which will only hurt you. Always remember, TV is a reverse game of snakes and ladders where you climb the snakes, and have to be charming and clever enough to do so, but then there are also plenty of people who cut the rungs of the ladders. So when you fall down one don't get bitter, or take it personally. Don't give up, just look for the next snake to climb. I have seen so many people not picking themselves up, realising it happens to all of us, and giving up.

Although your working hours may be long, think how lucky you are to be running round the country, or the world, being paid to poke your nose into other people's business and trying to understand it. If it makes you feel better, attempt if you can to add some meaning, as well as entertainment, to whatever you do. It makes films work better anyway. Most good entertainment can and should have content which illuminates the human predicament. Audiences are sophisticated enough to feel authenticity and truth within a storyline. Shows like *Jamie's School Dinners* and *The Boy Whose Skin Fell Off* are audience hits just because of this. It is lucky that nearly half the output on British TV is on public-service channels, as is much in Europe and the Commonwealth, and increasingly shows with content are breaking through to a hungry American audience. Cable channels increasingly find a bit of content helps win an audience, but don't eschew content-lite shows. They can be a great learning ground, and you can always try and squeeze in a bit of extra meaning to whatever you do.

The right production team is vital in marrying entertainment and meaning successfully. Journalists often ask me what the best moment was while making *Jamie's School Dinners*. They thought maybe when we found Nora, or a scene when Jamie and Nora were shouting at each other, or perhaps the moment Nora served the Secretary of State for Education a surprise junk-food lunch. But I reply that by far the best moment for me was when Jamie and the rest of the small production team sat down together in his restaurant, Fifteen, nearly at the end of the edit, a few weeks before transmission. We'd all been through it together, got on to the end, and become very close, which meant far more to me than anything else. None of us quite knew, or cared any more, who had done what – it was absolutely all of us who did it, we all made up for each other's weaknesses and listened to each other, and we all wanted to make the most entertaining programme we could that would make people care more about school dinners.

So I believe part of the secret of *Jamie's School Dinners* having touched people's hearts and won all its awards, was the genuine fun and teamwork and respect and love between everyone in making it: unusual in television, but a key ingredient of success.

However, love in productions can go too far. It is often problematic if members of the team start having sex on location, because when the liaison goes wrong, or people feel rejected, it can cause big problems. But a bit of passion and fancying – and even platonic love – can lead to a better film: the sort of production love that exists only in the passion of making the film, and you can't quite understand what it was about afterwards.

In my experience the winning films need love and passion of some sort: it is a key ingredient in making them. Everybody feels motivated in one direction, albeit in film-making, as in any passionate relationship, this can lead to shouting and argument too.

HOW TO GET INTO TV

A key requirement to enable good storytelling is to join a winning team. So how best to do so? First off, you need a basic job such as runner or secretary. Persistence is the key (and is important at all levels of TV). For although you may not be wanted one day, you may email or turn up to ask on another just when the runner has walked out, or there is an extra programme, or loads of rushes that need logging, or a producer is desperately needed.

At the start, write a CV that shows an intelligent interest in the medium (not just an interest in people or 'making TV') and ideally in a particular type of programme. At least break your interest down to factual or entertainment, drama or sport, and ideally demonstrate your passion with some evidence. Use any small thing that you have done before to the full. I was slightly interested in tape recorders and did a little work recording at university, which I exploited to the full on my first CV. But make sure you have done enough research into your alleged expertise to substantiate it.

Also try to find out something about the company or people you are applying to, make sure you know the programmes they make and have seen and have opinions on some of them. As well as looking on the website try to talk to another runner, if that is where you are beginning.

FROM RUNNER TO RESEARCHER

Moving on from runner to researcher is slightly easier, but still very tough – it took me nearly ten years! Getting on in TV is like getting through the eye of the needle, but it is the first stages that are hardest as you have nothing to show. I spent my first decade in TV pushing around trolleys of film, sitting in dubbing theatres, mixing sound and dreaming of my highest aspiration – of one day becoming a researcher or even an assistant producer. Imagining I wouldn't go far, I was amazed to have each job and be paid for it, which is a helpful attitude. Remember TV requires – in reverse order – cleverness, charm, hunger (and passion) and luck. But hunger and passion help make the luck, so they are the key things to demonstrate. I tried to do each lowly job as well as I could, while my colleagues at each stage were displeased with their lowly status, and showed it. Bosses like keen and contented staff, and most of all the hard-working and reliable ones who always come with a solution (or two) to their problems.

But that wasn't enough. I went for job interviews as a researcher, and failed. As I mentioned earlier, the BBC Education Department thought I would be too timid to talk to strangers on the phone – anyone who knows me knows that nothing could be less likely, but the interview on which my future depended terrified me. At this time I would try to get in the same lift as directors, and occasionally dare to say a few pithy words about their latest programme. And, even more rarely, sit with them in the bar or canteen.

After that long, long wait, it was a film editor dragging me into the canteen to eat with some scary Science directors that finally led to my move into production. I eventually struggled into a temporary contract as the only full-time researcher on a new business series in the Science Department by turning up at the interview with a couple of fully researched films for the potential series, with all the main contributors signed up and ready to go.

At last I was about to meet the gods who were directors. The series was staffed entirely with Science producers, and I was stunned when at the first meeting they all seemed to want to make films about growing wine in France with no business motivation, or much motivation of any sort. So, although I knew little of film-making, I differentiated myself by claiming and developing an expertise in business. No one else understood business, so it was easy to convince them. As you get on, branding yourself becomes ever more important.

As I learnt more about the craft, branding myself as the maker of business programmes continued to seem like a good plan. It would allow me to make story-driven documentaries about heroes – after all, we spend most of our waking hours at work, so workers are the modern knights. And best of all no one else wanted to make those programmes. But there was an immediate problem.

RESEARCHER TO PRODUCER/DIRECTOR

How are you going to get a chance of directing? My suggestion is first that you continue to do whatever job you are employed to do as happily and as well as possible. When there are inevitable problems, think through the solutions too, and present these to your boss. It is also good to remember that television is 90 per cent hard-working craft, and 10 per cent art and inspiration. You should aim to become like a good cabinet-maker, and remember that it takes time, and ideally being apprenticed to people who are already masters of the craft. So as a researcher try to choose the best directors to work with. If or when you get to direct, this will help you to make good films of your own.

Also as a researcher try to cultivate directors who you haven't yet worked with, and show intelligent interest in the films they have made. Help them a bit for nothing, talk about what is on TV – all this may help you hear of good films coming up you might be able to work on. As well as being hard-working and loyal, keep differentiating your area of expertise as far as possible. Also cultivate executive producers – remember they are lonely and don't get a lot of feedback or appreciation, and they might even get a kick out of mentoring. As they hit their forties many executives secretly hanker after mentoring someone. This is as well documented as the age-thirty crisis. And this mentoring research has shown (another of the few insightful things learnt at Wharton business school) that the mentee is half a generation younger – between ten and twenty years. So don't be afraid to write to the executive producer (or director, but the exec will have more jobs to give) on a film that has interested you. Amid the praise, give a view on something that could have been better, and best of all suggest as a result what this executive should be doing next.

Watch their programmes and talk to them at any opportune moment. Later on in my career, as I rose up the ladder, when my boss's boss was a channel controller or chief executive of a TV station, I would also cultivate their assistant – or even their driver (so I could end up saying that I was going in the same direction, and getting that crucial lift). There are large numbers of producers trying to get on, and the attrition rate is high. You need to be noticed.

STARTING OUT AS A DIRECTOR

My own move through the next tough eye-of-a-needle stage to finally winning that directing chance was hard, because most of the Science Department still thought that business, on which I had been researching, was a dirty word and money stank. The executive producer responsible for making business programmes moved on, and business was amalgamated with *Tomorrow's World*. But this in the event proved an opportunity to learn directing skills. Magazine programmes or cable make a great entry point, as this is where you can experiment. The former area has the benefit that you may be able to work with sharp and experienced presenters. Magazine shows, or short films, or unimportant series, are a great place to learn, as you get to direct alone, even when titled assistant producer. Short films are especially great to learn on because they are simple in structure, usually just one question and one answer, so like a single sequence in a big film. As it is simpler, you can almost tell the whole tale through pictures (and can even get addicted to this). But you shouldn't just want to learn directing your own short films, or long ones for that matter. It is also very useful to work as a shooting assistant producer for more advanced directors. I have seen so many top promo, advertising, and even magazine directors fail at long-form documentary because they were too keen on directing themselves, and spent all their learning doing it for themselves rather than also working as an assistant producer to an experienced director, and seeing what different directors did. You need to try to do both if you possibly can.

As you move on, have your next film but one, or next job but one, planned. It pays to look at the long term. It is as well to chat up different companies, or different series producers and executives in a broadcaster, so they want you when you become available. If you manage to get a job on a long-running magazine show, where you can really learn, try to have your escape route planned. Whenever I went to *Tomorrow's World* I would try to line up a research job on a full-length series for six months later. Continue to chat up executives who may give you that next job but one. The important thing is that you do not get stuck, and can plan your own destiny as you climb the greasy pole.

Perhaps the most important decision you can make in choosing jobs is who you work to, employing your director when an AP, or executive producer if you are a producer. As a director I always think it should be you who employs your exec, or at least you should think you are, rather than just worrying about who is working for you. Will they mentor and inspire you, rather than just being a manager and salesman? Will they be able to make up for your weaker sides, and teach you new skills? Or when they are doing the choosing, and employing others, will they take on whole teams of people just like them, which will make for an easier life and for worse television? If this is the case your deficiencies won't be covered by other members of the team, and the films won't be so good. Employ people who are different from you.

Real thought needs to be put into making up a complementary team. As I have said, I often describe my job now as a glorified employment exchange, particularly when involved in the beginning of a series like *Jamie's School Dinners*. The most important thing is getting the chemistry right, so the team will have different skills, which may grate, but may also inspire you to greater achievement.

NOT GETTING TOO CLOSE

There are some final tips for getting on with colleagues and contributors. It is usually good not to over-share. You are the equivalent of a psychotherapist in a professional relationship, so you need to appear to be hugely interested while working yet simultaneously to maintain your outside-work self. There is a line between getting on in TV and real life which you need to preserve. Remember this is work, and you get to go home . . . at least sometimes!

So although it helps to love your production staff and your contributors, you have to keep a distance while appearing close. Often contributors will think you are a very best friend, and so you are while filming; but you should always remember that you are trying to make an objective film. But bear in mind that, while most producers will meet hundreds of contributors, most contributors will meet only one producer. For each one you will be very special at the time, but at the end of filming you need to separate or you will drown under an everlasting sea of calls from needy contributors, for you have been their confessor during the filming – but don't want to be afterwards.

With all this relationship stuff, it helps to get right away from it sometimes. It is a hard thing to do, as television can be all-consuming. So it will be better if you have friends who help you do this. Many people make the mistake of socialising only with people in television, thinking that this will help them get on. But in fact, as you narrow your circle, it can have the opposite effect. The more you get around in more diverse company, the more you will be open to different ideas.

To make good television you need not to get too wound up and obsessed about it, so you need people to tell you that other things may be important too. To get new ideas you need not just to be reading in all sorts of things but, more important, to be getting out there in all sorts of places with all sorts of people. Although many TV obsessives would disagree, I believe you need to get away from television to stay sane, rather than spending your evenings with TV people, or even just watching it. I am lucky: my partners have always tried to keep me away from TV people. We even had a Christmas party every year with over a hundred guests and one rule: no TV producers. You do not need to know your peers too well, and your boss's boss, whom you could usefully cultivate, would probably not stoop to coming anyway. You will open yourself to different ideas the more sorts of people you know.

Even so, for non-TV partners it can be tough. I always consider it very important to take holidays with your partner, or best friend, when you can give them your full attention. I made a point of telling employees to take holidays at inconvenient times for the series, and for me, to show their partners that they were more important than television for once. One of mine took a lover, after ten years together, and I didn't notice as I was working so hard to make that first *Troubleshooter* series work. When I found out I was told it was only fair as I had one anyway – television, so do be careful.

Despite this, if you have no partner, holidays can be even more important for getting totally away from TV. But leave the phone behind, don't read email and don't watch TV at all if you really want to gain perspective. It may sound rather New Age, but with all this care for presenters, contributors and colleagues, you need to care for yourself too, and badly need to switch off and do some self-nurturing if you are to return and do it all over again.

Periodically try to take an even longer break if you possibly can, perhaps writing a book or doing something different. You will be a better film-maker when you return, as well as probably a better and more likeable person. Many of my very best programmes have been after one of these breaks. For if you have been following all these tips on how to get on, you may – like me at one time – have become something of a pushy git at work in pursuit of excellence. However much you smile and are charming, ultimately part of you becomes what you pretend to be. The really important thing is to realise when television is making you lose your very soul. And when it gets too much, and it almost certainly will, be brave and run away! More and more young TV people do. And in my view they are all the better for it.

People may want you to make films immediately one after another, but resist sometimes and at least try to take some holidays. If you only think of TV you will become very dull. This applies all through your career. Creating television is an intense business, and you must not get bored by it. For as you proceed (hopefully) you will find TV a highly competitive business, with a lot of other people wanting to get on too. Your colleagues may secretly rejoice in your failures, as theirs will then look better. So ignore them and just follow every tip you can to make better films. And try to be open, honest and straightforward, as this is one course of action that no one else will be able to read.

JANE ROOT

Former President, Discovery Networks, and Controller BBC2, now CEO Nutopia

My big slogan as an executive – it got me into a lot of trouble, but I still really believe it – is that if you don't have some really big failures you are not trying hard enough to push the boundaries.

Be brave and push harder. You are not likely to win unless you are taking risks and doing new and untried things, pushing TV forward. That is what Jane did and mostly she won big time.

PAY RISES

As you progress there is one final card you can play to get on. But not too often – and you will need to have done something well. Here's some advice based on long experience. If you are frustrated in your job and want to move on, or even if you want a large pay rise, you need to increase your apparent value. But don't in any circumstances *threaten* to resign – your bluff could be called. Instead choose someone you know can't keep secrets – in other words, almost anyone in TV – and tell them yours, i.e. that you've been approached to leave. Ask them to keep it confidential, of course. But they're all gossips at heart.

When I was stuck in *Tomorrow's World* I chose to tell my supposed secret, in confidence, to someone two layers above me in the hierarchy, an executive producer I had chatted up for future jobs. Shortly, as I expected, I was called in by the department head, and as luck would have it, there was after all something I could be offered. This was the Michael Grade idea of doing something on business, with Sir John Harvey-Jones. The *Tomorrow's World* boss, Richard Reisz, who was executive producer, might have thought I would have the talent, but I believe that the combination of my self-styled branding as business expert, the fear that I might leave, and other departments having refused to do it, led to my incredible 'luck'. I did just the same with pay rises every few years, though only after a success.

MANAGING YOUR BOSS'S BOSS

So after all this, you are managing your presenter, your contributors and the people you work with. There is one final person to manage successfully if you want your career to advance, and this requires even more tact. Although it is useful to cultivate your boss on the way up, it can be even more important to cultivate your boss's boss. If you are a researcher this could be the series producer, or executive producer, but if a producer you can aim higher: heads of department, company bosses, channel controllers and commissioning editors are people with a lot of luck to dispense. The challenge is to build a relationship with those at the top without threatening your immediate boss. This means you need to be careful not to outshine your boss when in meetings with both together, and somehow, sometimes, meet your boss's boss alone.

There are all sorts of tactics. First you can use your contributors to get at the boss's bosses. Strangely, like all people in TV, even big bosses seem to remain in awe of stars. When I finished editing the *Trouble at the Top* transmission pilot *Nightmare at Canary Wharf*, it suddenly became highly newsworthy as Kelvin MacKenzie replaced Janet Street-Porter. I wanted to transmit straight away, but my immediate bosses wanted to wait till the rest of the *Trouble at the Top* series was finished – which would be nearly a year later. I needed to get direct to the top, but without being threatening. So I invited the controllers of both BBC1 and BBC2 to the River Café for dinner with Sir John Harvey-Jones, from whom they were always keen to hear – he knew about business and it was becoming fashionable then. So I knew they'd be very keen to come as they were suddenly in awe of 'management' and a charismatic

business leader. Not surprisingly, my immediate bosses invited themselves along too.

However, used to the lateness of BBC mandarins, I kept Sir John in
a nearby pub and we arrived an hour late, as I didn't want him to have
to wait for them all. They looked very 'surprised' (if that's the right
word) as we entered and asked what had happened. They were not used
to being kept waiting, so I explained just why they had. Then Sir John
popped the question he had been primed for: 'Are you transmitting
Nightmare straight away? You really should.' And the assembled
controllers looked to my bosses, who had to say yes – and I had said
nothing! The programme transmitted just when it was timely, and won
a large audience, and made a lot of noise, partly because of the 'luck' of
its timely transmission.

In my time I have told a senior executive whom I needed to see that
I was happening to pass his country cottage, 150 miles from London,
so he had to say, 'Pop by for a cup of tea,' and then I drove all the way
specially. I've often told a channel controller that I was going in the
same direction as his taxi, and asked to jump in. Even as a junior
researcher I made a real point of getting in the right lift with a series
editor, and then complimenting his latest programme, with the odd
tiny but hopefully pertinent criticism – you have no idea how lonely
it is at the top or how few compliments even executive producers get.
It is as important 'loving' bosses and bosses' bosses as your team and
your contributors. So never forget that a key part of successful film-
making remains managing stars, contributors to your team, your bosses
and your career.

So far we have found strong CHARACTERS, we're thinking OUT OF
THE BOX to create a strong NARRATIVE DRIVE, we've worked out the
FRONT, identifying the heroes and their challenge, and we are LOVING
people into submission as we try to make our films and our careers.
Next come the INTERVIEWS and the writing of the commentary which
will give a voice to your edited film.

Six

INTERVIEWS

AND COMMENTARY WRITING

COMMENTARY, INTERVIEW OR ACTUALITY

When it comes to putting a voice on a film there is a simple hierarchy. Conversation is at the top; it is the most usual way for people to speak (other than lecturers, politicians or pontificating dinner-party bores). And thinking about drama again, usually a good inspiration for factual television and film, how do the people who spend hundreds of millions in Hollywood wrench the guts of viewers for around a hundred minutes, and give them a truly engrossing and cathartic experience? Partly because there is very little interview or commentary. Most Hollywood directors usually first use conversation, or actuality – but of course they have the advantage that they can write it, and they can spend years honing each word to write it more specifically. But for factual film-makers – with a thousandth of the budget and contributors, not actors – it isn't easy. Frequently our contributors have not said to each other quite what we need, or there is just one of them. Then we use the next kind of voice – *I*NTERVIEW. Even though many of us, me included, might want to make films with just actuality, because we all really want to make a Hollywood drama (you get paid a hell of a lot more and there's the pool in Malibu), most of us have to resort to *I*NTERVIEW because actuality won't tell the whole story. There are many techniques to help interview and it is a vital part of factual film-making.

Many documentaries are designed to be made with just these two voices, actuality and interview, as many factual directors aspire to make films where a combination of pictures, actuality, plus a few necessary bits of interview, tell the whole story – like in the movies. This is a great aim, and can sometimes work really well, but mostly it doesn't, particularly for European audiences. For conversation or actuality don't always do quite what you want, and interviewees, though more controllable, can be long-winded in explaining facts, unwilling to articulate the challenges, and unable to key up a scene with just the right motivation or give you the pregnant conclusion that will lead you in to the next scene.

So when you get to the cutting room and you find the contributors don't quite say what you need, and much in the interviews is long-winded and the film feels boring, incomprehensible, or both, then you will need commentary (sometimes called narration), whether from your contributor or a hired voice. In my experience you will very often need this in factual TV. So writing commentary or narration is one of the most important parts of factual film-making. Unfortunately commentary writing is surprisingly hard — all writing is, but while this is realised in drama, many factual films fail because it is overlooked as not too important — just something to add on at the end. But it is vital. When I ran my BBC unit this was what restricted growth. It was possible to find more directors and other talented people — the limit was the number of people who could write commentary. It is a rare skill, and one of the toughest aspects of film-making. So before we come on to interview technique let us first consider the challenges of commentary.

COMMENTARY

Writing commentary is an organic process. When should you write it? Start early, adding rough bits of linking commentary as soon as you have first assembled your film. This first commentary should try to make a route map through the labyrinth of the story, providing only succinct facts, but it needs to be very short, neutral and help build tension. Refine and refine this commentary as you recut, but also occasionally view your latest cut without the commentary to see in an open way that you have got right what the material is trying to tell you.

If a film is not great in itself — that is, almost all films — this succinct, sharp commentary can help advance the story, and make a lithe and narrow-boned skeleton for all the flesh of the film to hang on. It's a skeleton you are scarcely aware of, but it is what holds up the whole body of the film. In fact commentary writing can become the most important part of a film, driving why you are watching, and why you might care, articulating the big question and answer, and the smaller questions and answers that make the narrative.

The first bit of commentary, and usually the densest, is likely to be in the pre-title, though of course in the whole film the more you can get actuality and images to tell the story the better, as long as this grabs the audience — especially the subtext that commentary can only allude to. At the start of editing this pre-title I will write commentary to begin it, to try out the story. Later I will try to replace this with images and actuality that do the same thing, as I like to see if I can avoid commentary at the very start of the film. Remember the key dictum of film-making: 'show not tell'! It makes a film more filmic and convincing if you can begin by showing the evidence of the problem as an actuality and an adventure for the hero to embark on. A particularly good example is *The Boy Whose Skin Fell Off*, which opens with an utterly extraordinary sequence: a dressed dead figure in a wheelchair, then a coffin in the middle of a sitting room, then actuality from a pair of onlookers – before commentary comes in from the character in the wheelchair. As before, my notes for this book are on the left.

THE BOY WHOSE SKIN FELL OFF
YIPP FILMS FOR CHANNEL 4, AS TRANSMITTED, BUT SHORTENED SYNCH

Exterior of ordinary modern house. Title superimposed.

Evidence of the problem: simple bedroom. A woman is clearing clothes, a man comes in to fix a radiator, there is a static character in a wheelchair.

SYNCH MUM   He wanted that one on, his yellow on. He says I wanted my yellow shirt . . .

SYNCH BROTHER   I've cried but he's had enough . . . it's hard to say but I'm pleased he's gone.

Voice-over recorded before death from fully dressed figure in wheelchair.

JONNY (*voice-over*)   Welcome everybody my name is Jonny Kennedy, I'm thirty-six.

Upsound Mother.

JONNY   There's my mother.

And next to her is my brother.

Then we see character in wheelchair still dressed in an open coffin on the bed.

And that's me in the box.

I have come back in spirit. I'll tell you the story of my life and my death.

Only now do we have commentary (but not too much). First outlining the

COMMENTARY   *Jonny Kennedy is one of the most extraordinary people in Britain. For thirty-six years he has*

problem, and the quest which this time includes the big question here rather than at the end (rules are made to be broken).	*survived his very rare and painful skin condition. With time running out he wanted his last four months to be as uplifting as his strange life.*
	And asked us along for the ride.
Then the route map.	*It's going to be a busy summer. Jonny is determined to learn to fly, pay a call on No. 10 and have a huge house-warming party in his new dream home. But first there's the funeral to sort out.*
	JONNY Hello.
Then a lively actuality scene (in this film the title was at the front) of Jonny buying his coffin.	FUNERAL DIRECTOR Hello there.
	JONNY I'm Jonny Kennedy and interested in buying a coffin.

In most cases, even this, you are likely to need commentary pretty quickly within the first couple of minutes to focus up who the characters are, why you care and the challenge. Once you have grabbed the audience with this, hopefully following some great actuality evidence and judicious commentary which has set the big questions, the route map and who you should care about and why, then the film proper gets going. This is usually after the title or subtitle, a minute or two in, when you should be as filmic as possible, choosing some of your best actuality with minimal commentary.

In the wonderfully original *The Boy Whose Skin Fell Off*, instead of the first scene after the introduction being full of information about the miserable disease, in the finished film we went straight into a lively engaging sequence of actuality about Jonny buying his own coffin, in which he shows an engaging wit and charm. And the commentary into it? All it needs is: 'But first there's the funeral to sort out,' a line that very simply gets the story going in time.

At the end of this first lively and engaging coffin-purchasing scene we can have more information from commentary – but now nearly five minutes in.

THE BOY WHOSE SKIN FELL OFF
YIPP FILMS FOR CHANNEL 4, AS TRANSMITTED

COMMENTARY   *Jonny's rare genetic skin condition EB means his skin is constantly coming off and trying to regrow and eventually it develops terminal cancer.*

This is followed by an actuality scene which originally came first, in which Jonny outlines his painful disease on a radio show. We are only ready for it now we care.

After this each commentary link can provide the motivation into the next scene. But it shouldn't tell you what you have just heard and seen, nor what you are just about to see: it needs to tee up each scene with sparse fact and a reason for watching. It can also neatly suggest what you might be looking for in the upcoming scene, just as subliminal ads put an idea in your head without telling you just what you are going to see. And remember commentary too should come out of action.

When your commentary is all written, you have a structure and the key challenge has been overcome. You should now know exactly what the film is about and is trying to say. Then you can go back and rewrite your pre-title/cold open again – and no, this has not been wasted time. If you hadn't done a wrong pre-title in the first place you wouldn't have had a guide to get this far. It is like having to put on an undercoat of paint which you never see before putting on the layers of topcoat; without it, the topcoat would never look right. It is an iterative process.

USING SPOKEN ENGLISH

Commentary writing is an art, a hugely important part of factual film-making, but a few simple tips can help. The first thing to remember is that commentary will eventually be *spoken* by a narrator (or presenter), so it should be in spoken not written English. Although we may be aware that some languages utilise different constructions when written, such as Italian with all its complex subjunctives that are not used when speaking, it is worth remembering that English is different when written too. Just think of the policeman reading the notes from his notebook: 'As I was proceeding down the thoroughfare at a leisurely pace,

I observed some criminal activity being manifested by the two young individuals.' Ask him what happened: 'I was walking down the road and saw two thieves!' It is just the same in commentary. So often commentary is written in prolix language, so you ask the director what happened and scribble it down: there is your commentary. In fact I write much commentary by just scribbling down what the director says when I ask him or her what is going on.

One of the biggest problems I am left with in the cutting room is leaden 'written' commentary. When I view a film, I speak the lines that flow from the action I am seeing, and one of the most difficult things for directors working for me is that they have to write them down very fast, because I won't exactly remember what I have just said after the pictures stop. That is because I speak it, not write it, busking as I go.

So try to remember that spoken language is different from written language – notably, having less complicated constructions. Try to get into the habit of using spoken English when writing, and not finishing up with over-verbose and florid commentary. It can help if you try busking it in the first place, as I do, speaking it out loud and scribbling it down quickly, or using a small tape recorder.

NAMING CHARACTERS

Once you have worked out who your characters are, another valuable use of commentary is to give them their names. This also means giving them attributes that will fix them in our minds and signify that they are important, so we can identify the characters when we return to them. *Jamie's Ministry of Food* was transformed by describing Natasha 'whose five-year-old daughter has never had a home-cooked meal', and Clare, 'who has lived on twenty-seven packs of crisps a day and a diet of junk' so we remember them and care. Also remember that with characters, like everything else, to write commentary about them in action. Each week when I received a roughcut of *Sex with Mum and Dad* to help with structure and commentary, I would often find it started after the title by introducing the characters and telling us a bit about them before they did anything. Don't say: 'Rochelle's mum is a thirty-six-year-old cleaner.' Put it over a piece of action, not wallpaper: 'It's Saturday night and Rochelle's thirty-six-year-old mum won't let her out.' Then later: 'A cleaner by day, she has returned to find Rochelle out again.'

Faking It and *Wife Swap* were made not just by strong characters, but by a brilliantly written commentary that brought them out and made you care about them. In fact Stephen Lambert's format empire grew alongside mine, just because of his mastery of commentary and plot.

WIT, MUSICALITY AND BREVITY

While I believe that most commentary should be short, factual and not too flowery or contain too many adjectives, it helps if it is clever, even witty. After all, spoken English is often witty, although not usually too flowery. So where appropriate you should be witty, as you would be in speech, because wit and humour help in storytelling. Just think how a good dinner-party guest would tell the story. It is great to write a short line that gets a laugh – but short and deadpan is even better!

So you have short, lively, witty, factual, spoken, commentary. Now like any good orator you need to make it poetic too – not florid but musical. Especially in the pre–titles/cold open you can just go 'bla bla' for every syllable, and if it sounds poetic and musical it will probably work. My films almost always build at the end of the title sequence 'dum di di dum di di dum dum dum' or 'dum di dum di dum di dum'.

> Can she dum di dum –
> Dum di dum –
> And dum di di dum –
> Can she dum di dum, and dum di di dum –

Try saying your commentary with 'dum' and 'di' replacing the words and see how it sounds.

Once the commentary is all written, and the order is roughly right, you need to do something else most important which will make the biggest difference on the final passes: see if you can reduce it. First see if any commentary can be replaced with pictures, actuality or interview that will do the same thing throughout the film, because it is better if they do it rather than you! Then continually reduce the actual words.

Successful commentary writing is about saying something with fewer words in each pass. The final script should usually make sense if you read it just on its own – a succession of short, tight sentences that tell the story. These are a few from the third episode of *Jamie's Ministry of Food*, directed by Rita Daniels, that get us through a chunk of the film.

**JAMIE'S MINISTRY OF FOOD, FRESH ONE FOR CHANNEL 4
EPISODE 3, AS TRANSMITTED, COMMENTARY ONLY**

v/o   *With 'pass it on' not yet working fast enough, Jamie needs a complete rethink.*

Jamie wants to persuade businesses to allow his original class to come and teach their workers.

He needs to persuade companies all over this Yorkshire borough to allow his teachers in.

But it's not proving as easy as he'd hoped.

He might have got a venue but it's going to take a lot of companies to fill it.

ASD Lighting agree to see him. He starts by meeting the workers on the shop floor.

Soon, he has enough companies signed up for the experiment to begin.

However, it can also help to get detail into the commentary to make you feel as though you are really there and in the moment – as in the sequence of Jamie trying to turn a thousand people into cooking teachers later in the same episode. Without the detail, this sequence was dull. However, just as when you are introducing people, do not pause for the detail then restart the story, a very common mistake. Put the detail and the time within the action. (Not all commentary pieces are included below, just the ones referring to time, and again no synch.)

**JAMIE'S MINISTRY OF FOOD FRESH ONE FOR CHANNEL 4
EPISODE 3, FEEDING 1,000, SCENE AS TRANSMITTED**

v/o   *It's 8 a.m. and Jamie's class are arriving. In the space of a few hours, they'll have to teach every one of the thousand people, mostly non-cooks, to cook a new dish from scratch. Having only been cooking themselves for fifteen weeks it's their biggest challenge yet . . .*

It's 9 a.m. and the first fifty workers arrive. Jamie's groups each start teaching five of the Rotherham Council employees . . .

It's 10 a.m. and the fifty hospital workers have just ten minutes to savour their beef stir-fry before they in turn teach it to fifty construction workers.

Two hours later – five hundred workers have completed the stir-fry. There are ten more stages to go . . .

> *By 7 p.m. eight hundred people, mostly non-cooks, have successfully had one-on-one lessons.*
>
> *In the cold light of day, the real question is how many of the thousand will pass the recipe on back at work. Julie is worried what will happen when Jamie leaves.*

Commentary needs to continually build, with a motivation for each sequence, so: 'Having done something, our hero now has to . . .' If the next sequence doesn't have a motivation or a question, it probably shouldn't be there. We need to want to know what happened.

Here is another tip for shortening and improving commentary. As you hone it through various cuts, try just once watching your film without it. Then you will see what the film itself has to say, now that you have structured it with the aid of the commentary, and where more actuality might help. You will also see (sometimes frighteningly) where the film has nothing to say. Although commentary can never sufficiently make up for footage you have shot that has nothing to say, at least it can try – but the danger lies in still making it too long. It is better if possible to drop those sequences that don't say much and need to be created with commentary, and use commentary for what it is best at – linking and helping footage that does have something to say.

And one last point: it is surprising how often the most important things seem so obvious to you that you quite forget to mention them to the audience. You may remember the key point of that first series I ever worked on, *Commercial Breaks*, was that it followed stories over a year. We knew that so well that at first we forgot to say so in the commentary, so the audience didn't know!

CHOOSING THE NARRATOR

Finally you get to the end of your edit, with the commentary written. The last thing I do is to go through the commentary, and leaving exactly the same gaps for it in the film, shorten it once again throughout. It will feel better! Then is the time for the recording; hopefully you will have sorted out the right narrator in good time, for the right narrator is very important, so make sure you start looking early, and get them booked.

I like to find an intelligent actor who can give the reading a bit of humour, especially irony. Most films are improved by this — think dinner-party conversation again — unless they are about very dark or sensitive subjects. Listen to other voice-overs they have done, and ask other talented people, just as when searching for producers and stars. When I needed a sharp wry voice, for *Trouble at the Top*, I asked Stephen Lambert who he would recommend, and he suggested Robert Lindsay, famous then for *Citizen Smith*. Using Lindsay really made the series.

Employ the best you can. Famous actors are famous partly because they have better voices, so use them if you can afford it. Many will say no to start with. But actors are vain. Ring them or write to them and say how special your film is, and how it will only come alive with them. And I emphasise again: do it as far in advance as possible. Actors can be busy! Be prepared to work around their schedule, even going to where they might be working, or even where they live, to record. Tickle their tummies to make them want to sign up, again like everyone else. We went to Denham, near where Robert lived, to record the series. Make sure you send them a script and DVD in advance and try to interest them in the programme. The reading will be much better if they care, and understand what you are trying to get at.

PRESENTERS AS NARRATORS

However, what if you already have a presenter? If it is an Attenborough or Clarkson, a producer or journalist, they will probably narrate themselves, and all the above applies. But what if it is a boss in *Undercover Boss* or *Back to the Floor*? Or Jamie Oliver undergoing an unknown adventure? Should you write the voice-over for them, an actor, or both? If you do choose the presenter/main contributor to narrate, you should try to write the commentary in their style, and then get them to change it a bit into their own words, while keeping the length and sense.

But should you? In *Jamie's School Dinners* we tried it both ways. After cutting the first two programmes, and writing and recording guide commentary for a third-person narrator, we wondered what it would be like if Jamie were to narrate it all himself. Given that this was my test-bed, my first programme since leaving the BBC in which I could do everything just as I had always wanted, and I was desperate for it to succeed, I was happy to experiment. So we entirely rewrote the script in the first person, including our stabs at a few cheeky-chappy Jamie-isms, and did a rough record of it ourselves, pretending it was his voice, to see if it would be an improvement.

It was challenging, partly because this wasn't a presenter show where the presenter is there all the time, but a drama. In an animal show with David Attenborough, and many other presenter-led shows, we are with our presenter all the time, even when he is out of vision. There is no parallel action, but *School Dinners* was like a drama in which the main character – the hero – and the subsidiary character – the giant who will oppose him – are separate at the start, build to their meeting, and are separate again later as each plots alone.

So there was action that Jamie didn't know about, as Nora first went about her business at Kidbrooke before he met her. After they had met and argued there was further separate and parallel action, stuff Nora was doing that Jamie didn't know about. How could Jamie voice-over this? For all this a separate commentary and commentary voice would prove to be invaluable. It would just seem silly if Jamie was explaining what Nora was doing when he, Jamie, wasn't there. We could have got Nora to do that, and in American networks we probably would, but it wouldn't have been easy.

There is another reason why third-person commentary can help in films like these. If you are making a film with jeopardy, and all hero stories need jeopardy, a narrator can help tee this up in a way our hero can't. A narrator can say, 'Our hero is about to meet the most challenging giant in his life,' while our hero doesn't know this, or, 'Our boss has just lost three million pounds and signed a useless contract' – which our boss won't say. And what about, 'Our heroine is the most beautiful woman in the world'? Even if she has just won Miss World, she will sound a bit pleased with herself saying this.

Executive producers and commissioners have forever tried to persuade me to get presenters doing all the narration, right from *Troubleshooter* and Sir John. But for both the above reasons I mostly resisted. In *Troubleshooter* there was the usual hero's parallel action – the company worrying about Sir John's impending visit, and then their reaction; and plotting things Sir John couldn't know about, after he had gone away. There was even the problem of introducing our hero: 'Sir John Harvey-Jones is Britain's most famous businessman. He has been voted industrialist of the year for the last three years running.'

How would it sound if he said this?! In the ABC American series *Jamie's Food Revolution* (a combination of *School Dinners* and *Ministry of Food*) Jamie did all the voice-over himself, much to camera. We tried to temper him introducing himself and all he had done, so it didn't make him sound too pleased with himself, as with no narrator after the cold open there was no one else to take on the role.

JANE ROOT

Former President, Discovery Networks, and Controller BBC2, now CEO, Nutopia

In America much less commentary is used, but that is possibly something you are going to see change, because it is an underdeveloped art in America. There's much less experience and history of factual TV. For many years most talent worked in drama. Only since the reality boom of the last ten years have you started to see a lot of talent with a lot of depth in factual television in America. Which is one of the reasons so many Europeans are doing so well in the US.

STEPHEN LAMBERT

Executive Producer, *Undercover Boss*

On the whole they hate commentary on the broadcast networks in America. They associate commentary with documentary, and documentary they associate with worthy cable stations. I think that the big audiences associate narration, or commentary, with something that they might watch on PBS or Discovery, and they feel uncomfortable seeing it on the big networks, because a lot of people who watch the big networks would never watch PBS or Discovery. So they're going to go, 'I don't want this, this is not for me' — they have a much stronger sense that narration or commentary is pedagogic.

Commentary, whether from contributor or narrator, is a great way to make the questions clear, and although little used in the US I believe out-of-vision commentary is about to take off there, as more UK hits like *Wife Swap* and *Undercover Boss* are shown there. As we will see in the chapter on commentary, many US directors are now picking up the factual skills outlined here and overtaking Europeans at their own game. Hopefully this book will help this trend.

Which is why back when the commissioning editor for *Jamie's School Dinners*, Peter Dale, asked me to try both ways on one film, I was keen to try the experiment, even though it was challenging, to see what happened. He was a man of few words, but the few were invariably very wise. Was I right about sticking with a narrator for stories like this, and if so how does it affect a programme not to have one? Or might I be wrong, and can it actually improve it? Does it depend on how much *conflict* there is in the film?

So we tried Jamie's voice from end to end in *School Dinners*, but as expected it turned out dramatically to weaken the series. Also as expected, this was because it was particularly problematic in the scenes when Jamie wasn't there, as when Nora was struggling on without him. There was the need to tee up what Nora was thinking, but you couldn't, and as a result the whole film was softened.

So we decided that in *School Dinners* it would be wrong to have Jamie voice it himself, though we did keep the third-person narration short and terse. When the commissioner of *Jamie's Great Italian Escape* had the same idea, and asked again, we decided to try both ways once more. This was a softer feature series in which Jamie tried to get back to his cooking roots round Italy. The drama was mainly between Jamie and the food, but also between Jamie and a changing cast of Italians. This time there was no anti-hero, and Jamie was there from beginning to end. So this time when we tried writing the third-person voice-over into his first-person voice, it worked very well and we ended up using it.

So there is no absolute answer. It is something you wrestle with. Although Jamie's voice throughout was fine in *Jamie's Great Italian Escape*, because he was always there, it probably made it an even softer series, for better or worse, without the commentary to voice an opposing force and up the pressure, telling us things we could know and smile at, but the presenter didn't. The biggest difficulty for me was having Jamie introduce himself, which made it seem a little indulgent; so despite doing well it probably suffered from having his voice alone. The American networks often get round this by having at least a narrator in the cold open. So to sum up, using the presenter to narrate usually softens and warms the series, but it makes the drama less exciting, and the gaps are exposed. This is one reason, I think, why US versions of UK reality shows often do less well. So in my view it depends on the film.

In America, which has a different tradition of factual programme-making, they are not only scared of commentary from a narrator, they are even wary of commentary out of vision from a presenter, and mostly want him, or her, in vision.

STEPHEN LAMBERT

Executive Producer, *Undercover Boss*

We were going to do pick-ups with the boss afterwards, in editing, and the expectation of the Americans that we worked with was that we would film those. But I said no, we're just going to do them with the sound recordist. Of course, it's really difficult. It's a dominant mindset. It's a paradigm that they're operating with – they may be right, may be wrong, but they don't half believe it!

The American series *Jamie's Food Revolution*, combining *School Dinners* and *Ministry of Food*, aimed to transform the food eaten in Huntingdon, West Virginia, particularly in its schools. Huntingdon had been labelled America's unhealthiest town. The Ryan Seacrest production team filmed endless interviews with Jamie designed to link the sequences. These links that interrupt the action might not work for a European audience, but the US consumes TV in a different way: viewers haven't been brought up on the European diet of factual stories; factual has grown instead out of light entertainment, so needs lots of dramatic magic moments. It doesn't matter so much how they are linked.

However, I believe that the drama of *Jamie's Food Revolution*, although successful, didn't take off quite as well as the UK version partly because of luck, partly characters, but also because the drama was a little weaker without a narrator to harden it. It also had to overcome being more diffuse – remember, more of less is always better in TV – and unlike *School Dinners* it was following different stories, so did not have a consistent antagonist like Nora. But the point as regards commentary is that we are doing more and more in Europe in the presenter's voice,

STEPHEN LAMBERT

Executive Producer, *Undercover Boss*

I mean, the crucial point here is that American broadcast networks don't have the tradition of popular observational documentary. Their broadcast networks, until ten years ago, didn't have anything on them apart from scripted television, news and news features programmes, and maybe the occasional awards show, like the Oscars or the Grammys. And that was it. That was American television.

On the West Coast was entertainment – which on the networks included both drama and scripted comedy – and on the East Coast were the news divisions. And that whole genre on our most popular networks, BBC1 and ITV1, that is popular observational documentary – the stuff that generates docu-soaps – never existed on the broadcast networks, though it did exist to some extent on cable. So it's been a very long process getting the broadcast networks to accept anything like that. And certainly, the idea of commentary is something they don't like at all. On Undercover Boss *we only have commentary in the cold open, the pre-title, and then we have a little bit at the beginning of each part.*

while America, which did it almost entirely without third-person narration on network TV, is going the other way. If you want to win in America, hone your commentary-writing skills, because commentary is about to make US factual shows more dramatic, and as it does so more will be wanted, and in Britain reduce your commentary further.

After all these experiences I think that the best solution for commentary may be a compromise. First, film as many links as you can on location, then write some pieces for your hero to read later, especially as Europe moves faster in the US direction (as well as the other way round). But also write some narration for a separate narrator, the pre-title, the route map, and some judicious bits in the film, upping the jeopardy, suggesting what you might look for in a scene, making gear changes between scenes, and reflections on the hero that the hero could never make. Split this way, you can use the separate narrator to move the film up a level (most useful in commentary), as in, 'Now Jamie has successfully beaten off the dragon he has to cross the chasm on a rope bridge that is about to snap before he can beat the giant,' or, 'Jamie is about to undertake the hardest task of his life.' If Jamie says it himself it sounds a bit pathetic. But you can use your presenter to voice feeling as the action is happening. It helps increasingly if these voiced hero bits start in vision, so you begin when your hero is in the action, and that they are impressions and emotions that only the hero could have.

It can be even tougher when you have an inexperienced presenter like Sir John Harvey-Jones. New presenters are rarely good actors, so it can work badly if an inexperienced hero reads your commentary from a script in a booth. Even if it is in spoken English and you have used the hero's tone of voice, it will usually still sound stilted — particularly if they are not that good at reading.

So with non-professionals I write it out myself, in their language, but I don't get them to read this. Instead I write myself a list of questions which will get just the sort of answers we need. Then I ask questions in the commentary booth, or by taking a sound recordist to their home. For instance, we wanted Sir John Harvey-Jones to say, 'When I first get on a factory floor I can feel the pulse of a company and get an instant view of why it is or isn't working.' But instead of getting him to read this line I would ask him a leading question: 'Tell me about how you feel just getting on the factory floor for the first time, and what does it tell you about the company?' I would put more of the words I wanted in the question if necessary. As a result it would feel busked and natural rather than read — in fact so natural that the editor of the long-running documentary strand *Forty Minutes* and the king of BAFTA awards, Eddie Mirzoeff, asked me enviously how it had been done. He thought Sir John's naturalness had made the series, but couldn't work out how it had been achieved. With Jamie we did a bit of the same, but he being more experienced, I let him see the lines we had written, and then made him look away from the paper so he could busk it in his own words, and with his experience, in the commentary booth.

So most often with a presenter or main character driving the story, I record the presenter busking or answering questions, either in a booth or perhaps, even more relaxed, with a tape recorder at home, but there is still the commentary record with short bits of narration from an actor, your voice of God. Finally, more films are now voiced by the director, but this depends on your voice and if you want it to be your opinionated journey.

THE RECORDING

When you are using a narrator, or a presenter who will just read lines, make sure that when you reach the recording booth you have written a commentary script that is grammatically correct and includes plenty of commas to avoid ambiguity and help with the flow of the read. It is hard to read a script which contains errors in punctuation or spelling. To aid reading, also make sure no sentences are split between pages, and include time-codes for each cue.

When you give your commentary a final read-through prior to recording, it should be the short, tight and succinct story of the film; in fact if it is right it should read like a story and usually make sense in its own right. If it isn't succinct, tighten it a bit more. Try to be consistent in how you introduce characters in your script; don't for instance introduce posh people with surnames and others without, unless you are making a point. But do vary the style of names occasionally – sometimes just the first, sometimes including both first and last. Even Nora was called Nora Sands sometimes. Finally check through the tenses. Use present tense where you possibly can. It puts the audience in the action. The timeframe at any moment is the time you were filming the sequence. So not only is this present tense, but the presenter's age and the factory's status is what it was at the time of filming.

Make sure the script you bring to the recording is double-spaced, with a hefty left-hand margin, to leave room for changes. Make it legible and easy to read. Send your narrator the script and a tape beforehand, but do not be disappointed when they don't even look at it.

The recording is a thrilling moment, when the Frankenstein's monster you have created comes alive, and you see how marvellous or monstrous it is. To help the process, praise and encourage your actor or presenter. Try to get them to put life into the read, but without overacting, which can be a real problem, especially with actors who have not done it before. The ideal actor is one who has the intelligence to bring out any humour or irony in your script, to understand your film and, without overacting, to provide an energy that can lift the audience into the coming scene. So direct your actor or actress neither to overact nor to be too flat, but just read, and most important not to come down in pitch at the end of a sentence. This may be normal in reading out loud, but in commentary you need to be lifted into the incoming scene.

Commentary should almost always end on an up, pregnant note so the pitch should rise or at least stay flat at the end of each piece but definitely not fall. If it has energy it will do this naturally. Try just listening.

Finally, listen to the artist and rewrite a little as you go. They will like to be involved and may have bright suggestions. But I always keep to the rule that changes are fine from the narrator as long as they make it better – and most importantly don't make it longer. Likewise I say the director can rewrite anything, as long as it comes back shorter. Last of all, when you get to the end always go back and record the first three (not two) minutes as the actor will have warmed up and know what it's about. The dubbing theatre is a vital part of film-making. Sound can make a film, both in choosing the right emotional soundtrack and the music to enhance your film and its effects. But in my years as a TV troubleshooter I have found it is writing decent commentary above all that can get me out of most messes. Put the material in a logical order, with a narrative driven by commentary, and you can make any film adequate, and you can sometimes make a potentially good film that isn't working into a great one.

INTERVIEWS

However, while commentary is excellent at tersely conveying fact and motivation, I believe it is usually less so when used to impute emotions to people, so it should rarely be used for this purpose. I could say by this point that you have got pretty bored reading all this, that it has annoyed you (not bad, as you can think why I am wrong), or even that you are enjoying it – all commentary, from me. But it would be far more convincing if you said so yourself, which is interview, and we saw your expression as you said so. Which is why interview can be so useful.

Halfway through *Jamie's School Dinners* we were off, early on a Monday morning, to Jamie's uncle's pub near Southend for our first and only awayday to discuss how the series was going, and where next. I arrived at the office to discover that Jamie was late. I was told that he had had a terrible weekend. He had held a big Sunday-evening staff meeting at his restaurant, Fifteen, where his cooks and waiters had told him of their worries that he was away too much, partly because of filming *School Dinners*. It really surprised and upset him, particularly that he hadn't quite realised their concern. He was distraught as we set off to the pub. It also seemed at the time that he might never succeed in transforming school dinners and, worst of all, the papers were full of untrue stories about his marriage. So although it wasn't in the script, thinking out of the box we grabbed a DV camera to take with us, and then interviewed him in the van en route. He was about to have to feed twenty thousand kids, was at a low ebb and worried.

There was no one in the van for him to have an in-vision conversation with, only the production team, and even if there had been they might not have been willing to plumb the depths of his emotion. That left interview or commentary. Interview could extract emotion, and his face and the silences could say as much as the words. Only if he hadn't been available, unwilling to answer, long-winded, or you hadn't asked the right question would you resort to commentary for this. Even then you could never say how worried Jamie was about feeding twenty thousand kids as convincingly as he could himself. You could just state the bald fact that he had to do so. This is what he said in the interview. It expresses what he needed to do *and* how he felt about it.

JAMIE'S SCHOOL DINNERS, FRESH ONE FOR CHANNEL 4, PROG 3 AS TRANSMITTED 26.10–26.40

In vision   I have nothing but fear for the future of dinner ladies, because I am genuinely scared and quite out of my depth.

Out of vision   The thing is, the next month and a half is about taking over the whole borough.

In vision   So I don't know quite how I'm going to feed twenty thousand kids every day. (*Pause.*) Erm, but I'm definitely going to do it, I'm definitely going to do it.

Commentary could have said something like: 'Mentally life is really tough right now. Jamie has nothing but fear for the future of dinner ladies, because he is genuinely quite scared and out of his depth. The next month and a half is about taking over the whole borough so Jamie doesn't quite know how he is going to feed twenty thousand kids every day.' But you needed to see his eyes to believe the fear. After all, there is little worse in modern commentary than artificial stakes and worries imputing jeopardy and worry when you can see none is there.

INTERVIEW FOR FEELING

Interview can provide the emotional drive of the story when actuality hasn't, so try to make sure it contains as much emotion as possible. In interview you don't only want to know what Jamie is going to cook for lunch, but also how worried he is, raising the stakes. You don't want to just know how many people ate his lunch, but how many ate it, *and* how bad he feels about it. Put 'feel' into every single question till you get used to extracting emotion, for emotion is the fuel of film. Don't ask, 'What documentaries are you going to make next year?' but, 'What documentaries are you going to make – and how do you feel about it?'

If some volcano is going to explode, an interviewee could ramble on about the science and say there is a certain percentage chance that it will explode in five years, but commentary can often say this distinctly and briefly. After all, you can work on commentary, hone it to just what the audience needs to know. What commentary can't do is say how scared the interviewee is; only the interviewee can do that!

Perhaps the best way to get emotion into an interview is to turn it into something that as far as possible feels like a conversation with you. To appear relaxed before the interview, prepare and prepare again. Write down questions that will provide the emotional motivation for a scene and an emotional conclusion that moves you on. Give the interview a structure. Divide the questions into subject areas, and then make sub-questions. Try to amalgamate them so that you have fewer. Then when you have really focused the questions so that they will elicit the answers you need, learn them and put them in your pocket, if you possibly can, or at least try to avoid looking at them, so you appear to the interviewee to be having that casual conversation. Think hard about them, but don't let the interviewer notice this under any circumstances. And keep it relaxed and natural. Don't ask the interviewee to stop and say it a different way because their answer was no good – you wouldn't do this in conversation, but carry on and say, 'Sorry, I don't quite understand. Could you explain that again?' If interviewees think they are conversing with you they will be more natural and less guarded.

There is a bad old rule that interviewees need to start their answer with your question, as you will be cut out, so the question will not be heard; and I hear many directors interrupt endlessly to try to get contributors answering in this unnatural way, but: (a) it is unnecessary for a modern sophisticated audience; (b) where it is necessary your question can be left in the film; and (c) asking interviewees to redo their answer starting with your question totally disrupts the flow of a natural conversation – the whole point of your putting your notes in your pocket and appearing spontaneous and relaxed.

When interviewing Peter Mandelson at his home my questions were so casual that after the first few he asked if we were filming. Yes, we were, I said, but I had already got in his first answers to my 'Why did you do it?' with the bluff 'Why did I get involved in the Dome? Because I was a minister and I was told to and, you know, would be a good fall guy if it all went wrong and the fickle finger of fate pointed at me.'

Unless challenging an Alan Sugar, try to make an interview feel quiet, gentle and intimate. Again it is not a bad idea to appear a bit incredulous, even silly. Often interviewees can be a bit flat. Many, from engineers to businesspeople, have learnt to say that whatever they do is unrisky. When we filmed that Danish bridge builder for instance, he was determined to say all bridges were utterly safe. Then you need to put provocative questions like, 'You really don't worry in the least about it?', asked on a rising note, which should hopefully glean the answer, 'Of course I worry . . .' When that fails, I say, 'So even my mother could do it?' or, 'What *do* you worry about in the bath in the evening?' Keep pushing. Remember the secret of a successful producer in TV is to be a terrier, the dog that always wags its tail, smiles and never lets go!

There is another problem that can hit you with interviews: interviewees who tell it one way off camera and then become more wooden once the camera rolls. Even Sir John Harvey-Jones would tell me a factory boss was totally useless over lunch, and then somehow conveniently forget this when being interviewed immediately afterwards. In fact on our very first filming day at the Tri-ang toy factory he did just that in the local pub and I ran to get the crew to film him before he had finished eating, to grab the moment, hoping he would still be loquacious. But if, even then, your contributor clams up, I am quite happy to suggest to them what they just said before the camera rolled, with a leading question like: 'Tell me how you feel as you first get on the factory floor – how the layout looks wrong, the machinery's run down and the whole floor doesn't seem to work, and you need to find out more.' The key point is to start every scene with a question either implicit or, even better, explicit.

And don't be afraid of asking difficult questions. Pop them into the middle of an interview – contributors seldom pull out.

SIMON DICKSON

Deputy Head of Documentaries, Channel 4, commissioner of many award-winning films

If you go all the way through a film only telling people what they want to hear, the film will only ever be B+. For every great film a die has been cast when the film-maker has crossed over into a different space with their lead character and has told them or asked them something that has changed the relationship between the film-maker and the subject. And it comes down in the end to bravery on the film-maker's part, and mutual trust between the contributor and the film-maker. And timing – there's no point in going in and asking an earth-shattering question on day one. A documentary that doesn't ask that million-dollar question isn't a documentary, it's just another television programme.

Don't stop to give pieces of direction – such as 'You can make the answer a bit shorter' – but include them in the conversation. For you must keep the flow and the feeling of a conversation going all the time if you can. So add them within questions, such as 'Tell me in a livelier and slightly briefer way,' but only in the middle of the question, so the flow keeps going. When our headmistress of Benenden School in *Back to the Floor* told us, in a rather dull and pedestrian way, that she was excited about going to the school, and I knew that she *was* excited, I was quite happy to ask, 'Tell me how excited you are about going to the school – tell me in a livelier way, and a bit more briefly, how really excited you are, and what you are going to do.' Present tense can be useful in some questions, as it is dynamic, and puts you right in there. And make sure that you ask what everyone wants to know. Add it in the middle of an interview and don't let on how special it is for you, and then move on. Above all be brave: however famous or important the contributor is, contributors very seldom pull out, but lack of bravery can wreck your film.

SIMON DICKSON

Deputy Head of Documentaries, Channel 4

One of the things that you would be driven bonkers by in the cutting room, and which I find difficult and challenging when I'm in your shoes, is when you know that the film would be dignified or elevated by the existence of one particular question – which is often the key question – and you'll say to the production team, did you ask your key character X or Y or Z. And the director will turn to you and say, 'No, I didn't ask that, I didn't go there.' And I will say, 'Why didn't you go there?' and the director's reply would be, 'Well, I thought it might jeopardise the access. I thought it might upset him. I was worried that the access might go down.' The best film-makers don't worry about that in the way that the less experienced do.

If there's a catastrophic falling out between the director and the key contributor, fine. If it happens on camera, but the approach by the film-maker has been well-intentioned and sincere and they haven't been trying to trip up the main character for the sake of it, then that's even better. Because documentary's about truth. It's about getting to the heart of people by asking them questions. If you let them tell you just what they want to tell you about themselves, they never tell you the one thing that is really fundamental to who they are. It has to be teased out of them by someone who is curious and persistent and brave, and isn't afraid of the whole house of cards falling down if they ask that million-dollar question.

THE IMPORTANCE OF SILENCE

The most powerful tool in an interview can be doing nothing at all, being brave enough to be silent, for silence and the look that goes with it can be the very best part of an interview. So always let a contributor finish, and then often just wait, especially if it has been an emotional response. Their look may say it all, and even better, after a long pause, they may feel compelled to add a coda, and those give you the very best bits. Interview is just like scriptwriting: you must write out your questions and plan meticulously, and then be willing to go in another direction when your interviewee surprises you. Again, think out of the box. The very worst interviews are those in which the interviewer doesn't even listen to the answer but is thinking only about racing on to their next question and what it is, showing they're not even listening. There will be no time for any silences, and worse, it will not feel like a conversation to your contributor. So always listen, keep it feeling natural, while remembering that question list in the back of your head. No one said film-making was easy – almost all aspects require parallel activity.

The location of your interview can also make a difference. Dullest are interviews in chairs in offices. At home is better. Doing something can be even better still – even washing up. If there are interruptions from children, animals, the phone, etc., allow them and film them, even encourage them. It will feel more natural. Best of all, film interviews when someone is doing something that is active, involves movement and perhaps even concentration, such as sailing a boat. In the *Millennium Dome* series we interviewed the leading designer, Derrick Tuke-Hastings, as he swam round his yacht. I stayed on it to ask the questions, shouting them down.

The favourite interview I did was another grabbed one, that I never expected to film, and I use it to show yet again how important thinking 'out of the box' is. It was just eighteen months till the new millennium, but at least the structure of the Millennium Dome was now complete, even if nobody had quite worked out exactly what was to go inside. Tony Blair came down for a big topping-out ceremony, to encourage the workforce and signal how important it was, along with his minister responsible, Peter Mandelson. This was before the scene when I tried to accompany him as he was called hurriedly back to No. 10 and left the job. I was just leaving, with the ceremony over, when we came across Mandelson, who had left the entourage and was getting a bacon sandwich in an outlying part of the Dome. Thinking out of the box, I just started chatting to him, and quietly signalled the cameraman, who understood and started filming. Sandwich in hand, Mandelson set off down some stairs across the empty Dome and through its endless outskirts.

The cameraman kept filming Mandelson all the way to his ministerial car as the Dome turned from the place we were filming in, to full-scale background, until, as we got further away, we could see it all, and it got progressively smaller as Mandelson kept walking. It became a single very long shot, that told not only the story of the building, but at the same time became an interview about emotion. It worked by letting Mandelson carry on, with me only interjecting tiny encouragements, as any avid listener would, that could later be removed. Leave the silences, let contributors fill them and just add the odd interjection to keep them going – it is their voice the audience wants to hear. So, with my encouraging questions cut out, it ended up as a shot which slowly revealed the enormity of the Dome in the background, and the enormity of the challenge both emotionally and physically in very emotional words. It lasted two and a half minutes on transmission, which is a very long time for a shot and someone answering one question.

The only commentary that preceded it was: 'After a year on the job Peter Mandelson is desperate to get some things off his chest.' Once again it is short, gives us a time-check, and tells us in what emotional state we might approach what we are about to see.

So remember the best interview has feeling and emotion as well as fact. It should feel natural and like a conversation, and you should let it breathe with silences and let it just go on, if an answer is working like the Mandelson walk, encouraging it with smiles and tiny interjections.

ACTUALITY

Dialogue – two or more people talking to each other – is by far the most frequent way words are used in movies, and it is the way most people talk! So when directing a documentary, or factual programmes, as well as using pictures, try to tell as much of the story as you can with actuality or dialogue. It is more natural to life if contributors tell other contributors, rather than the director, or if they interact with a presenter like a Jamie or Sir John. So, ideally, rather than interviewing someone, you should be trying to film two or more people conversing.

But for your film the slight problem is that they need to be conversing about something to do with the story. Often that means you will need to get them talking about what you need to move the plot on. This means you often need to focus what a sequence is about for the contributors, just before it begins. After all, if you are trying to film a sequence about why kids are now more constipated, it is not very useful if Jamie and the doctor only talk about where they both went on holiday, unless you were to think 'out of the box' and turn the sequence, for instance, into one on the dangers of holiday breakfasts as a result of learnt behaviour at school. Of course you should always be open to re-editing on the hoof, but this storyline does not seem very likely.

FOCUSING ACTUALITY

Presenters are easier than contributors, for they should have an idea of what is required of the sequence, but you need to help even them, focusing on where they have come from in the film, and where they are going, maybe reading back to them the three salient points of the previous scene that will motivate the one you are about to shoot.

When, as an assistant producer, I was making my first *Troubleshooter* film at Tri-ang toys, Sir John Harvey-Jones needed a lot of help – it was his first actuality film too. Partly as a result of the time spent up at the factory before filming began, doing research and gaining the confidence of the workforce, we were able to spend just eight hours going round the factory, shooting the body of the film. I pointed Sir John in the right direction and, more important, propelled workers and middle managers into his path, for some very lively dialogue. These contributors would be reminded moments before of the key points that they themselves had told me earlier, in my research, and encouraged to tell this truth.

This technique of 'coming across' workers who had something to say, and would actually say it in a relatively focused way, was also a key part of *Trouble at the Top*, and even more important on *Back to the Floor*. In the Sainsbury episode, for instance, we persuaded the workforce to ask Dino Adriano what his salary was – a fact that they didn't know, although we did. He was asked on camera, so he really had to tell them his salary, and then justify it – it was nearly fifty times some of theirs.

HUGH DEHN

Series Producer and Director, *Back to the Floor*

It was in the staff canteen sitting at those tables – and talking about everything to do with Sainsbury, and I suddenly thought this is a perfect moment to see if they can get the boss to tell them what he earns. I'd won their trust, so I gave one of the staff, who I thought the bravest, a little piece of paper saying could you please ask Dino how much money he earns.

> *It was the most incredible moment, because half a million pounds to them was the most enormous amount. It was a look of complete and utter astonishment – the picture that told the story, used in publicity. Afterwards I said to Dino, 'It's in the public record,' and he just took it on the chin.*

The workforce then went on to break a rule: they weren't allowed to talk on the night shift, stacking shelves. They opened their mouths 'illegally' and told the gobsmacked chief as he stacked shelves with them, so he promised to change the rule. It takes a lot of persuasion to get people to be honest, especially when their jobs could even be at risk. The advantage is they are saying what they believe, partly protected by the cloak of TV publicity. But they will still need a bit of encouragement just before they take the plunge. Most people are decent and honest and actually keen to say and do the right and honest thing. The director was adept at persuading bosses and difficult important people to take part and, equally important, to be honest.

HUGH DEHN

Series Producer and Director, *Back to the Floor*

To win their trust, don't mislead contributors. Before filming spend as much time as you can where they work, to know what's going on, but you don't want to spend too much time and bore them. Don't let anyone know what you have discovered because you want spontaneity. You can chase something very small and ruin the whole thing, so you have to choose which subjects you are going to deal with very carefully .

The bosses have got to trust you, and know that you are trying to show what is going on, so when you tell them to walk through the door, and look to the right, they've got to trust that you are taking them through it because you really want to show something that is valid business-wise, not an oil slick they're going to trip on.

When it came to filming the conclusion of that first *Troubleshooter* on Tri-ang toys, the actuality was even more important. I needed Sir John to tell bosses the truth about themselves and their company for the very first time. I had no idea how it would work, nor if I could encourage him to be strong enough. Even finding time in the busy magnate of industry's schedule proved tough. Eventually I found a couple of hours – a short break between engagements he had in the Midlands, a hundred miles south of the Tri-ang factory. I would have to persuade the Tri-ang bosses to come in. Sir John was not displeased. He taught me that whose ground you choose for a confrontation is very important: best to do it away from where people feel too comfortable.

So I was happy it would be away from the Tri-ang factory, their home ground – but where? I wanted a location they would actually agree to come to, and most important not a boring office. In fact the more boring the subject matter the wackier the location should be, especially when it comes to business. The Tri-ang bosses happened to mention a garden furniture distributor in Redditch for whom they made plastic chairs. It sounded an unusual location so, on a grey February day, I arrived at an indoor swimming pool surrounded by plastic palms and parasols near Birmingham, the showroom of this garden-furniture supplier. It seemed a suitably unlikely, out-of-the-box place to film a big business bust-up. Which is how I came to film the denouement on which my career would depend round an exotic swimming pool.

Only filming didn't go as planned, and the expected bust-up didn't happen. Sir John had been full of bluster as I briefed him beforehand. Not surprising really: he had been shocked, on camera, going round the factory – shocked by what middle managers told him, and shocked in interview, describing the boss as old-fashioned and autocratic (and that was when he was being generous). Now he had the chance to tell the boss just what he told me . . . but he didn't. Because it is not a usual thing for people to do, especially the British. Often people will be critical in interview but not actuality, which isn't good enough. I felt my film, which was so important to me, slipping away. Remember I was still titled assistant producer and paid the princely salary of £16,000, and this felt like my one and only chance, and a fluke at that.

So I pretended there was a telephone call for Sir John, and called him out. I reminded him once more that there were three salient points he had been telling me: (1) the factory is old, and old-fashioned; (2) the flow of plastic and toys round it is a mess; and (3) something is going to have to change fast if the business is to survive. He wasn't saying these things to the bosses on camera. All I was doing was reminding him what he had been saying to me in the form of a brief list, always useful to presenters.

As Sir John went back in and filming recommenced, I was hopeful. But unfortunately he continued just as softly as before, without saying what he really thought, as the film so badly needed. Confrontation and saying what you think is hard, and easy to avoid – a bit like writing scripts. So I interrupted filming again, saying there was another call for him. I then told him three more things. If he didn't go back in, and say what he meant, the very truth he had been telling me, then: (1) we wouldn't have a series, as this was only a pilot; (2) he would be finished as a presenter; and worst (3) he would be wrecking my future. This was my great opportunity to prove I could direct, and if I failed I would be returning to that Portobello Market stall.

This combination of self-advancement and altruism should be an irresitible package. Throughout the process it is also helpful to appeal to the presenter's vanity – that this is the chance to show their expertise, their specialness, to a world sceptical of business/engineering/science, and convince them that by advancing themselves they would be doing the charitable thing for their profession. So with a combination of the carrot of ego and the stick of what we might lose, I tried again on Sir John. And after a final push at last it worked. He did say to the new investor, Howard, and the struggling chairman and part ex-owner, Sidney, what he had been saying to me all along, and we got a very strong sequence. The extract below from the film as transmitted began with a commentary sentence from Sir John, recorded as an answer to a question, not written.

TROUBLE AT THE TOP: IN THE NUTCRACKERS
BBC TV, AS TRANSMITTED

SIR JOHN (*voice-over*)   Now I want to meet Howard and Sidney together. I've chosen the neutral ground of Tri-ang's garden-furniture distributor, where I hope to convince them of the size of the changes they need to make.

SYNCH SIR JOHN   You are not going to be able to compete in the long haul with the factory as it is at the present moment; ultimately the factory is in

---

my judgement fairly inefficient, the plant is old and non-competitive, as Sidney knows. The layout is –

SYNCH   I don't agree with you Sir John –

SYNCH SIR JOHN   I don't give a damn if anyone agrees with me. I am not attacking you for being bad – what we are talking about is the future of the business. I do not believe the factory can survive as it is at the present moment.

Not long after that fateful final filming Mr Sid, the chief executive, left the struggling toy company and a new team took over. It was a real makeover.

So in actuality, just as in interview and commentary, you need to be very clear what you want out of the scene. Like Sir John, almost all contributors need focusing to a greater or lesser degree, though they may need less 'encouraging' than Sir John did in that scary denouement (though I have often found that the more important the people presenters come up against, the more encouraging they need). However, even simple scenes need focusing, and Jamie and Nora were no exceptions. After all they are not the ones cutting the film in their heads as it goes along, or arranging the next day's shoot, although they will have some blinding insights. Your job is to fit them into the story, which means your contributors will need to know what a sequence is about, especially contributors who have not been involved in the scripting.

For instance, when Jamie was ordering the ingredients for his first recipes, it was important that Nora should ask him the right questions. It would be no good if she talked about holidays! With focus it turned into a lively conversation about the right subject (note the brevity of the opening commentary) with Nora ticking off the new kitchen worker.

**JAMIE'S SCHOOL DINNERS, FRESH ONE FOR CHANNEL 4
PROGRAMME 1, AS TRANSMITTED**

COMMENTARY   *Jamie's making up recipes as he goes along, but Nora's the one who'll have to reproduce his dishes when he's gone.*

NORA   So what are you putting in the curry, what veg?

JAMIE   I went through that with you yesterday.

NORA   You didn't for the curry.

JAMIE   I did – I was talking about turkey, and you said, 'I haven't got any turkey, I've got chicken.'

NORA   I've got the chicken, yeah. I said you got chicken but we shouldn't have chicken coming in this morning for what you wanted today – it should have been in the day before.

JAMIE   I found out yesterday when you told me I couldn't have the turkey, you said I've got chicken.

NORA   Yesterday's too late to be planning for today.

JAMIE   Right.

NORA   There's got to be a plan of each day and what you want and it comes in the day before.

JAMIE   Yes.

NORA   That way when you come to your fridge in the morning I can take everything out on a trolley. I know you laugh at the trolleys when I go to the freezer in the morning.

JAMIE   I don't have a problem with the trolleys.

NORA   So in the morning I could come in, you want two kilo of carrots, it could all be done.

JAMIE   Well, I promise it won't happen again. I can't do any better than that.

NORA   But you promised me that two days ago but it still happens.

Despite your best efforts, often contributors (more so than presenters) may prove unable to articulate quite the dialogue you need to advance your story of what is really happening, especially if they are not professional presenters, and on camera for the first time. And often your contributor will ignore the three things you said you need, unwilling to articulate them in dialogue. Then you will need to be provocative, and may even have to join in the conversation. If you don't, contributors will sometimes continue to say what they actually don't feel.

I believe it's a question of doing your research really well, and then using every trick to get back to what people were saying to you in the first place. I consider this to be moral and authentic, digging out the real truth. It can be a game of cat-and-mouse, and it can sometimes help to catch contributors unawares, articulating the points as your camera begins rolling rather than beforehand, especially if you don't have a presenter to use, and especially if your contributors are powerful people, such as politicians, who are experienced at hiding what they think. So I have always found that it helps to appear confused, while being ordered and in control.

CONFUSION IN THE CAUSE OF HONESTY

Don't make a show of beginning to film — just slip into it. Otherwise contributors will take 'turn over' to mean 'now make your voices and conversation more boring'. As contributors get comfy and chat away, just quietly start filming, of course saying in advance that this is what you will do. This can be particularly tough for a film crew, so before you begin shooting actuality you need to explain to your film crew how you work. Don't let everyone get settled, but get a lively conversation going as you set up, then just plough in and have the crew start filming what is already going on as soon as they are ready. The more of a muddle it is as you get going, the less the contributors will be able to worry about what they are going to say, and this is just what you want. In fact confusion is a way of putting contributors at their ease and gaining energy, which is what most filming needs. The alternative is to be very quiet and formal, and have a long pause before filming actually begins, which will give your contributors time to worry and clam up.

We had a particularly difficult challenge as we set up to film a master interview for a film on the South Yorkshire police, with the Chief Constable. He tried hard to be warm, but he was a very controlled man indeed, and the police are well used to interviews — usually with suspects. As we were setting up I got into arguments with the crew; they got more and more upset. As we began filming the Chief Constable was really off guard. Government ministers can be even tougher. In *Jamie's School Dinners* the then Secretary of State for Education, Charles Clarke, agreed to meet him at his restaurant, Fifteen. We began filming as they talked, but instead of the fine lunch he was expecting, the waitress who arrived at the table was Nora, who served him the sort of standard processed school food that Jamie was trying to get rid of — rice crispy-encrusted processed meat and smiley faces. It was a shocking moment, but as he was on camera he could do nothing but smile, then say how helpful Jamie had been, and of course that these would have to disappear from the menu. Jamie is luckily fantastic at pieces like these.

Eighteen months, and two Secretaries of State later, we came to film the update, *Jamie's Return to School Dinners*. This time, perhaps not surprisingly, the PR people didn't want the new Secretary of State to come to Fifteen, and said it would be in the minister's office, on his territory. Fine, we thought, Nora and Jamie can bring dinner from Nora's kitchen in an insulated bag – after all a lot of this update film had been about schools that had no kitchens, so school dinners were being cooked in a pub before being carted round Lincolnshire to the schools.

Unfortunately Nora was also now being 'looked after' by Greenwich PR and they knew she might prepare dinner for the minister. There were Whitehall PR as well, and they rang to say no food allowed in our filming. Perhaps Clarke had been upset at seeing what British kids ate (he didn't seem so at the time and it had, I think, come over excellently) and the new minister certainly wasn't about to be! So we thought we'd failed, as I often do, but when you fail you always need to see it as an opportunity ('when it's right it's wrong'), and try to think of a way to use it. The other problem Jamie faced in this update programme was that despite healthy food now being served in the school canteens, kids were going to the local shops to buy their junk. So we took Jamie shopping just before the meeting and popped what many British kids eat at lunch in his bag – crisps and chocolate.

BEWARE OFF-CAMERA CONVERSATION

We were only allowed a short meeting in front of a phalanx of PRs and managers – a very uncomfortable situation. We were also told the minister would need a private conversation with Jamie first. If you allow this, then it becomes the place where the real discussion happens, off camera, so I never allow it if it can be avoided, saying that I need to film the moment they meet, then they can have the private conversation. This later private conversation hardly ever happens because once they've got going on camera they won't stop.

This is what happened with the minister. We filmed them first meeting, from the initial greeting as Jamie walked in – 'Hello, I'm this week's Secretary of State' – and then just kept going as the minister and Jamie chatted amicably, then started talking about school meals. In the car on the way down I had focused Jamie on just what we needed to get from this meeting. There were three key things which commentary would be able to tee: (1) that banning junk meals in schools was not enough, kids also needed to stop buying junk outside and bringing it in; (2) that more money was needed, particularly to rebuild kitchens for schools without them; and (3) a commitment to continued funding.

But ministers can be intimidating and these points didn't come up easily. Jamie needed help not just to remember the points, but also to confront the minister, almost showing that the tough questioning was not just his fault but ours. The only way of doing this, again, is to join in the conversation. There are three ways of doing this, and surprisingly most directors still use the first, which works least well: this is just interrupting, which stops the flow. A better way is – without any 'excuse me' or stopping filming – just joining in the conversation and then leaving it.

Then there is a third way, and this can be the best of all. I had just gone up and whispered in Jamie's ear, 'Remember you've got the junk in your bag, get it out, say it's what most kids eat and ask for more money.' Soon the PR told us to stop, as we had been given little time and we were running late, but we continued till we were asked again, and really had to leave. I had briefed the cameraman to catch anything the PR said, we had filmed every word from beginning to end, and Jamie had asked all the right questions of a tough minister.

So when in doubt focus your contributors, and even presenters if they are doing something unusual, on three or four key things you need from each actuality sequence. Even when Jamie met Tony Blair at No. 10 I was quite happy to whisper in his ear as the camera was rolling – as long as it was on the Prime Minister, who was in the middle of answering a question, not on Jamie – reinforcing my star's strength and focus in pushing the next point, and challenging an intimidating opponent in an intimidating place.

THE TONE OF ACTUALITY

You can almost always tell at once when the actuality you are filming is good. And it is often because of the tone, not the content. Louder has more energy and passion – softer can be because your contributors are thinking they are hiding what they are saying. I sometimes think you could edit actuality with a sound-level meter alone. When contributors' voices get louder and rise a couple of notes up the scale, they are passionate, heated and arguing, which is good. When they get very quiet, at the end, they are being conspiratorial, which is good too. When they are on a middle note of middle loudness, it is middling and boring. And sometimes this is all they are, as they strenuously avoid saying what they really think and, if they do, say it in an unwieldy and unfocused way. To overcome this you can try temporarily to become one of the contributors yourself, and join in the conversation more. After all, you are in the conversation when interviewing – in fact you are half of it!

So if it sounds dull, do everything to liven it up. Use your energy and facial expression to encourage your presenter – with silent praise as they get tougher, and despondent looks as they weaken. If necessary engage in the conversation, and get it going, stir it, interject – 'So all the kids hated your meals, did they?' – get everyone arguing about the subject, expressing their views strongly, which they may be loath to do. Try to communicate with your cameraman to be on the other people while you engage, and be aware of how to edge out of the dialogue once it gets going, without the contributors noticing. You should try to move gently out of their eyeline, so no one can look at you or talk to you. Preferably get behind whoever you have just argued with! And avoid eye contact if they look round for you, even by just lowering your eyes to the floor, so they have to talk to the person they see in front. Then from behind gesticulate to the person who has had to take over your point, encourage them with facial movement to say what they think, and smile when they do, and once they've got going gently leave them to it. They are now talking truthfully and emotionally – a tough thing to get people to do.

Not everyone agrees with this method, but it is only to get a conversation on the right track of the story of your film rather than about something completely different. It is certainly not designed to get contributors to say something they don't think or feel. In fact it is designed to get them to do just the opposite.

You can cut yourself out in the cutting room, but the audience is sophisticated and understands that there is a director, so it doesn't matter that much whether you're there in the film or not. Many of the best film-makers – Molly Dineen, Nick Broomfield, Michael Moore, Adam Curtis – are now in their films, either in sound or vision or both, and perhaps it is more honest rather than less to acknowledge your presence. But most documentary-makers try to pop in just occasionally, to help the dialogue between others, and then cut themselves out again as far as possible.

Similarly, at the end of filming a piece of actuality, make sure your camera isn't put away but is still at the ready. Even better, say we just need to film a few shots of you listening to each other, mentioning the sound will still be on if they ask. Even though they know you are filming, the contributors will be partly relieved it is over, and desperate to say what they have wanted to all along. Because the camera is focused on the listening face, they feel freer. And the voices quieten down, they start saying the truth, and the camera can begin to move again. It is very often the filming before and after a conversation that can be best.

To sum up, it is great if you can get all the information out of pictures and dialogue within the film, just as in Hollywood drama, as it is almost always better if you can get someone talking to someone else about a subject, rather than just speaking to you in an interview. Real life isn't full of interviews, but conversations. But sadly in documentary, unlike drama, we cannot write the dialogue, so sometimes contributors don't talk about quite the right thing in conversation. Despite your help they will digress all over the place, and even worse they won't express emotion: so use interview when actuality has failed, but remember to try to get emotion within it if you can. And as a last resort use commentary. Just remember that although it may be a last resort it is often what makes a factual film – just as long as it is short!

Seven

CARE

AND GETTING THE PROGRAMME ON AIR

When you have finally edited your film you need to get people to watch it. And when they have seen your work, it is not just the audience who need to feel pleased, but also your peers in TV and the critics, so it is deemed a success and you get to pitch and make your next film. Usually, if the audience or critics love it your TV peers will follow suit, but if the audience hates your film it is even more vital that your TV peers love it.

This chapter is all about making people CARE. It is about how you position, promote and sell your finished film, to help the viewers to CARE and convince schedulers and marketeers to help you. For there is little point in choosing the right story, and making it perfectly, if it doesn't get the audience it deserves, and it can be miserable if it goes out unpromoted at the wrong time and no one watches. The most important thing in film-making is to make the audience really care, memorably CARE. Because if they don't, why should they bother watching? But before that this chapter is also about pitching your next story so the buyer cares and gives you the money to make it.

Making people care is the most important thing in film-making, and perhaps the only test. Everything we have talked about so far has been designed to help. If you have followed the story so far you'll have found:

CHARACTERS about whom the audience should care; thought

OUT OF THE BOX to follow their real adventures, so the audience care even more; used

NARRATIVE DRIVE to pose a big question, so that the audience really care about your characters pursuing their quest, complete with small questions with real jeopardy that make sure they still care en route; cut your film with a strong

FRONT that sets up who the characters are, and is a route map to the film so the audience cares from the off; made sure you

LOVED your characters into submission, so they are happy to have taken part and told you the truth, and been shown in domestic situations that show their real emotional stakes and make you care even more; and you have

INTERVIEWED them for feeling and written a commentary for terse fact, teeing up scenes and helping the narrative drive along, all designed to make the audience care most of all.

All these techniques are used during the film-making process, so that you will have done everything possible to make the audience care deeply and memorably about your story. But they won't be of any use if you can't sell it. So before we move on to the thorny subjects of press, marketing and promotion, let's start at the beginning of the care process, choosing and pitching your story just right so the broadcaster (or your boss) will care enough to buy it.

As you go towards the finish of your programme you should already be thinking of the next film, or next but one, because commissioning takes so long. And the first thing in this process is to make sure you have a story that the commissioner will care about, and pitch it to maximise this care.

MAKING COMMISSIONERS CARE

Although you may sometimes just be handed a film to make, many times you will be trying to develop ideas either out of the blue or within limits, such as being asked to pitch for a particular slot or to make a story within a strand. Whichever you are doing, you are working within constraints. You need to think of a time-slot or a subject area. It helps if it is an area for which you have branded yourself. It is unlikely the buyer will take a light-entertainment extravaganza from a person or company known for very serious documentaries. It also helps if you find something from your own experience.

Peter Bazalgette was in a queue at a garden centre and suddenly thought: 'All these people are trying to make gardens, why not do it in forty-eight hours?' And so began *Ground Force*. My family used to be in business and I was intrigued at what wickedness they had got up to – hence my business programmes. *The Boy Whose Skin Fell Off* came from the director's heart: he had suffered from cancer himself, and the film was local to Newcastle, his home town. It resonated with him, it became his passion.

So now you have found a great story (not a subject), with potential for conflict, even a clash of cultures, that may take you into a hidden world. But whatever route you take to finding a subject in today's increasingly competitive and derivative world, to sell programmes needs ambition, and you can never be too ambitious, or create too original a twist. Look at *Walking with Dinosaurs* or *Human Body* or the first *Big*

JON ROWLANDS

Former Head of Development, BBC Factual,
Creative Director, Renegade Pictures, responsible for
format hits *Don't Tell the Bride* and *Man About the House*.
He recently got married and set up home . . .

Look for things in your own life that have universality. We all get married, all buy a house, all do up a house. The biggest domestic arguments take place in Ikea. Buying things for the house is an incredibly intense personal thing. Traditionally it's the woman's job to make the home, so we decided to pitch an idea putting the guy in charge, and put the man at the centre of Man About the House *and* Don't Tell the Bride. *What does he want, but also what does he think she wants and what do they both want? A very, very simple situation with a twist to make it very compelling.*

I have a very simple development credo: what would happen if X did Y? What would happen if a man organised a wedding? What would happen if you gave teenagers a baby? What would happen if your boss came and worked next to you? If you know the answer, that's not interesting. If the answer is 'I don't know', that's the right answer.

Brother, with the ambition of a closed house rigged with cameras, and the twist of the confession and the evictions. Or the ambition can be as simple as new technology. Paul Watson's adaptation of *The Family* of the early 1970s, and its precursor the US series *An American Family*, are often said to have created fly-on-the-wall reality TV. Recently this has been reinvented under the same name, with a family's house rigged with cameras and the gallery next door, the ultimate reality TV.

So before you can convince the viewers, the first thing is convincing someone who runs a TV channel, or your bosses, that the audience will care. Clearly you need to pitch it. Whether you need to pitch to or within a production company, or to a commissioning editor, the same rules apply. First you need to plan how to make this, the all-important recipient, care – because if they don't care, no one else will get the chance to!

SIMON DICKSON

Deputy Head of Documentaries, Channel 4,
commissioner of *The Family* and *One Born Every Minute*

*For me to get really excited about something it's got to carry a substantial
risk of failure. I had admired* Going Cold Turkey [which followed
heroin addicts through withdrawal twenty-four hours a day] *but it
didn't really move me. So I wondered if we could apply the* Big Brother/
Going Cold Turkey *technology, the multiple-cameras approach, to
subject areas the audience would be more inclined to watch. My first
suggestion was that we put multiple cameras in a family home, and we
did. I'd rather take a substantial leap into the unknown with a
production company that I trust than go in baby steps in a linear way
from one thing I know has worked to another thing that is likely to work.*

*The evolution of a new sub-genre of documentary can rumble on for
years. It's three years since a conversation with Nick Curwin and
Magnus Temple over a plate of Vietnamese mackerel in a restaurant in
Shoreditch to where we are now with* One Born Every Minute –
[successor to *The Family*, set in a maternity hospital] *riding high
in the charts and the channel's most successful, highest-rated programme.*

THE PITCH

There is a chance, of course, that you'll run into the head of development, a company chief or commissioning editor before you've sent
anything on paper to their office. You might run into them at an awards
ceremony, in a cutting room or in the corridor as you go in to visit one
of their colleagues. Don't miss your chance! Tantalise them with a few
snippets, but not too much. Do it quickly, so when they see the proposal on paper it still has something exciting and new to entice and
surprise them (and be aware of where you are doing it and how wary
commissioners are of being assaulted).

And here's another tip: when you write the actual proposal, leave a
little out. Leave room for surprise in the discussion that will happen
when you formally meet. Don't forget to watch the commissioner's

latest programmes and have an intelligent view on them. Finally, remember to lay out the idea briefly and punchily. I would suggest that you create a short front page that says what it is about, what is different or special, who it is for, and why the target audience should watch it. As in making a film, form a short focused outline from a mound of research. This may be all the commissioning editor will read! But as long as the idea is half decent, hopefully it will at least get you a meeting.

HARRY LANSDOWNE

Commissioning Editor, BBC 3

Don't doorstep me, as someone once tried to do at breakfast in Edinburgh, or hand me a newspaper cutting without thinking how it might translate into original, compelling TV. If it feels daring, I don't expect to have it all on a plate. Do try to watch the channel a bit before. And do email me just a key paragraph that sums up the idea.

Within the main broadcasters there are mostly a host of factual departments. Do you go for Features, Factual, Entertainment, Documentaries, Specialist Factual . . . and what is the difference? Well, they often overlap, but in Britain if it is cookery, like *River Cottage*, it is likely to be Features. As you move towards stronger formats with more content, like *Heston's Michelin Impossible* in which he solves a company's cookery problem each week, it could be Features, Factual Entertainment or even Documentaries. If you become more serious, as in *Jamie's School Dinners*, *The Family* or especially *Cutting Edge*, you move fully into the world of Documentaries – but then Jamie's later *Ministry of Food* was Factual Entertainment (maybe that was why the content was a little lighter). Finally as content grows, and science and history come in, you move into Specialist Factual, which can depend even more on research. So it can take longer to develop the pitch for programmes such as *Henry VIII*, since you need in-depth knowledge, unlike a Features idea like *Don't Tell the Bride*, though both still take thinking through. But in the end they are all factual programming, so choose who you like. And stay focused not just on the idea, but what you are pitching overall.

VICTORIA DUMMER

Senior Vice President ABC Alternative Series,
Specials and Late Night, USA

Just have a very clear, concise idea. Often if people are coming over from England they use the opportunity to pitch several ideas. We'd rather hear one very focused idea than several, because that really shows your passion, and that you've put in a lot of effort. So it's 'This is the one,' rather than 'Here is our laundry list of four or five shows, and would you like one of them?' It's better for us if they show they have thought about the shows, thought about the market, and decided 'This is the show for you.' It's just a much stronger position to pitch on.

ANDREA WONG

Former Chief Executive, Lifetime Networks

There's more competition in the US, because you're competing against fifty to seventy widely distributed channels, so you have to carve out your brand and your niche, certainly in cable. To be successful as a cable station you have to understand what your audience, flipping among all those channels, is going to choose you for. Then it's really important to execute and create shows against that clearly defined brand. So on Bravo the audience knows it's going to get reality shows and a certain kind of real show. Lifetime is a clear brand because you know you're going to get fiction, movies and drama. So are channels like the Food Network and Discovery. So if you're selling, don't waste your time going to the ones that aren't interested in your wares, because it's a waste of your time and theirs.

Finally the time-slot makes a difference to how you pitch a story, getting weightier through the day and evening. Look at the sort of thing that is on in daytime, and at 7.00, 8.00, 9.00 and 10.00. Think what your audience might like to watch then. There are also a host of channels showing factual, from cable through the terrestrials. Again look at what they are showing and think what they might need. Remember, even if you are a runner trying to pitch an idea within a company, you need to think who the audience might be, which channel and what time-slot, how long and how many episodes. All of this is vital if you are to focus what you are doing.

FRONT PAGE

As said, I would suggest that you take a short front page that says what your proposal is about, what is different or special, who it is for, and why the target audience should watch it. This is, in truth, probably all the commissioning editor will read – a short piece that sums your pitch up, with a wealth of research behind it. As long as the idea is half decent, hopefully this will at least get you a meeting. Then you've got to be really prepared. Would the following example make a real or an unreal project? You can decide. What are the problems with it?

KID SQUAD
(6 x 60 mins, 9 p.m.)

THE BACKGROUND

As kids become ever more sophisticated, bombarded with information, targeted ever more by advertisers and increasingly savvy shoppers, could it be kids who can solve the problems of businesses, and institutions, which are struggling to change and to keep up with the kids who use them?

Five charismatic clever kids set out to solve everyday problems in public and private sector businesses that kids use. Each week a new place, a new challenge. Without the baggage it's time for kids to discover what's wrong, and what could be done.

THE PREMISE

Why is the toy shop losing money so fast, the local theme park failing, and how should the record company react to downloads? What can a struggling toy company or British football clubs do to make money, and why is no one going to the restaurant? And what about the failing fashion shop? Each week we send a group of five kids to a different business that has kids as customers to find out.

If this works they could even challenge why the trains don't work, come up with obvious (to kids) solutions to some of the problems of hospitals. And who better to come up with solutions to why a failing school is not run right – and how about exams?

This famous five are carefully chosen for charisma, brains and innocent wit. They include the hyper-precocious specs, the sports fanatic, the cool, the emotionally sensitive and the freckly.

Then the fun begins, as the kids ask the questions adults wouldn't dare, or even think of, identify and approach the problems from first principles.

THE STORY

The Start
A young fashion clothes store is going bust. The boss wants help. He needs to understand his market. The kids visit to see what he thinks the problem might be.

The Research
The kids talk to friends. One gets a weekend job in the local Next, a couple go on an intensive two-day course at Philip Green's retail academy. The final two, setting off on their bikes, meet staff at rivals, secretly film, talk to the public, and advertisers, spy, discover and then . . .

Meet the Store
With their new-found knowledge, all five set to work all over the store, selling, meeting suppliers, talking to customers and managers to find out and agree the real question.

Final Denouement
The kids set out their plan for change. The merchandise needs to be transformed, and especially set out quite differently, they need a DJ to attract the local kids and a party evening. The store could be run quite differently so their friends would love it.

The Aftermath
As the shop puts some of this into action – will it work?

AUTHENTICITY

Authenticity is becoming so important now that I have a created a checklist for pitches round the acronym A.U.T.H.E.N.[T.]I.C. The word is carefully chosen because so many series fail, despite having plenty of conflict, because they are not authentic – the situations, or challenges, in which we put our heroes are not true to the characters. Let's apply this to the programme, *Kid Squad*, we have just pitched.

AMBITION – Is it ambitious enough? What is the most kids could do?

UNDERPINNINGS – The research. Can kids really change businesses? This is like the foundations of a house. What is below the surface keeps it up. In television you need ten times more knowledge than the viewer will see in the finished programme for it to ring true.

TOP – Have you worked out a reason for making the film? Are there companies that are serving kids and are in trouble?

HURDLES – Have you worked out a set of challenges for the kids? What will they do? How do you break it into sequences which are these challenges, or questions?

END – Hugely important: how do we know if our heroes have succeeded or not? How do we quantify this?

NOMENCLATURE – How do we cast our kids so that each is memorable, and what characteristics do they need?

IN THE MOMENT – How do we keep that clock ticking, and the audience really wanting to know what happens next – from the beginning?

CARE – Good old care again. The million-dollar question: will we care?

I don't know. Would you commission it?

TASTERS

It can also be useful to make a taster tape for the pitch. With DV cameras and self-shooting assistant producers this need not cost an arm and a leg. It can be a small but crucial investment, particularly in showing off a new presenter or range of characters, and sometimes even the quality of access to a tricky institution. It's like offering a sample in another business. But at all costs, make sure it is good, though not over-polished, and with a punch.

Selling a programme idea is like selling anything. You need to hook the buyer – understand their needs, the pressures on them, what they like and what they hate. Then systematically try to correlate their needs with the strengths of your programme idea that meet those needs. But don't over-sell. The knack is to avoid the buyer feeling that you have told them too much, and to get them to ask you to tell them more! And always listen: they may have suggestions of their own. And if these are good, they will begin to feel ownership of the idea − to 'buy in'.

AXEL ARNO

Chairman, Eurovision Documentary Group,
and Commissioning Editor, SVT, Sweden − a king
of international documentaries

It's very rarely that I jump off my chair because I am just told something. I feel really excited when I see great footage, like from Last Train Home, *the film that went on to win IDFA. The footage was just from the research trip, but of one hundred million people migrating in China. This material had an amazing quality and I was just sure it would be a fantastic film, and it became a really good film that we bought.*

A taster has to tick one of the boxes, saying that the film will be truly unique, access-wise or picture-wise, or show something I've never seen before. Or it should show a fresh take on something I have seen before with a new angle or some new thought that hasn't struck me before. Put in the strongest scene you have − something that will actually connect.

Inevitably when you actually move into production and begin to research characters and storylines, and try telling them in the pub, you will find that the project becomes different to precisely what you had pitched. (It certainly will if you have made a lot of it up, as many people do in proposals!)

But don't worry too much. Remember that the commissioner is unlikely to remember what they have commissioned, and if it eventually works will think it is just what they asked you for. It will figure in their proud list of annual achievements! In 2001 Mark Thompson, Managing Director of BBC Television, introduced me to the new Director General, Greg Dyke, saying, 'Robert Thirkell is the man who makes programmes when they are not commissioned.'

Keep going and those commissioners and controllers may eventually relent. Then they will be proud of what 'they' made, a bit like presenters

STEPHEN LAMBERT

Chief Executive, Studio Lambert,
creator of *Wife Swap*, *Secret Millionaire* and *Undercover Boss*

When Wife Swap *was pitched and sold it was largely a personal finance show. It sort of came from an ideas meeting where we were looking at those daily features that you often get in the newspapers, like with six or seven women, breaking down their income and what they spent their money on, and thinking, wouldn't it be interesting to have the nurse live on the income of the high-powered lawyer and spend the money the way she's spending it, and for the high-powered lawyer to do the same with the nurse's income. So initially it was a personal finance idea. But because it was women, swapping and living on each other's income, we had the idea of calling it* Wife Swap. *And everybody said, 'Oh no, we can't call it that because people can't swap wives.' And I thought, 'Why not?' and said, 'They don't have to go and sleep in each other's bedrooms, but they can do everything else.'*

really – they often don't know quite what they want, just get them to own it in the end. In reality they just want hits, and you will be judged only on this, certainly not on whether you played by the rules.

STEPHEN LAMBERT

Chief Executive, Studio Lambert,
creator of *Wife Swap*, *Secret Millionaire* and *Undercover Boss*

I think the biggest stumbling block to a lot of good ideas is that you're expected to work it out in ridiculous detail before you get the commission. And that often isn't the best way to work out how a format works. The best thing is for there to be something that is inherently interesting. And it's the interplay between starting to cast it and working out once you've got the potential cast and the reality of their situation, that enables you to start thinking about how to make the programme. The secret of making a show is to find a commissioning editor who falls in love with the basic concept and then you work it out when you're making it.

DO THE OPPOSITE OF WHAT THEY ASK

There's another thing to remember: network commissioners and channel controllers don't usually stay long in their jobs – no more than three or four years – so there's a good chance that they will have been fired or promoted by the time your series or programme is finished. Especially if you take a long time to make it! Then it will end up as a positive benefit if you can prove that what you have made has little to do with the original commission or commissioner. If it is too close to the original, and so to the current incumbent's predecessor, it may get shunted to the back of the schedule. Unless of course you can convince the new commissioner that it is actually their idea.

It's not just TV commissioners who don't usually stay long in their jobs. There may well also be a new channel or network controller in post, their boss, who will want nothing to do with a show that is derivative of a success commissioned by his predecessor. Then it will end up as a positive benefit if your show is entirely original, not derivative at all, and in fact has little in common with the original commission. And if your controller and commissioner *have* survived, they will almost certainly have forgotten quite why they commissioned your show in the first place – they'll be focused on their latest hit. Best of all, if you have ignored them and are making something that others are not, you stand a better chance of surprising and pleasing those people who really count: the audience.

To help this process I sometimes think: whatever is asked for, do the opposite. This applies to anything from duration to genre. Everyone looks at last week's success and wants to make new versions of it at once. Following the success of *Jamie's School Dinners* I was asked to make social and political makeover shows about everything from prisons to hospitals (with the addition of Trinny and Susannah). And if I was given a penny for every show I was asked to do following *The Apprentice* in which 'contestants' are knocked out week by week, my pockets would be weighed down with pennies. So eighteen months to two years after any big hit there will be a glut of copycats that the controllers have commissioned, such as *Tycoon* or the many other knockout competitions. But by then there will be a new 'last week's hit' that is all the rage and everyone is being asked to copy. So whatever is asked for, it can help to do the exact opposite! Even when or if you become a commissioner. So my advice is straightforward: to succeed keep away from derivative series, unless you are reviving something years later, in which case the form will have advanced so much it will in practice be new.

The success of my BBC Business Unit could partly have been the result of my decision to make programmes of forty-minute duration, just at the point when we were being told that, for controllers and schedulers hour-long programmes were all the rage, and that the forty-minute slot was a thing of the past. In fact nobody was allowed to make them any more. So two years later there was a dearth of forty-minute films, but – irony of ironies – BBC2 controllers were still importing hour-long American series, which without the ad breaks ran for considerably less than fifty minutes. These normally began at 9.00, and there was then a fixed junction before the politically immoveable *Newsnight* at 10.30. Consequently, following the US imports, even with a few trailers and links thrown in, there was a near forty-minute gap to fill! The only other solution for this 'problem' was a thirty-minute programme followed by a ten-minute programme, but there were not enough of these either. As I had managed to ignore the rule, and was still making forty-minute films, my programmes were suddenly very popular; they were almost the only such programmes on offer. (These were *Back to the Floor*, *Blood on the Carpet* and *Trouble at the Top*.)

Best of all, if you end up making what other people aren't, inevitably you stand a better chance of surprising and pleasing the people who really count – the audience.

If in any way you can get commissioners or companies fighting over you, make them care even more. Having completed my first series of *Troubleshooter* I had the challenge of finding something to come up with next. I made my business programmes in a specialist factual department, Science, so when I was given a stark choice – *Horizon* or *QED* – I was very worried. I might have been just about all right at new inventions – working on *Tomorrow's World* I could do car engines and making stuff – but science? I only just passed a combined Physics with Chemistry O-level, and had never done a second of Biology in my life.

Unaware of this dismal failing, the two editors of *Horizon* and *QED* competed over me. I was told that one even burst into tears in front of the head of the Science Department as she thought she was losing.

I appreciated that (needy as ever) and decided to work for her. But the reason she had burst into tears wasn't to get me, it was to get anyone. She was one story down in her upcoming strand of science stories, and there were just fourteen weeks to find a story, gain access, research it, make it and edit it. Normally, with the story already found, there would be nearly half as much time again.

When I had signed up and found this out I nearly burst into tears too. I was a non-scientist, with a record short turnaround to make a film, having to live up to the BAFTA, and I didn't have a story. So how to find one about which my commissioner and my audience would care?

First I needed to look for one, but where? Just as in the original *Troubleshooter*, I needed to narrow the search with a likely subject area. Asking friends and contacts is always a good start. So I confided in a close friend over dinner, a psychiatrist. Now psychiatry I might be able to understand a bit; it wasn't pure science. Great, I said, as she talked, let's follow someone's cure – remember I like to tell the story of heroes. Excellent she said, have you got a few years? I was despondent again. Then she remembered a new course at Guy's Hospital in quick cognitive analytic therapy. It took place over six weeks. By now I didn't actually have six weeks left for filming, but I went along to see it anyway. Boring, I didn't care. Back to the drawing board.

But often you hear one bit of information about a story, and then another, and although both on their own might not excite you, they can illuminate each other. Now I was thinking about the subject I was on the lookout, and going to as many dinner parties with psychiatrists as possible. I didn't need to. I'd forgotten I lived with one, who mentioned a four-week course at the Maudsley, Britain's leading psychiatric hospital. Their 'Parent Child Game' aimed to transform disruptive children, with a team of psychologists instructing the parents on how to react to difficult children, using a microphone and earpiece and hidden behind a two-way mirror. I wouldn't have picked up on this if psychiatry hadn't been in my mind from the dinner. Very often the right story will come at you at least two ways – and sometimes this is just what makes it right.

After some rapid persuasion, the Maudsley Hospital agreed I could follow it, but not with one of their own patients, which they felt would be morally questionable. If I could find a suitable child myself, I could make the film, following them through the 'game', which suited my purposes perfectly as I could do the casting. It was another big advantage for me that the parents took part too, as it would create more conflict. Better still, there was one key psychiatrist and one key psychologist – a hero and anti-hero – who watched the parents interacting with the child through a two-way mirror, and gave instructions through a hidden earpiece in each parent's ear. It was all a recipe for conflict.

Unfortunately I no longer had four weeks left to film it, and I didn't have a suitable family to follow. So I persuaded the Maudsley to run their course for a fortnight and advertised for a family immediately. I used a separate Maudsley psychiatrist to give me advice on what might happen, showing him tapes of potential candidates. It is always worth asking for a 'second opinion', someone independent who won't be in the film, when making any scientific, academic or technical films.

I had succeeded in dusting off my old story in new clothes and turned this into following one of the naughtiest (superlative again) children in Britain – a five-year-old we had found in Neath. Would we care? This was just after the James Bulger case and the opening was:

QED FAMILY GAME, BBC TV, PRE-TITLE AS TRANSMITTED

Andrew writhing on floor in superstore aisle.	Andrew screaming.
	DAD *Embarrassed, very very embarrassed, when he's in his tantrums, you've got people looking at you as if to say, can you control that child, but he's very very difficult to control.*
People looking on.	
Dad attempting to get shoe on screaming son in superstore aisle.	Andrew more screaming.
	COMMENTARY Most children have tantrums, but one in ten outbursts like this are the mark of a seriously disruptive child, whose parents have completely lost control. At five, such children are infuriating, at fifteen they may well be making headlines as juvenile delinquents.
Outside school.	Andrew Weber's already left two schools because of his behaviour. He would bully his

Andrew banging on car roof.	classmates, bite his teachers and turn over the desks.
Dad outside school.	DAD *My wife was threatened by one parent that if something's not done about him they're going to do something about him, so in the end we just took him from the school.*
	COMMENTARY Since early February, while his eight-year-old sister Joanna goes to school he's been at home with his parents. Clive and Amanda Weber have reached breaking point.
Dad and Mum at home.	DAD AND MUM *He goes in people's gardens, he's ringing people's doorbells, he's just a nag all the time. A lot of the wicked things he gets up to, he's flooded our house out, he's hitting his sister, he breaks things, he's tortured the animals, he's just a waster, a total waster. We are just at our wits' end with him. He's at an age now if something's not done what's he going to be like when he gets into his teens?*

There was just synch: pictures of strong evidence of the child Andrew misbehaving in various locations from the street to the supermarket, and a strong interview from the embarrassed parents at their wits' ends, desperate for the treatment to get Andrew to change, which took one or two minutes, and a small amount of commentary that could have been less. Post-title there was more parent synch of their challenge to control him and desperation for change from the therapy and a journey from south Wales to London and the treatment to get the story going.

Then in the treatment the psychologist viewed the behaviour of parent and child using two-way mirrors and cameras, as using hidden earpieces they told the parents to praise their son when he was good and ignore him when he was bad rather than giving him the attention he craved when he was naughty. (Just like directors, really, who function best on lots of praise, and boundaries.) The outcome was dramatic. He had tantrums; he stormed out and ran off across the hospital grounds, with us following. But slowly and magically the therapy began to work.

Remember my favourite recipe – conflict leading to transformation and if possible redemption. I had it all as the whole family was transformed by his improvement. His mum's last words were over Andrew peacefully playing an electric organ with a very touching tune – again a bit of luck that was spotted by a superb researcher, Charlotte Howarth.

QED, THE FAMILY GAME FOR BBC, FINAL WORDS AS TRANSMITTED

MUM AT HOME   We got so wound up with him being so naughty and everything, we thought nothing would work. It's just incredible, it's gobsmacking, we can't get over it.

It was genuinely moving – and timely, so it managed to pick up nearly nine million viewers, nearly a 40 per cent share, and a couple of awards. The lady running it, Sue Jenner, was in effect Supernanny and a new genre had been born. I had managed to find, pitch and make a transformation story again and survived - but, as always in TV, for how long?

COMMISSIONING

Eventually I made the shift from pitching films to commissioning them, so what tips can I give you about pitching from the other end? For when I finally persuaded the BBC I could make more business documentaries I was already an executive producer, so I now had the challenge not just of coming up with stories but of commissioning them. I started with my own 'strand' of single documentaries, *Trouble at the Top*, competing with the likes of *Horizon* (or *Nova* in the US) and *QED*. It would end up running for eight seasons, and had numerous spin-off series like *Trouble Between the Covers* (a magazine, not a bed) and *Trouble at the Big Top* (the Dome, not a circus). But which programmes to commission? Surprisingly the job is not, as you might imagine, sifting through hundreds of good ideas and then choosing a few. Rather it is desperately wanting anything original that jumps out at you.

One of my criteria was star quality in the name, subject or topicality that I had used myself when pitching. Another, something people could identify with. A third, the surprising view or behind-the-scenes discovery. But often more important than any of these was the desperation of someone to make the film combined with the potential for some kind of transformation, because, remember, good stories often follow people under pressure through transformation, ideally to redemption. For in the end, as my employees continued to say, to make me care there were only three important things: conflict, conflict and conflict.

Because conflict reveals character, and so the universal truths we all want to know. Seeing a hero having a gentle and peaceful existence does not advance any story. But where do you best find conflict? We have discussed looming death as a motivator of drama, as in many gangster films, or perils such as earthquakes when the tectonic plates bang together. But, as I said earlier, business doesn't have much looming death, except perhaps in southern Italy and the Bronx.

However, there are other things that create conflict: family, war, but best of all for our purposes is where different mindsets bang into each other. The advantage here is you have the potential for humour too, with those tectonic plates of Britain banging together: north *vs* south, modern *vs* old-fashioned, rich *vs* poor – and best of all, class.

As I searched for stories for my new strand *Trouble at the Top*, I thought back to *Troubleshooter*, when I was one story down at the end of the first series, with time running out till transmission. Desperate to find this final *Troubleshooter*, I was sitting staring at my dinner and thought of pottery. People use pottery every day, and it was made till recently in old-fashioned British factories – dozens of factories in one town, Stoke on Trent. Now it was about to move to China. So I wrote to just about every factory, and one actually said yes. Churchill China was Britain's biggest potter, employing around a thousand staff. It was owned and run by three brothers – a great ingredient for conflict. They were lovely, but making hardly any money, another fine ingredient. And the reasons why became obvious, and could prove a source of pressure and disagreement. For instance, when we went round we were able to have Sir John 'bump into' the firm's design team and ask how much this massive business, making more plates than anyone else in Britain, spent on design. 'Five hundred pounds a year.' Not surprising that it was a bit naff, till it all changed following Sir John's visit.

It was a great story of tectonic plates banging into each other. Now, as series editor of *Trouble at the Top*, with people pitching stories to me, I still suggested looking for subject areas with potential heroes and conflict, where those tectonic plates of modern Britain were banging into each other, and was thrilled when stories like the *Kinky Boot Factory* were brought to me. For as a commissioning editor the very best thing is to be surprised with a simple idea or conceit that jumps straight off the page. When the upcoming documentary-maker Hughie Dehn offered me *Back to the Floor*, I was thrilled instantly; it did just what it said on the tin. Just like the *Kinky Boot Factory*.

DOMINIQUE WALKER

Commissioning Editor, Channel 4, Factual Entertainment

Start off with the thing you know you'll never be able to achieve, and then work backwards – with an idea that is so ambitious you think either no one will commission it or no one will let you do it, rather than starting with the thing you think you can achieve and then trying to make it seem a bit more ambitious.

ROY ACKERMAN

Managing Director, Fresh One

I have a theory, which I call arrowhead commissioning. When you shoot an arrow into the body of a victim one of the reasons it kills them is they can't take it out; if they take it out lumps of flesh come with it and they die. So to some extent you have to shoot an arrow into the body of a broadcaster, which might mean them spending development money on it. It could be a talent, or a completely new way of looking at the world, or a territory they've never looked at. It could be a title.

The arrowhead idea means you do what you have to, to convince them to take the risk on the idea. If you can persuade them to spend time and money on development then they've got something to lose. Once they have decided to do the idea they are much more relaxed about working with you, trying to make it better. Once they've lost their cherry, so to speak, they want to make a good show, and you are on the same side.

But even if you have made the commissioner care enough to buy your film or series, and tugged on all the levers of production with enough skill and determination to make a totally compelling tale, this is still not enough to ensure success.

PROMOTION AND SCHEDULING

Promoting and positioning your programmes is as important as making them brilliantly. There are three parts to this: scheduling, press and publicity, and trailers.

It is worth thinking of press and publicity from the start – taking photographs, thinking of potential diary pieces, or even bringing a journalist along on your shoot – but you are unlikely to want anything published till a few weeks before transmission as you build to that all-important moment. But this all depends on when your film is scheduled, so getting it the right slot is the first step in promoting your film.

Scheduling is a dark art. Mixed in the cauldron are: which day of the week, what time, following what, and against what? Success depends a lot on how good the schedulers feel your programme is and whether they think, if put in a good position, it is capable of winning the channel a decent audience and/or noise, or if they shunt it to a back-yard alley. If your film is decent it is definitely worth winning a decent slot for it. If it goes out unannounced, in the middle of the night, the audience may care, but few will watch, and it will be missed by many potential viewers who might have cared too if they had seen it, including the TV bosses who you'd like to be familiar with your work. So the first thing in positioning is to get the right time-slot.

I once bumped into the BBC Head of Documentaries at a fashionable restaurant to which I had invited the BBC2 scheduler for lunch. He was very surprised to see us both there – I was a hectic person, so why, he wondered, was I bothering with someone so relatively 'unimportant' in the key commissioning decisions as a mere scheduler. (This was before schedulers became *much more important*!) Then it dawned on him: suddenly he understood why all my films went out in peak slots between 9.00 and 10.30 p.m. I was wining and dining the scheduler because getting the best slot is very important. Of course what the programme is like will affect this, but your relationship is also vital. The schedulers will believe you more if you are honest – if you have an occasional pup, a film you cannot fix, tell them so; they'll respect you for it, and can cleverly bury it. Then when you have something you really want to push, they will believe you and help you even more.

Cultivate not only the top scheduler but their juniors as well. In fact cultivate anyone in a scheduler's office. Show interest in them if you visit a broadcaster, and you might learn something too. Scheduling and time-slots matter. Just look at the success of *Undercover Boss*. By winning a placing after the *Superbowl*, which won an audience of 100 million, it managed to retain 38 million of them, making it the highest factual launch and a superhit. Without that slot it would not have done so well, but the film was good enough and its makers clever enough to get the full weight of the CBS publicity machine behind it.

CECILE FROT-COUTAZ *and* JULIE URIBE

Respectively CEO and Senior Vice President,
Fremantle Media, North America

The thing that's been missing is another big field competition. You've had Survivor *and it still works,* Big Brother *still does OK, and* Amazing Race, *but there hasn't been another of those field-based competition shows with high stakes. A lot have been tried in the last eighteen months, and prime-time networks have been struggling.*

It's not to say shows without competition will not work, but it's much harder to (a) sell them and (b) launch them. It's usually either big talent or big jeopardy or things that will give you your stakes in a very obvious way, though that's not what Undercover Boss *is. If it hadn't been for the lead-in [from Superbowl] that show probably would have failed. It was critical to getting it off the ground. It all came together at the right time and right place, with that right lead-in.*

The thing about US shows is you have to rise above the noise level. The last show that was a hit as a new launch, before Undercover Boss, *was* Are You Smarter Than a Fifth Grader *in 2007.*

There is one more thing you can do – with the scheduler's help – if you are transmitting a series. Get your running order right. If you have a series of individual films, put your best programme first, your second best second, your third best last, and place the rest in between. The first of a series, like the front of a film, is vital. Many professional people in TV, on whose judgement you depend, will only watch first films. Just as films fail because they start too slowly, with a long intro-duction, many series, as we have seen, fail because the first programme was an introduction to the whole series. In new formats like *Back to the Floor* we never put the film we actually shot first at the front, because it was never the best. Inevitably we hadn't worked out what we were really doing until partway through shooting the series.

Each programme in a series should be self-contained. An audience is extremely unlikely religiously to watch every episode of your series. In fact you may have a mostly new set of viewers each week – and many won't watch your whole programme as they come and go. But a few viewers will have watched earlier episodes, so if you feel that you need a history or recap sequence, keep it very brief at the top. Again, start in real time, and bring in backstory later. Make each programme self-contained, but not repetitive for those who watched last week. The same goes for all important recaps through your film. In one-off contemporary documentaries the tendency to tell the backstory at the front should be resisted.

MARKETING

Cultivating marketing people is equally important, and it is worth doing so if possible right from the start of a series, or even for a one-off film. Because the marketeers know the audience. They can help focus what your programme is about and who it is for, and you can help them in this too. They will also decide whether your series gets no promotion or lots. *The Boy Whose Skin Fell Off* and *Jamie's School Dinners* both had great 9 p.m. slots from the schedulers, and great promotional budgets from the marketeers. That helped the audience at least to get to the starting block, where the front of the film we had so painstakingly designed would have the chance of grabbing them. As a one-off *The Boy Whose Skin Fell Off* would never have been the hit it was, without this help. After all, one-offs can be particularly hard to get a channel to promote. But a new head of programmes at Channel 4 saw it and decided to push it, and we were lucky he did. Schedulers, marketeers and controllers are all important – and you can learn from them. They are intelligent and in far closer contact with the audience than you are.

Marketeers, with their wealth of audience research and other information, may even know why your programmes are working – or not – even better than you do. They certainly told me why the first roughcut of *Jamie's School Dinners* I sent them wasn't working, because I bothered to ask. When I showed them the near-finished film, you may remember they worried the audience didn't care enough, so we changed it. But they were invaluable all the way through.

I first met the marketing and publicity teams at the very beginning of *Jamie's School Dinners*, which is in my experience unusual but very helpful. They were the first to tell me that making the audience care about Jamie again would be a big challenge, and what to beware of.

When we first spoke to them at the start of the project, their research, if you remember, showed that many viewers still thought of Jamie as that millionaire with a fantastic life who made loads of Sainsbury ads. Some of the public, they reported, were even quite anti-Jamie, as was some of the press, who were giving him a hard time. Because I had talked to the marketeers from the beginning, they were the ones who continued to warn me that it might appear to these critics that Jamie just had a Channel 4 contract to fulfil and didn't much care how. In fact he couldn't have cared more. But the challenge now we had shot the film with this in mind was to get the audience to come to the series to see that. They worried that *School Dinners* might be seen as just another self-promoting television series.

So how to make these anti-Jamie people give a stuff? That was our challenge. We would need to pull their heartstrings. Because of these warnings from our marketing and publicity colleagues, we had done everything we could from the start to make people care about Jamie, to make him a David against a Goliath during filming. We had, as we discussed in Fronts, changed the pre-title of this series so as to begin not with Jamie but with evidence of the problem – kids being exposed to repulsive-looking food. Even so, when we had the finished programme, the marketeers' new question to me was: why should the audience know what we had done? Why should they even watch the film?

So working closely with us, they came up with a campaign of ads and trailers to ensure that the public might at least be tempted to try the series. The marketeers were the most talented I had ever worked with, and their trailers and ads not only helped make the series the hit it was, but brought a large audience along in the right mood. They understood instinctively that we needed our hero to be heroic and overcome tough obstacles. This applies right through filming, but is especially important in positioning. So the marketing people came up with an unusually brave ad campaign that would show what pressure Jamie was under, with kids saying how he couldn't cook as he soldiered on oblivious. It needed to be funny.

It is often as hard to persuade a contributor of the need for a trailer that makes him look bad as it is to film a sequence in which he suffers in order to make him heroic. Jamie had a large entourage devoted to promoting what a good cook he is, but they were more used to making books than TV, so selling them a campaign alleging he couldn't cook would normally not be easy. The marketeers worried that they might find it hard to understand that only if we gave him a tough time would the public come to love him again.

On location he was usually away from them and, being a savvy character, was game to film challenging scenes. But when it came to the tricky trailer, we were supposed to convince him back at his restaurant in Hackney, surrounded by his team. Instead I needed to engineer Channel 4 marketeers bumping into Jamie when he was alone and off-site. Even then convincing him would be touch and go. I used all the arguments about heroes, and, savvy as ever, he bought it, as did his wonderful No. 2, Louise Holland, who behind the scenes was making the whole school dinners campaign happen. This marketing campaign, which undermined Jamie but later made him into a David and the government a Goliath, helped make the public care for him again, and so make the series the success it was.

NICK STRINGER

Marketeer for *Jamie's School Dinners*, now at ad agency BBH

We struggled to work out what our creative brief should be. What we struck on was that Jamie was not just taking on the government and school dinners but he was doing it for a group who didn't give a monkey's who he was. His toughest audience was going to be kids, because a shepherd's pie cooked by Jamie Oliver is still a shepherd's pie. So the marketing was about kids drawing graffiti all over his face and throwing food at him.

Jamie needed to be brave enough to buy this campaign, but he was surrounded by people who were fiercely protective, so there was bravery on all fronts. That's what marketing done well and advertising done well does: it doesn't give you the conventions, it makes you think differently.

There were billboards on the streets which looked as though kids had covered them with graffiti – like the trailer in which big breasts had been drawn, as though with a crayon or chalk, over Jamie's apron, and insults scrawled across them such as 'This bloke can't cook' or 'Your food is minging'. Then there were similar newspaper ads, and most important, undermining trailers, like this, in which the pictures wittily fought the words:

JAMIE'S SCHOOL DINNERS, TRAILER, CHANNEL 4

Jamie in chef's whites surrounded by veg. He doesn't see kids behind in playground staring through window at him.

When I first got to the school, I got to be honest, I was really nervous.

But I couldn't have been more wrong. The kids have been absolutely fantastic, they've welcomed me into the school, you know. If I had been a kid at the school and someone like me had come along I probably would have given them a bit of grief but not at all, and when I took away their junk food, you know, I got rid of the chips and the burgers and the pizzas every day, got rid of the junk . . .

Hand-drawn thick crayon moustache begins to animate on his upper lip as he continues to talk, oblivious of it.

Beard begins to animate.

Graffiti *Rank* animates on pointing at veg. Jamie is unaware.

On to the fresh produce and getting the dinner ladies to cook again. It was fantastic, not a single problem; they were supportive, they were eating it up, they were spreading the message. You know there's basically a lot of love in this school now and a lot of mutual respect.

Your food is minging animates the other side.

Pulls back to reveal breasts now drawn on his whites. *This bloke can't cook* on window behind. Jamie is still oblivious.

What? What?

Just like everything else, always check your trailer. Discuss it in detail with promotions before it is cut, read the script, and if you are not happy when it is done, insist it is recut! I cannot believe how many directors complain to me of a weak trailer, who did nothing about it and didn't even talk to promotions about making it! Recently I had some friends who made a brilliant pilot for a new format. On its transmission would depend the fate of their series idea. Unfortunately it was not highly promoted and had a weak trailer. All that work for nothing. I always view my trailers before transmission.

However, more often than not you will not have been able to win trailers or ads – they cost a lot – but there is still a lot you can do, with the press. Viewers are savvy and often see on-air promotion just as an ad, whereas press articles are usually more objective. So whether you have trailers or not, press is vital.

PRESS

Timing is everything with the press; if you are too early people may either have forgotten or become bored with the subject. So press campaigns need handling with military precision. When I was making *Troubleshooter* I first created an elaborate schedule of press deadlines. The series mattered to me hugely, being my big break, and I was desperate that it should receive publicity. If you make a first film you should be too.

First off are features that have to be written months in advance (for some magazines three months). To help this I would cultivate friends who write features – they are always looking for something to write and are less likely to 'do you over'. If you don't have friends as journalists, cultivate friendly journalists. Many feature writers have a hard time, so my advice is – help them and flatter them! Then tell your boss or the press office what you are doing.

It can be scary opening up to journalists for a story on your programme. So give them every good reason not to 'do you over'. Be as open and honest as you can without bringing up things that could reflect badly on you or your film. Offer them the possibility of future stories on your TV shows, or inside gossip from the TV industry. Even hold out the hope of one day getting them on TV themselves! It is always possible. At least tell them how you envy and admire print journalists; I really do, so that's easy. And if they seem loyal and sensible, even take them on location. I took a friend of mine, the psychologist Oliver James, filming with *Troubleshooter* and his double-page feature in a big national daily got the whole press ball rolling. But make sure they don't go to print straight after their location visit – make it a condition that they get their pieces out two or three weeks before transmission.

If you are telephoned unexpectedly by a journalist while making your film, say you are too busy and will call back, especially if you do not know the caller. Refer to your boss and the broadcasters, who will have an idea of who the journalist might be. Discuss what they might want, and think through what you might say before calling them back. You don't want to be responsible for the latest *Daily Mail* exposé, especially without talking to anyone else about it.

As well as persuading feature writers to follow your story directly, try to find an angle for them, which may not be your story directly, but theirs. Get your contributors in columns with names like *A Day in the Life*, *Relative Values* or something relevant to your contributor, in magazines wherever you live. Many broadcasting press officers will not approve of your entrepreneurship; they have a bigger message to get out, for the whole network, and will want to control access to the press. Don't let them, especially when your programme is a low priority. If this is the case, you will need to do it all yourself, but you will also need to chat up the press officers so they won't get too angry about you making press noise for your programme that could detract from some of theirs.

And if, as is quite likely, they get furious – smile sweetly and say you didn't quite understand. Many of the most successful documentary-makers are great at publicising both their films and themselves. They would be unlikely to be recognised as great documentary-makers if they weren't.

My schedule of press deadlines usually began with these long lead-time features, worked on during filming for colour supplements and magazines with perhaps a two-month deadline. Next, a month before transmission, I would speak to all the listings magazines. Around three weeks before transmission was the important deadline for the pre-viewers in the Sunday newspapers. Finally, with a couple of weeks to go, came the important previewers for the dailies.

With these, it is just getting 'picks of the day' in the TV listings that counted as much as what was said in the previews. So with dedicated obsession I would ring every previewer, apologising for bothering them but just to 'check' if they'd got the DVD (or maybe now seen it online), and if they had any questions, such as doubtful spellings. I liked to give them a titbit about the programme, and ask their opinion about its strengths and weaknesses, because 'I really value your opinion.' And of course I really do – they are often the first neutral people to see it.

Finally, at the end of this long press road, there are the reviewers, quite different animals who are proud of their independence and have to be treated very gently, far more so than previewers. Previews are usually nicer than reviews, that is why you find so many in the résumés of producers, directors and executive producers. If you phone a TV reviewer, just ask quietly if they got the DVD or have seen it, and then only say more if they appear to want you to say more. Otherwise they will think you are trying to manipulate them (which of course you are).

One last thing is becoming ever more important – a strong and original web presence. Again, employ the best you can to create your own site, or even do it yourself, but use it to add to what you have done, not repeat it. And try to use other sites to create a buzz. Look how well Jamie does from his sophisticated and continuously updated web presence and iPhone apps such as his twenty-minute meals, which in a reversal are leading to a new TV series!

PICTURE PUBLICITY

Photographs can be at least as important as words, and can help you get features and publicity on the net, as well as arresting readers. If you are lucky enough to have a photographer, make time for them. An hour when they can go to work alone while you pause your filming will be worth eight trying to grab photographs as you shoot, when you don't give them a moment to do what they do properly, and you just annoy one another. If you don't have a photographer, take stills yourself, as they are invaluable publicity. And remember in 'picks of the day' news-paper previews photographs will be used at a very small size, so keep the content and your presenter big and arresting.

With *Jamie's School Dinners* we had the excellent Channel 4 Press Office fully behind us from the start. Matthew Robinson worked in conjunction with Jamie's PR, Peter Berry, who is also very sharp. It was a military campaign in which they knew what they wanted and, with our help, made sure that there was as little publicity as possible early on. Then they arranged for features to be written well before, but only with an agreement that they would be printed according to a precise schedule, starting a couple of weeks before transmission. There is little more annoying than a small feature 'spiking' a big one. This publicity then built through a host of interviews, some live on radio and TV, to a news event we created. We had had professional photographers along during filming, and made sure we gave them enough private Jamie time. But at the end, shortly before transmission, we wanted a good photographic occasion, something that would make the news. We first planned to dump a truckload of chips outside Parliament, then to have a load of Greenwich kids march on Westminster. Finally we took Jamie, Nora and the Kidbrooke kitchen team to Leicester Square to cook their new dinners in a trailer and offer them to passers by.

Press officers, just like marketeers, spend their lives watching programmes intelligently and thinking what they are about, so use their

---

MATTHEW ROBINSON

Publicist for *Jamie's School Dinners*, Channel 4

It really helps if the film is answering a question people might like to know the answer to. We spend a lot of our time asking 'What is this programme about, what's new here and why would people care?' It's always great when you can lift the first few lines of commentary from a script for your press release – it shows that the programme-makers really understand the story they are telling. So often TV programmes are inspired by stories in the newspapers and magazines, so you are effectively selling the same story back to them, which is tough.

You need to understand not just what will hook viewers, but also what will grab journalists. Producers who read and engage with newspapers and have an understanding of how news is made are far more effective at getting attention for their programmes.

Features and news are very different. News pages can have high impact, but you are at the mercy of the news agenda and the stories can be double-edged. On the other hand, features give you greater certainty that they will appear, but need more planning. The best guarantee of a positive story is to work with a writer you trust – or even write a piece yourself if you have the skills. It's always wise to check previous pieces by a journalist online if you are uncertain about them.

opinions. They can be excellent storytellers. It helps if you can show them a roughcut. On the Friday of editing of *Jamie's Return to School Dinners* – the follow-up to the original series – the Channel 4 press officer rang me up just as I was leaving the cutting room at 6 p.m. with eight people expected for dinner at home, and still to cook for. He is very perceptive about films and told me it was rubbish. So much so that he hadn't bothered to watch it to the end. He was speaking excessively, I am pleased to say, to make me actually listen. The film, he said, had failed to mention Jamie's huge success in the previous series, and concentrated only on what had gone wrong.

He had felt something was missing, and although he might not have identified it quite correctly, he had done what was most important – recognised a fault and made me think. I immediately returned to the cutting room and added a scene. Dinner was very late! The next evening I invited my two favourite film editors to dinner, and at 11.00 sat them down to watch the film. They saw the real fault: it wasn't that there was a lack of celebration, the problem was that in our cut Jamie appeared to be judging what was wrong before he saw it. So the next day we got an assistant editor to move two scenes and rerecord some commentary, just before Jamie was to see it.

BROADCAST PUBLICITY

Radio can also be a useful tool to publicise your film. You can get your contributors on a host of local and national radio shows in the UK, from breakfast slots to *Front Row*, from *Start the Week* to *Woman's Hour*, and on stations round the country; there are similar openings around the world. *Jamie's Food Revolution* was helped hugely by Ryan Seacrest. If you manage to win a really important interview, especially if you are the producer/director, remember to tell your boss and offer to let them do it, but agree to a horrible location at a horrible time (which with local radio it is likely to be anyway). Almost certainly they won't want to put themselves out, and the field will be clear for you.

Finally, at the top of the publicity tree is TV itself – again, not only for your contributors but for you too, which is great. Don't be scared if you get the opportunity to go on a TV show to push your own film. Many people who *make* TV are lousy performers on it – most often because they are very controlling types who inevitably come across as rather guarded. In fact they can be very hard to interview. But many of us will end up appearing on TV one way or another, so best get the hang of it. Given the likeliest programme you will end up on is a complaints show, you need to learn to start by agreeing with everything everyone else says when you are being challenged, or even insulted. In general I've learned that when attacked by the press, or by a hostile crowd, always at first agree that they have a point – and only then try to turn the tables with a 'But . . .'

Lorraine Heggessey is now CEO of *Talkback Thames*; before that she was a very successful Controller of BBC1. Not so long before her stratospheric rise, I was executive producer on the very last programme which she made. It was in the *Minders* series, on location following a community mental health team in south London. She'd been filming a patient under their care who had been in and out of hospital and had sometimes been sectioned under the Mental Health Act. His family had not wanted him to be filmed, but he had agreed, as had the psychiatrist who said he could give informed consent, so Lorraine and her team went ahead. Later he withdrew consent, but for us it was too late – we were well into editing, and the consent he had given earlier was considered by our lawyers to be legally robust.

Subsequently critics were invited to appear on Channel 4's *Right to Reply* where I had to defend our decision to transmit. I was roundly attacked for allowing the film to be shown in circumstances in which the subject had given his consent while ill. I was on weak ground, you're probably thinking . . . So how did I respond?

'Of course you are right,' I began. 'We all feel very bad about it. But surely we would feel even worse if the mentally ill were denied the freedom to be on TV just because of their illness.' It worked, and the studio was with me. Always tell people they are right before you tell them they are wrong.

Never underestimate how important all these people are to you – the schedulers, marketeers, publicists and press. You will live or die because of them. If all has gone right with them, and finally you have won the slot, the trails and the press, at least you can be fairly sure that the audience will know about your film, and you should start with the biggest possible audience for that particular kind of subject. Inevitably some subjects – however well made or marketed – are of interest to a relatively small audience. They are nonetheless still worth doing. The point is to ensure that as many people as possible who might be interested get to see and enjoy the sort of programme this is.

AUDIENCES

If you want to understand what is working and what is not working, you should try to get hold of the audience share tables, known as BARB in the UK (but there are equivalents in every country). This is how nearly every controller, scheduler, commissioning editor and executive producer start their day. BARB figures, called overnights, which are available around broadcasters and most production companies the morning after transmission, tell you the total audience and, equally important, the share of the total TV audience attracted by each programme transmitted through the previous day. (You can also find figures for the more important programmes every day in the *Guardian* online media section.)

As the day turns to evening, the total audience rises, and then inevitably falls as people go to bed. But the total audience isn't the only thing that counts. The percentage share of those watching who switch to you is what counts most. A high share of the total viewing audience at that particular time can also be considered a real hit.

Compare programmes first with how programmes on other channels in the same time-slot and day are doing. Look not only at the total audience, but at which programmes are gaining and losing during transmission, quarter-hour by quarter-hour. Then see how they are doing compared with the programme that went before – whether they have picked up or lost audience. Perhaps most important of all, compare the programme's performance with the programmes on the same channel and time-slot on different days, and how other films performed in this time-slot in previous weeks. Try to discern trends in order to understand the audience better.

If you do this regularly it will give you more of a feeling for what the audience really wants – and when it prefers to watch this particular kind of programme. It may even hearten you to discover that the audience is more intelligent and discerning than many suggest.

Always remember that although you need to please your bosses, your peers and the press, at the end of the day your real paymaster is the audience – you are working for them. In the end they will be the harshest and most intelligent critics, and all the others will follow them. Learn to judge potential audience size for the sort of programme you are making. You should be judged, and you should judge yourself, by your ability to get the maximum audience and impact for your kind of film. It is not the total audience size that counts, but it helps.

In my unit at the BBC we would all guess what audience each of our upcoming programmes might get, and we became surprisingly accurate. Once we had the slot, knew the opposition and what was coming before on other channels, the result would be a combination of the subject and how well the film was made. Unlikely subjects, very well made, could win through, while what sounded like winning subjects could fail in the wrong hands. We didn't mind doing some lower-audience subjects in the mix, but we did mind succeeding in making the audience care, not only through the character selection, the script and the edit, but then through painstaking attention to everything to do with the promotion, scheduling and marketing, and getting the most people to view – for whatever it was.

PERSONAL PUBLICITY

There is one last point to mention about publicity. Even if you have done all this – even more so if you have successfully done all this – there is one more trick to follow. Even if you have successfully pub-licised and branded your programmes, there's still more press you can get – the publicity for yourself which will help to brand you. If you have been successful, or even more are on your way up, media inter-views can be of great help. In Britain the *Guardian* media section is best, other media sections second best, and then there's the industry trade papers such as *Broadcast*, which are always looking for stories. In the US there are a host of trade papers, and there are lots of other magazines around the world. Try to chat up journalists and get to know them as you progress in your career. They are all looking for stories, and you never know when you will need them.

Although no one may be ready to do a story just on you when you are starting out on your career, you can get pieces in the trade press that are about the making of the programme – including, of course, a bit on you. But be careful to tell your bosses. Otherwise they may be offended and even jealous – but most will be pleased rather than livid as long as they get some glory. You could also write diary pieces for the national press about what you have made. Diarists are always on the lookout for TV stories, and there are a whole range of specialist diaries dotted about the papers, so be imaginative! And don't worry too much about how the diarists will rewrite what you say – it's the publicity that counts.

Sir John Harvey-Jones had a good deal of experience of the press, so back when I did my very first newspaper interview he taught me that as soon as you talk to the press they may say anything and even re-cut your words, but don't worry, even critical publicity can turn out useful. If you have decided to go with a particular journalist, just suck up to them as much as possible, seem as humble as possible, compliment them as much as possible, and hope for the best.

When I started out, many of the producers I worked with in Britain thought that they were artists and above the mucky business of pro-moting their films. But a strong tip for success remains to court schedulers, marketeers and the press. With more and more programmes and channels, making a noise becomes ever more important. Always remember there is no point in making the programmes if you don't sell them!

Eight

TIMELINE

TITLE AND TRUTH

TRUTH, TITLE AND TIMELINE

We end with three of the most important aspects of film-making. The TIMELINE is a great organising principle that you need to start right and keep going. It can get you out of many messes, and it applies not just to your film but your career. It is not surprising that the oldest stories, fairy tales and the Bible start with 'Once upon a time . . .' or 'In the beginning . . .'

The right TITLE is also crucial. I have seen many programmes and series fail because of the wrong one, and win through with the right one.

And TRUTH in factual film-making is both vital and fraught. It is a large and controversial subject, and we can only touch on it here. The challenge is navigating honestly while making a brave and watchable film. And there are a host of lawyers, regulators and editorial policy specialists to help or hinder you, depending how you use them.

TRUTH

First to TRUTH, a complex and fraught subject for factual film-makers, particularly with all the well-publicised scandals of recent years. Film-making can be more like painting than photography, and you need to use the techniques you have mastered to reveal the truth you found. Some purists might believe that the only true ninety-minute documentary would be one in which the director turned on a locked-off camera, and without moving it, turned it off again ninety minutes later. But even then, choosing which ninety minute to film would make a difference: as soon as you decide to film one thing rather than another, or even put in a single cut or cutaway, you are changing reality. And the very fact that you are filming will change the way people behave. You may have selected particularly untypical people on a particularly untypical day – after all, if we had been filming you reading this book for the last hour, would that be typical of you, and really show what you are like? Wouldn't it be better if the film-maker researched who you are really well, and then organised a beguiling story to reveal it?

Remember a story is what viewers are paying you to make for them – a story that helps them to make sense of the world and tell their own story, but a story that feels real and reveals the truth behind a character. So I firmly believe that truth is not to be claimed by simply filming what is in front of you, but in honestly 'representing' what you saw in your research.

As soon as you put in a single edit, choose to film from one angle rather than another, choose to shoot one character or scene rather than another, you change reality. In fact Heisenberg's uncertainty principle, and the observer effect, which says that just by observing an experiment you change it, seems to apply to film-making, so it is important to realise this and use the techniques of film-making to get back to conveying an unobserved reality – what you found when you just hung out, and your contributors forgot you were there. The aim is to get back to how they spoke, what they said, and how they behaved. There are two aspects that matter very much in film-making: the small truth of the detail you show, and the big truth of what you are conveying.

More and more I come to think that the films I want to work on, and the films that work, need to be truthful to three things: the story, the contributors, and you. And they will only be any good if truthful, because the audience can smell lies and they stop a film feeling right.

STEFAN RONOWICZ

Editor of many award-winning films

In the cutting room you don't make a good film by lying, you'd get hammered. People know. You have to follow the truth however difficult it may be. The only path to making a successful film is to follow the truth, and only the material you shot, the film, will tell the story. People think they can lie with film but they can't. Film is really bad at lying.

Success is about finding your own story and telling it, truthfully. If I am asked to make films that follow quite a different sort of story to the ones I am truly passionate about, I try to say no, because they are not true to me. For instance when I was in the Science Department I would avoid science subjects without a story that I just didn't understand or care about. Now when I am asked to executive produce a film 'looking at' another odd family, but with no story or reason other than to gawp, I say no. What is the big question, where is the story, what is heroic, where is the quest? I am not sure; they didn't tell me. But without these it is not my film. Sometimes I do agree to help nearly finished films which are not true to me, without a story or question, in which absolutely nothing happens. As I struggle to find the question, I am just glad that I didn't spend six months of my life making the film. I don't like making films about subjects without stories, especially subjects I don't care about or understand. So they don't end up true to me. You need to find out which films are true to you.

It is not just yourself, and 'your film' you need to be true to, but your presenter, contributor and subject matter. I am often asked to make films about two teams, in which one character gets eliminated week by week. Someone suggested I do a show like this with Jamie Oliver. But it is just not true to his character to fire people unnecessarily, just to make a show. *Jamie's Kitchen* came from somewhere very different. Jamie was trying to help deprived kids become chefs. They only dropped out if they were really incapable. And he tried to save them if he could. He wanted to help them, not humiliate them. This is his character and his brand. This is why it worked. When Shaquille O'Neal set out to help Florida schoolchildren lose weight in *Shaq's Big Challenge*, another Stephen Lambert creation, he just didn't seem to be as involved or care as much as Jamie, so it didn't work as well.

You also of course need to have strong characters that you bring out and make people care about, the narrative drive of small questions and answers, and all that we have been talking about to make the audience care and help a show to break through. But go against your presenter's 'truth' at your peril. *Jamie's School Dinners* fitted with my view too. I cared too, which is why Jamie and I got on so well making it, and it won so many awards. It was true to both of us, and I made sure to employ a team to whom it was true as well.

Sometimes I think I helped unleash a monster in 'reality' television, but then there is nothing wrong if it is real – just that so often it puts people in situations that are not true to themselves, pushes them falsely, and then doesn't work. Conflict gets you a long way, but not if it does not ring true. The audience is a lot cleverer than many think. So it is important to keep in mind the A.U.T.H.E.N.[T.]I.C. acronym as well.

On location you may often need to set up challenges for your presenter but make sure, from your detailed research, that these are the sorts of things that might really happen. Would a school class bet Jamie that if they all ate his meal he would dress up in a 'sweetcorn' outfit and parade across their sports pitch? And would he really do it? The answer was yes to both, it worked, and felt moving and real.

In *Jamie's Return to School Dinners* we had another idea. Pubs in Lincolnshire would attempt to make school dinners, because there were no kitchens, with varying degrees of success. Should Jamie organise a 'cook off' among these pubs, and then fire the worst? No, he wouldn't, we decided; that would be naff. Documentaries like *Jamie's School Dinners* fail as soon as challenges feel set up rather than growing organically and naturally out of the action and being true to how the characters would behave.

Truth includes daring to be critical of characters in your film. You can, and should, give them a hard time, as long as it is honest. Back at the time of my very first newspaper interview (with the *Observer*) to publicise *Troubleshooter*, I was worried about how the boss of the Tri-ang factory had been criticised, and had ultimately lost his job. Before the interview began, I had decided to share this fear with the *Observer* journalist who had come to see me at BBC Television Centre. I had wanted to show vulnerability – to get him on side. He replied, wisely I thought, that people never truly object to criticism when it is fair, only when it is unfair.

Sidney Orchant left his job as Tri-ang's Chief Executive following transmission of the programme, as did Ken Morris, Chief Executive of Shropshire Health Authority, following completion of the *Troubleshooter* featuring him. But both felt they had been fairly treated – so much so that both agreed to be followed again, in an update programme a year later, in their new jobs. Often directors are scared of being tough with contributors, but be brave – as long as you are also being honest. It is extremely rare for contributors to pull out.

There are a number of ways to make sure that people feel they have been dealt with fairly. First of all, never lie to them. You may not need to cross every 't' and dot every 'i', but you must not give them a false impression. I get furious if I am with a producer who promises to a contributor he will not make them look bad, as he tries to reel them in, or that, for instance, we will never criticise the dreadful food in a restaurant, if that is the subject of the programme, just to get access. I get even angrier if the producer commits on paper not to make a contributor look bad. How do you know what will happen? If you feel compelled to say something like this, say you will give an honest impression rather than using the word 'positive'. It can also help to give contributors so much detail they become bored. It is worth remembering Simon Dickson's talk of doom in which he tells contributors the downside when they have agreed to take part, before filming starts.

SIMON DICKSON

Deputy Head of Documentaries and Commissioner, Channel 4

When you go through the Talk of Doom, either the contributors realise that this production is not right for them or a cloud starts to lift, because you go from a pregnant feeling of abstract trepidation to a mutual sensation that every conceivable bad thing that could happen has been visualised and talked through. And once you've done the Talk of Doom with the people that you're looking to film, you've got on to the next step, and the relationship that you have with people from that point on is typically much stronger.

It is important not only to gain the trust of the contributors before filming, but also during the process – and afterwards, if you can. Once you have contributors hooked at the start, remember to tell them the downside – they will like and trust you more for this. Then during filming keep them informed of what you are doing as much as possible. Tell them about other things you are shooting, without them, as much as possible too, so they don't find out unannounced. Though you do not need to spell out every detail. At the Millennium Dome, for instance, Jennie Page, the Chief Executive, and Peter Mandelson, the minister, didn't see eye to eye, but it was important that we informed each that we were filming with the other.

As with friends or lovers, they can be shocked if they discover things that you have intentionally hidden from them, and even more betrayed if they feel that you have lied. It is always better to tell at least part of the story that is true, than it is to lie, which you should always avoid.

CHECKING EVERY FACT INSIDE OUT

As the editing process nears completion and your commentary is written, ring the contributors often to keep them updated about what you are doing and to check small facts. Involve them, but only on your terms. Tell them the rough structure, how they are looking, worry them a little. Even take them into your confidence and tell them that all is not good about the film (then the finished film may actually be a relief). Ask them lots of questions of fact, entreat their help.

And check every fact inside out. I probably try to instil this into production teams more than any other rule: if your film is factually accurate as well as honest, it will not only convince the contributors, but will be a better film. I strongly believe that factual accuracy, obsessive concern with detail and quality go hand in hand. Just as a house feels *right* if everything, from the light switches to the door handles, is in the right place, so a film in which every detail is accurate will feel a much better film. The more accurate detail you can put in, the more you will believe you are in the story.

If the audience feels deceived just once, or notices a single mistake, they will lose trust in the film. How do you recover from this? It is interesting that the people in this book who sailed closest to the wind, are also considered the most brilliant just for their daring. When they were found out in scandals like Queensgate (with its misleading editing of a quote from the Queen) and passports for the Hindujas, both filmmakers and contributors suffered badly, but just those daring and driven characteristics have brought such people back from the dead to the pinnacles of their profession. Again, stuff happens to everyone; it is how you deal with it that counts.

Bear Grylls is a presenter who is a daredevil adventurer, brilliant at surviving in the wild. And this is just what he did in his excellent series *Man vs Wild*. Unfortunately, despite enduring great suffering in pursuit of his adventures, he made a couple of slips, perhaps from hubris. He went back to a hotel in Hawaii while he was enduring being stranded on a desert island and tried to ride a 'wild horse' that had in fact been hired from a trekking station nearby. I was asked by Discovery and Channel 4 to help make sure his next film was excellent, which meant being especially solid. The footage shot by director Alexis Giradet of the derring-do of his record attempt to soar over Everest was stunning –

but it turned out his altimeter had broken en route before he had beaten the peak. We needed to be careful with the commentary, as well as the footage. As ever, when you go from an early draft to the final thing, keep checking. What follows was an early draft.

BEAR GRYLLS' MISSION EVEREST
DIVERSE FOR CHANNEL 4 AND DISCOVERY. EARLY DRAFT PRE-TITLE

BEAR   On 14 May 2007 Gilo Cardozo and I, Bear Grylls, attempted what everyone claimed was impossible, to smash a world record by flying above the height of the world's highest mountain, Everest. Our plan: to fly above the 29,000-foot colossus using nothing more than thin silk parachutes, with engines literally strapped to our backs. We'd be flying in the world's biggest and deadliest mountain range, the Himalayas. Flying above the height of the windiest place on earth.

GILO   I've never climbed a really high mountain. I've never done anything this challenging before. All these things are totally new to me – jetstream winds of 200 mph, temperatures down to minus 60 degrees and a breathless altitude at 30,000 feet could kill us in seconds.

I'm scared but because I'm scared that's why I'm doing it. One in six climbers dies on Everest, so what are the chances of survival if we push the limits even further? One mistake up there and we'd die.

BEAR   Have I really thought about the possibility of dying out there? In the few dark moments, yes. This is our story. Of an amazing journey that we took to the edge of the planet as we risked our lives to achieve a dream and to shatter a world record.

Everybody should use the strongest actuality and write the strongest commentary for the pre-title and then later, as the film comes in to land, check it out. As we did so, there were two worries. One: that it said in the opening sentence that he attempted to smash a world record flying above Everest. Two: that it said in the final sentence that he achieved his dream and shattered it. Both worried the powers that be. But the first was what in storytelling terms had inspired the adventure. And it was true. It was what he had attempted. Only the big question at the end needed changing. As his altimeter had broken, he hadn't provably flown higher than Everest. Moreover, in storytelling terms it gave the game away.

So the first claim had to be defended. We won on this, and changed the pre-title to one that suggested more the jeopardy of the story and why we were watching. And we put in a third-person narrator who could be harder and more objective. My additions are on the left.

BEAR GRYLLS' MISSION EVEREST, DIVERSE FOR CHANNEL 4 AND DISCOVERY, NEAR-FINAL PRE-TITLE

The Problem (with evidence)	v/o Mount Everest – the Himalayas.
	(Pause.)
	Adventurers come not just to climb, but also to balloon, glide and ski down the highest mountain in the world.
	They face temperatures of minus 40 degrees, a breathless altitude and winds of up to 175 mph.
	Everest has claimed over two hundred lives.
	BEAR *Have I really thought about the possibility of dying out there? In the few dark moments, yes.*
The Quest	Now two British daredevils, Bear Grylls and Gilo Cardozo, are planning to do something most adventurers think impossible. To fly higher than Everest using only backpack engines and nylon parachutes – paramotors.
	GILO *Just that image of looking down on the peak of the world really captured my imagination.*
	BEAR *If we fail, then at least we fail while daring greatly.*
The Route Map/Challenges	But before they can even begin, they've got to build a new engine that will fly higher than any paramotor has gone before . . .
	BEAR *These mountains are completely unconquerable. We don't conquer these*

> *mountains, we're allowed there, by their kind of grace.*
>
> *. . . train their bodies and minds to stare death in the face . . .*
>
> GILO   *I'm scared of being at 30,000 feet, but scared of doing it.*
>
> *. . . and persuade their wives and children to let them go.*
>
> Shara cries.

The Big Question   Can the two friends fulfil their dream and come home alive?

> BEAR   *I always planned this project to be safe and ambitious, bottom line is it's still ambitious, but not safe.*

All this is true. It adheres now to all our rules for fronts of films. (Though I hasten to add yet again this is a default position when I use the toolkit. If someone comes up with a more surprising opening that does the same, I am thrilled.) But more importantly it only says Bear wants to fly over Everest, not that he does so. So we have a big question and we have jeopardy.

But then at the very end of the film we added a truth that didn't spoil the story at all.

> v/o His ultimate height cannot be officially verified, but to the two pilots this was never about records but about pushing the limits of human possibilities.

It turned out to be a very successful film – it had no need to be otherwise because what actually happened had been thrilling and dangerous, and it had been well shot. Bear's scandal is as far away as the others.

KEEPING CONTRIBUTORS' TRUST

Getting it right is so important that, although you will have checked facts, there are some that only your contributors will know. So when your commentary is written, read through the relevant bits to them on the phone (in my view it is not necessary to include adjectives as they are not material fact). This is the very opposite of what most directors are advised to do, but it has worked for me. It will help give you a band of happy ex-contributors who, in the gossipy six-degrees-of-separation world we live in, will tell new potential contributors how straight you were in dealing with them. In this way you will be able to get access to places that other people (who either have not read this book or if they have, do not apply its lessons) cannot.

One final piece of advice for maintaining trust with contributors. I have always shown finished films to main contributors before trans-mission, which is again unusual. I make sure the contributors are told that this is not for editorial input, but to check for factual accuracy and to help them feel a little less apprehensive as transmission looms. I insist to them that they cannot change the film editorially, but only point out any errors of fact – and if you have checked your facts well there shouldn't be any. They find it very comforting. In twenty-five years of film-making, and attending such viewings with hundreds of producers, I have had only one misspelled name pointed out to me by a contri-butor . . . so far.

Showing the film is all part of caring. After all, you have got close to the contributors, they have given you a lot, and you owe it to them. I tell the contributors that as well as checking for factual accuracy it is so that they will know how to react to the film when it goes out – and they can decide whether or not to tell their friends to watch. It also gives them an opportunity to make any complaints to my face. This is a formal occasion, so use a viewing theatre, perhaps one owned by the editing company, or at least a proper production office.

And here's an important sub-rule. In my career I find that I am often dealing with very rich and litigious contributors. Do not take the film to *them* if you can possibly help it – remember, choosing territory matters. Ideally the copy of the film that you show to them will be in a professional format, or appear to be. If you use a DVD make sure it is in the player already. The last thing I want to do is put a DVD in a machine and then have somebody ask to walk away with it at the end. And never, if you can help it, send out copies before transmission for this purpose; then the contributor will look at it and look at it, and show their friends, who will have every interest in suggesting changes.

JAN TOMALIN

Former Controller, Legal and Compliance, Channel 4,
now Managing Director, Media Law Consultancy

Contributors' previews must be handled with the utmost sensitivity and there should be a clear agreement in writing (email is fine) setting out the basis of the preview. It must be understood by the contributor that they have no editorial control or veto and the purpose of the viewing is to ensure factual accuracy and fairness. If possible get them to come to you and never let them have a copy of the programme. The next time you see it may be in court!

Another mistake, I believe, is to show the film to contributors while you are still working on it, so that, if they object, their changes can be incorporated into the programme. For this opens up the possibility of negotiation. Consequently I like to show the film when it is as finished as possible rather than work in progress, complete with title and ideally the commentary voice, so it looks done although it may still have a guide commentary in the director's voice, and may be recorded slightly fuzzily straight from the offline computer; but the main point is to say that editing is finished, and this is it. The director should have the confidence to correct all the mistakes themselves *before* it is shown. If it is a difficult, scientific or technical, film they may want to check it first privately with an independent expert, perhaps one who advised them before filming, or a friend who is an expert in the field. I made an entire and controversial series following a psychiatric team, and showed it to a fellow psychiatrist, who luckily even knew them, to make sure the criticisms were true and fair, before the contributors' viewing. Particularly in such a specialised area it helps to have a specialist look it over.

It also helps to try to get someone in authority – the series producer or the executive producer – to attend the screening. It shows the contributors that they are important – and the high-ups can fend off the difficult questions! I serve alcohol to make it a 'gentler' and more social experience, and an occasion for a little quiet celebration. It must be done with real warmth, because you need to continue to care for contributors up to *and* after transmission. They are the ones who may criticise you harshly in public or sue you. As long as you have been honest and open they will find it harder to complain, and if you have been warm too they are less likely to want to try.

Smile, giggle, reminisce about the problems of filming the particular scene you are watching. Pour drinks at moments in the film you are most worried about. But you will be surprised. The contributors will worry about minor things like how big their arse looks or what they are wearing, totally missing the character faults you were so scared of showing them.

Occasionally, and not surprisingly, people may not be happy with your film, but it will invariably be the ones who hardly took part or didn't at all. For example, we made a short series on a new government initiative of the early Blair years, another new kind of school led by a 'super head'. True to our heroic tale and search for narrative stories, we followed one such super head as he tried to transform the Islington Arts and Media School. But it was not a success, and the new super head was edged out while we were filming, in 2000. However, worry after the broadcast of the film came from governors of the school, who barely figured in the programme and whom I had not even met.

Sometimes the private screening works so well that contributors actually like the film and say they approve of it – only to change their mind after transmission as a result of what other people say. Dino Adriano, then boss of Sainsbury, viewed his *Back to the Floor* and liked it for its honesty. After transmission, others members of his mighty empire were surprised that there were things he didn't know about, like workers not being allowed to talk while stacking shelves at night. He maybe became less sure about the programme too, especially when he left Sainsbury and some newspapers cited as a reason his performance in *Back to the Floor*.

So why, you may ask, am I writing all this down? How will I ever deal with a contributor again? Because actually I do believe that the truth is best, and fair dealing is important. As well as this there are strict regulations, and not just about being fair with contributors. In Britain all independent production companies have to give contractual warranties to broadcasters that their programmes will be made in compliance with broadcasting regulations, so there is a heavy price to pay for a serious breach of the rules. That means you need to be familiar with and follow the BBC's Editorial Guidelines and the rules in the Ofcom Broadcasting Code – which applies to all UK broadcasters. Most broadcasters will have their own guidelines and protocols for different programme genres. Channels 4 and 5 have helpfully combined most of their guidelines and they have been published as the *Independent Producer Handbook* <www.independentproducerhandbook.co.uk> which gives a practical guide to the main areas of law and regulation affecting programme-making and broadcasting.

There are similar guidelines around the world. Wherever you are, as well as being familiar with the rules and codes make sure you refer up any concerns and doubts and involve your immediate bosses in any difficult decisions. Always keep good, up-to-date and clear records and note key points in an email, or on paper, before you film where possible, to help protect you if there is a complaint or a legal claim. And remember you need to take even more care when you're planning to film with children or vulnerable adults. In most countries, including the UK, when filming children you are likely to need written consent from the person who has parental responsibility, and take extra care.

LAWYERS

Lawyers can be particularly useful if there is anything at all that might challenge programme-making guidelines. Seek their advice early, even when just embarking on the project, and stay in contact with them throughout filming. You can only ever be blamed for not informing them of danger points or not seeking their advice. Just like contributors, they are very important to keep on side. Don't just involve them in the process, try to get to know them too, ideally delivering and collecting the script or DVD in person. The more they trust you, understand and are involved, the more they may allow. I will therefore always try to ask lawyers their editorial opinions and talk to them about other programmes that are on. After all, they are intelligent people who spend a lot of time watching television, and their editorial opinions might even be useful. They might be the first objective viewer of your script or roughcut. If you have managed to build a relationship they will better understand what you mean, and trust what you are trying to do. In a challenging film, or one in which you are worried what contributors may say, or what you say about your contributors, involve the lawyer at roughcut stage. Even if you have not needed a legal view early, unless your programme is utterly innocuous book the lawyers for a couple of days before editing finishes so there is time to make changes. Do this well in advance as you will then need the lawyer to view and respond immediately, so a decent amount of notice is not only courteous but often vital.

JAN TOMALIN

Former Controller, Legal and Compliance, Channel 4,
now Managing Director, Media Law Consultancy

The astute programme-maker will find that a subtle blend of meticulous research, clever argument and politeness will go a long way in getting the lawyers to stick their necks out. I often find that production company clients are surprised to learn that they can go further than they had thought. No one wants to get sued or have an upheld Ofcom complaint, and being tied up in litigation can ruin a small company, so you need to know how best to achieve your creative objectives while protecting your reputation and your pocket.

The cardinal principle is: lawyers advise and editors decide. Broadcast lawyers can be control freaks, so in gaining their support you must not let them take over your film. In the end you are the one with whom the buck stops if there is an Ofcom complaint or a libel action, so take ownership of the issues, but be guided by your lawyer's expert advice. Self-censorship is not conducive to creative risk-taking, which needs expert and enabling legal advice from an early stage.

TIMELINE

The TIMELINE, the next 't' we come to, is something we have skated over frequently in this book, for it is hugely helpful to films; it is a way of making stories develop narratively so that one thing happens after another and events are causally linked. But most important, as the TV Troubleshooter, I have found it can get you out of many difficulties. It amazes me how often all I have to do, when I am asked to a cutting room to help a film, is to put the material into the correct and logical order, usually just the order in which it happened, removing many intercuts. It is worth reiterating that time can be the greatest organising principle of a film, just as it can be in life. Even more worth reiterating, get that time clock going immediately. If your film has the advantage of being shot over time, as most do, the first thing is to take advantage of this and put everything in roughly correct order. Time can create a driving narrative, almost on its own. It does in our lives.

STEFAN RONOWICZ

Film Editor – a last word

Film, being an imitation of life, should have a timeline because we all live our lives with a timeline. Now a timeline is great; three-quarters of your structure is taken care of. The most difficult film is an issue-led film which doesn't have a timeline – it's an argument, you might as well sit down and write a book. You haven't got a chance in hell of making a successful film without a timeline, unless you find people who will make this film work for you because you are interested in them and their lives and their views. Even then a timeline helps!

Even more important is starting your timeline straight after the subtitle at the very latest. I get more work just doing this (and making that pre-title front) than anything else (and then unravelling those inter-cuts when one character is in two times at once, which we will come to shortly). It is then a question of seeing what is important, and making a story in time out of this. So many films I get called to see are spoilt by lack of adherence to this logic.

Of course, in the interests of storytelling and structure, some things filmed at different times have to move earlier or later. You should allow this only so long as they are timeless events whose moving does not affect the larger truth, and as long as you do not put something before the event that caused it, nor after an event it went on to cause – for instance a screaming row and a threat of divorce. It is very different if the one is the cause or the result of the other. Often the thorniest subject when it comes to truth in factual editing is timeline. But the simple rule here is this: if where a sequence happens in the order of a film makes a difference, don't move it; if it makes no difference, you can.

If someone learns to cook, then opens a restaurant, and you reverse these two events, you also completely reverse the sense. Swapping them would be misleading and false, just as you would get into terrible problems of causality with a time machine. However, if they are interviewing potential employees, and then go shopping for supplies, and the one is totally unrelated to the other, then it doesn't matter which order they are in. So you must be brave and swap scenes that could go anywhere to make the story stronger. After all, if you left every shot in the order you filmed it, you couldn't have a film, since you couldn't use a single cutaway. Again it comes down to you understanding the truth and choosing the techniques of film to show it, rather than just some rules.

However, many directors try to be too clever, moving time and intercutting so you see people in one place, then another, then back in the one, all in a single scene, which just makes the story harder to understand, and is always confusing. In fact the likeliest way for the film to work is in the right order. For instance, in *House of Obsessive Compulsives* we see the sufferers first at home, *then* en route, *then* in therapy. We will have seen the best dramatic scenes from later in the pre-title, to get us hooked. But if the sufferer at home is too boring, shorten it or just lose it. Because always remember as long as it is in the right story order you can lose time, especially at the front where there is always that temptation to put in too much, and keep in sequences shot early even though they are usually more boring.

So get that time clock going, and then either spell out time in the narration or through captions. If it is narration, it doesn't have to be just 'next week' and the like, but can be as simple as 'Now our character has done this, he needs to do that.'

SIMON DICKSON

Deputy Head of Documentaries, Channel 4

When I was starting out as a director, I remember there were certain things that I didn't always get right and one of them was timelining. I think, like all new directors, I was sometimes caught up with the thrill of a particular moment in a story rather than being disciplined and subordinating that moment to the overall narrative. Robert would always grind out a better result from my films, and those of my colleagues, by constantly reminding us that the truth is important and the timeline is important and the order in which things happen is significant. And while there may be good arguments for playing a scene out of strict chronological sequence from time to time, the overall narrative is better, more truthful, more satisfying and more revealing, if you retain a close association between the scenes that you're playing out and the time when they took place.

If you use a clock, then it must be consistent, either counting up, or down, not both. Which is better? If you have a deadline – and timelines work best with deadlines – then counting down towards that deadline generally works better, as in '25 JANUARY 2010: THREE WEEKS TO GO' or just the date or time period. You can also use captions that count up such as 'THREE WEEKS LATER' but they are harder to work out as you tend to forget the previous one. But try not to confuse the audience by counting time in two directions at once. Although you can start counting up, and then as you close in on the deadline count down. After the deadline, if the film continues, of course you count up again.

Either way, putting timelines on sequences, either in words or captions, can really help aid their understanding. It is extraordinary how a sequence that is not at first working, not engaging as well as it should, like Bear Grylls's final flight over Everest, can be brought alive by a clock and some detail, and the audience can be taken right into the moment, making it a winning scene, just as putting a clock and detail on the feeding of a thousand in *Jamie's Ministry of Food* brought that alive and made you feel right in there. My thoughts are again down the left.

BEAR GRYLLS' MISSION EVEREST,
DIVERSE FOR CHANNEL 4 AND DISCOVERY.
RECORD-BREAKING SEQUENCE, COMMENTARY AS TRANSMITTED

Time clock starts immediately. Time counting up.

Fourteen minutes in, at 18,000 feet, the first problems appear.

Their radio comms are breaking up.

Yes is three clicks, no is two.

After 18 minutes the GPS records showed that Bear was already at 19,000 feet.

As they fly up, they're heading into thinner air. If their single breathing system fails at the height of Everest, they'll pass out from oxygen deprivation within seconds. Unconscious and alone, flying amongst these giant peaks, their chance of survival would be near zero. But they can't carry the weight of a second emergency system.

Also adding detail of height.

6,000 metres – that's just below 20,000 feet.

(*Pause.*)

They're already one mile vertically above base camp.

(*Pause.*)

All the team on ground can do is look and pray.

7,000 metres is 23,000 feet. Every foot climbed is breaking new ground.

They are now 4.5 miles vertically above sea level and above most of the mountains around base camp. Everest is becoming far clearer beyond the Nuptse Wall.

They become more and more vulnerable. Alone, depending only on their skill, training, and Gilo's precious machines.

There's a problem. Gilo's descending, no one knows why . . .

At 9.22 a.m. the flight's over for Gilo. His untested Everest machine has failed.

Bear carries on up alone.

Still true.   Bear's flying even higher into the unknown.

Still true.   At 9.33, 72 minutes into his journey, Bear is as high as he ever hoped to go – staring Everest in the face.

This it has done even if Bear hasn't t beaten the record (we still don't know this).

The original Everest machine has worked in the thin air and the freezing cold.

The journey back, gliding with the engine off, should bring him down to a small village, one mile away from base camp.

Still concentrating on what they have done, so we have a real emotional climax now.

The Everest machine and their friendship have survived failures, disasters and near-fatal crash landings.

They've broken the engine and frozen it.

But in the end Bear and Gilo's machine flew where no other has ever flown before.

And only now do we throw in the failure to fly higher than Everest, but then we never said he had succeeded in doing so.

Finally with Gilo already safely on the ground, at 10.11 on the 14th May 2007, his friend Bear lands too . . . alive and in one piece.

Later analysis showed that Bear's GPS froze at 25,005 feet, 44 minutes into his journey. He was still climbing at over 250 feet per minute. He continued to climb for another 28 minutes before turning back. His ultimate height cannot be officially verified, but to the two pilots this was never about records, but about pushing the limits of human possibilities.

The programme didn't need to lie to tell a good story. It won a great audience, the baying press didn't attack Bear for not doing what he had set out to do or for lying again, but rather sympathised with him because of the storytelling and the way the timeline drew us in. Bear was back in business.

Make sure you put your time captions over sequences that were truly shot at the time you are saying, even if others that are insignificant in relation to cause and effect may have been moved around. So if you are having any problems with your film, do try getting your clock going, if your film is told in time, and do it bravely and honestly.

CAREER TIMELINE

Getting the time clock going and managing time applies not only to your film but to your career. Making TV can be the best job in the world. Being allowed – and, even better, paid – to travel the world, meeting whoever interests you and asking them the sort of questions no friend, let alone stranger, might dare to ask, is fun and a real privilege.

In this timeline of a career it can help to start late, so take heart if you are still a runner, or yet to be one! As long as you are working around the fringes of the business, learning and watching others tell stories, it will mean you are all the better prepared when you actually get to make a film, not only technically, but in what you can do morally as well. You will be amazed what you have picked up.

When I pushed those trolleys of film around in Lime Grove, then home of BBC Current Affairs, bringing film to researchers to illustrate items in their daily shows, the height of my aspiration was to be one of them. It took me more than another decade sound-mixing and eventually researching till I struggled to get my first film transmitted at the age of thirty-seven. By then I was so hungry, and had seen so much, it is perhaps not surprising the film won a BAFTA. And remember, as you struggle along, that the first rungs are often the toughest, and it gets easier to get someone to give you a job the further up the ladder you get.

If you have a long wait and are then lucky enough to have a hit, hold your nerve. The same applies, only more so, if you don't even have to wait and success comes early. Don't become a one-hit wonder. I see so many directors make their first film, achieve their first hit, and then get forgotten again. Often it is because they are too young. They may win 'best newcomer' at the Grierson, or the Royal Television Society, awards. And then they are treated like gods, so that no one dares continue to teach them the craft, executives fear telling them what to do, and they never develop. So they disappear again, often too bitter to make it back. So don't be in too much of a rush to direct – you can learn a lot of craft as a researcher or AP, particularly if you choose the right director. And when you do begin to direct, don't worry about working on format shows. Formats give a structure in which you can express your individuality, just like a symphony, or a five-act drama, or a Greek tragedy that is the same every time, with a new cast and subtle changes. They are great places to develop programme-making skills.

If you are lucky enough to have hits, then it can be very tough when your next film doesn't break through, but the important thing is not to despair. In my experience, good films are like buses. They come along in a bunch, and then there are none. After my first hits with *Trouble-shooter* quickly followed by the *QED Family Game* in the early 1990s I had a gap of three or four years which seemed like for ever. Then in quick succession along came *Trouble at the Top*, *Blood on the Carpet* and *Back to the Floor*, and another string of awards. The next year, 2001, when I wasn't nominated for a BAFTA, the boss of BBC2 asked me why, and what had gone wrong. Not being one of the four nominees, out of every programme in Britain for my category, was failure. Someone else had advanced my formatted story with *Faking It* and won the Features category that had till then been mine. I was considered a disappointment. It is then that you have to hold your nerve.

TV is a fashion business, so although you may win sometimes, every career will dive at some point. When it does, the important thing is not to lose your nerve, but hold on and determine to come back even bigger. There are a few people who when the hits have come in a row and then gone, reinvent their new story. They sit out the gap learning more, and come back better. So the admirable people in TV are those like Pat Llewellyn who, when knocked back, rise even farther.

It helps in the fashion stakes if you claim that you are still fresh and inexperienced for as long as possible. You can spend surprisingly long on this – I managed fifteen years as the new young thing. TV loves raw young talent, but in the end it becomes impossible to keep up.

BECOMING A MANAGER

As they get promoted, managers who are ex-film-makers attend more and more meetings, and need to learn the strange rules that govern them. I'll let you in on some. They apply through much of the business world, especially in large institutions, and nowhere more than in the public sector. First off, TV meetings are often like dinner parties. If you are invited for 2 p.m. it will really be 2 for 2.30, when they will usually start. But beware! There may be something critical to you on the agenda, in which case others may cheat and start on time.

Then there is the geometric rule of the agenda, which means that the first third of the agenda will be discussed in two-thirds of the time, the next third in a sixth of the time and so on. In fact in the BBC Science Department the executive producers thought that we should do more to develop the careers of the researchers, APs and producers for whom we were responsible, so we had an annual discussion about each person, and where they might flourish next. This was fine, except that the discussion was organised alphabetically. Each year the A to Ds would have well-planned careers and great opportunities. Unfortunately it would be just too late for the S to Zs, who would be rushed through at the end of the day. So if at the BBC you find more successful people with names beginning high up in the alphabet it is hardly surprising. As I write, the upper ranks of British TV, certainly in factual television, are dominated by those with surnames from the first half of the alphabet. Current and recent BBC and Channel 4 controllers are: Jay Hunt, who recently replaced Lorraine Heggessey; Janice Hadlow, who recently replaced Roly Keating; Richard Klein, who recently replaced Janice Hadlow and George Entwhistle; Danny Cohen, who recently replaced Julian Bellamy; and Julian Bellamy, who recently replaced Kevin Lygo. And those in power at the top of the pro-gramming tree are Glenwyn Benson, George Entwhistle, Jana Bennett and Kevin Lygo. So ignore the book and change your name by deed poll if you are not lucky enough to be in that alphabetic first half. In fact taking the highest place in the alphabet is probably the biggest predictor of success of all.

And if you are a film-maker who gets to manage (and in the end that is most film-makers, even if we have the wrong surnames to reach the loftiest management heights, for we still have our own small teams on location), try to be different and avoid gobbledygook and the latest fashion. For executive producers or even producers there will be meetings on performance review, equal opportunities and international sales of natural history that may have nothing to do with you. And then there are the latest management fads and endless meetings on strategy. The only worthwhile meetings of this sort are, first, the ones you are not at, when others want to knife you; and, second, those involving a 'new' television strategy, since that may give you the chance to write your own career plan. When I sat on John Birt's performance strategy review Jana Bennett wrote up what should happen to science, and got to run it, and I wrote up what should happen to part of education and used its money to make business documentaries. But more often strategy reviews end up as another endlessly time-consuming TV chess game. And if you look back at the grand strategies of five years ago, they rarely have much connection with reality today, which has probably already reversed them.

Bureaucracy can drive storytellers mad. There are three main reasons people leave broadcasting organisations of their own choice: money, ability to work on more kinds of programmes, and exhaustion with bureaucracy. The BBC's bureaucracy is probably why so many of the most talented people went into the independent sector originally, because they did so before the big money for selling the company was on the table. Freed up, they could make many more kinds of films.

Unfortunately much television has been run by people who have spent five weeks at business school, and think management is about implementing whichever fad the rest of business is about to dispose of. John Birt was at least a manager in his heart, a rare exception to the rule, which is probably why the BBC is a rare thriving public-service broadcaster, even if his people skills weren't great, and there was still an awful lot of strategy. And paradoxically who would want to work for such a successful manager because what would they ever teach you about film-making? Networks around the world have similar bureaucracies.

However, the BBC's next Director General, Greg Dyke, was in a different mould. He wanted to 'let a hundred flowers bloom'. Birt's BBC had been of its time when Mrs Thatcher was in power, trying to bring business practice to the BBC, and dividing it into buyers and sellers like the NHS, monetising everything, and empowering managers. Greg's BBC was very New Labour. It was supposed to be a lot more democratic, with ideas coming from everywhere, but there was still the same obsession with control, and using ideas from business.

I made one last film before joining the herd out of the BBC. I picked up a DV camera, never having used one before, and headed to Heathrow. There I joined Greg and twenty senior members of the senior BBC management team. I was going to film their journey to visit a series of top US companies in an attempt to find the secret formula for 'change'. It was a fascinating and shattering experience as we shot around the USA from Ritz Carlton hotels in California to South West Airlines in Dallas, and Alberto Shampoo in Chicago. I not only had to endure the bosses, the travel, the factory tours, and take part in the discussions afterwards, but film it too, never having shot a frame before. It was my very own *Back to the Floor*. I even used the title sequence from *Back to the Floor* for the film, showing the descent from the heavens to hell.

Before I began I emphasised that if I made the film it would be honest. I don't think they quite believed me, but it was. I showed it secretly to a few junior people in my office. They were touched; the bosses were not just names but human beings who cared desperately. They were mostly committed programme-makers just like us. They had put away their John Birt suits and now they all wore jeans. Many had once played in a band, and even inhaled. They were shocked by some of the tough and ruthless practices of business; they wanted to make people feel better. The most extraordinary thing was that, when asked, all of them – mostly ex-creatives – said they felt like outsiders themselves, and it was other people who were 'the BBC', even though they were now the ones running it!

Sadly it turned out that no more of the BBC staff were to see this side of their bosses. I showed the finished film to the senior managers who had bonded so much on the trip, at a Jewish Passover supper in the Broadcasting House boardroom. We played it at the end of an evening of singing and prayers from the mostly Christian and agnostic company – maybe a symbol of the way they had bonded and of the new BBC. I was showing the very first film I had shot and narrated all by myself to the only lot of contributors who had full editorial control and a veto on whether it would ever see the light of day (thus contradicting much of what I have said in this chapter). It was supposed to be a prelude to a grand showing at a big BBC management awayday in a big conference centre, but sadly the Queen Mother died, and the occasion was postponed for a few weeks. By which time the management, although they agreed it was honest, told me it would not be shown as the moment for screening it had gone, and it never was. It was the first time this had happened to me, because it is important to get your films shown; without this, you don't have a chance of getting to the best bit.

As I have emphasised, we all have setbacks. Don't moan and feel sorry for yourself, but use them to drive you on. I was still being driven by remembering the whisper of my executive producer as I went up on the BAFTA stage for the first time with *Troubleshooter*: 'Savour this moment, as it will never happen again.' It wasn't meant nastily, but had driven me for more than a decade as I tried to prove him wrong again and again. I had been driven further by being called a failure for not getting nominated in 2001. I was even more determined to reinvent and return, bigger and better, but it could no longer be as an upcoming young thing, the position I had maintained for more than a decade.

BECOMING A GRAND OLD MAN

Finally, if you follow all the rules, are passionate and lucky there may come a point in your own story when you are no longer convincingly the small hero, fighting your way up, or fighting your way back up. Then you have to turn on a sixpence, from hungry young Turk to grand old man in one pirouette. As well as film-making, mentoring helps in this. I give talks, write and use this toolbox, I am working on being that grand old man. But I still get it wrong. Because all this is only a template to be broken. Television remains an art as well as a science.

Shortly after I left the BBC I wrote to the boss of Channel 4, who invited me to lunch. He kindly discussed which independent I might join, and even offered to help me set up one of my own. I told him that the first thing I needed was a very long break – I wanted to get right away. I had been married to the BBC for a quarter of a century. It was a marriage that had been quite convenient, and we had had some great award-winning offspring, but it was just one of those relationships in which you have got bored and can't remember quite why you ever got married in the first place. Now I was free and single the last thing I wanted to do was marry again straight away. I didn't mind sleeping with any broadcaster or independent production company a few nights a week, but I was determined to keep my own home and my freedom.

When I returned from searching for ideas, writing, and teaching in the Far East and Australia, I had another lunch, excellent and Italian, with Channel 4's Director of Programmes. He asked me how many hours of output I would like, and how much turnover I would want to set up my own independent production company. His opening offer was just a few hundred thousand pounds. When I wasn't interested, the figure went steadily up above a million, as the courses came and went. Each time I said 'no' he thought it was because I wanted more, and increased the offer, but to no avail. So at the end of the lunch of increasing offers he asked what I would really like, and I replied that all I wanted was to sort out a few films for him.

Becoming a grand old man is very different to becoming a manager; eventually you may have to choose, carefully, which, and it may depend which of your sides you want to pursue. In making television, as we get further up the tree there comes a time when, hopefully, we have to ask ourselves why we are doing it, whether it is selfish or worthwhile, good or bad. We have to deal with two sides of ourselves. On the one hand there's the softer, gentler person who wants to get at the truth. But then there's the ambitious, pushy, manipulative terrier who is needed to wheedle out that truth and get it on screen. The very skills you need to succeed in making films – obsession, painstaking attention to detail, drive and manipulation – mean that you can lose touch with your more caring self, the one who wanted to pursue truth and make television programmes in the first place. It is why television is often such a poorly managed industry. People who are obsessive about making good films are promoted, but their skills are not necessarily the right ones to manage a major industry. They can even be counter-productive.

Managers, if they rise to the very top, need to give their channel a successful identity, with a strong brand strategy and delegate. To accomplish this, they need some talked-about hits which will mark out 'their' channel, particularly if they fit in with its strategy and its identity. Then they need to win a decent audience across much of their remaining output, but of course they also need to find and empower the right people – which can be difficult for ex-creatives. Many TV bosses, mainly promoted from the ranks, still display obsessive concern over every detail, and also really enjoy asserting their power in doing so. The competition and politicking of clever people with no common goal is fascinating to behold – especially their pleasure when colleagues fail.

CONCLUSION

So eschewing management and trying to become a Grand Old Man, the very first film I was asked to help wasn't as compelling as it should be in the cutting room, as are many films, although it had some wonderful material struggling to get out. It is a film that summed up everything this book has been about, and I used all its techniques, showing that this toolkit on storytelling can be applied successfully to all kinds of films. It became a surprise hit, winning the international Emmy for world's best documentary of the year, along with a host of other awards. It sums up the C.O.N.F.L.I.C.T toolbox.

SIMON DICKSON

Commissioning Editor, *The Boy Whose Skin Fell Off*

One day he's in my diary and then there he is in front of me – nice chap. I turned the idea down at first. The way Patrick tells the story, I turned it down once a month for six months before I finally decided to do it, and he's probably right. Because I hadn't cracked in my own head why people would come to it. I thought on the face of it the story of a young man dying a painful, horrible, premature death wouldn't be a big ratings winner. To a man, everybody else in Channel 4 who had been offered that film had turned it down too. That doesn't mean that they were wrong to turn it down, it just means that I was right to do it. We've all turned down things that have gone on to be hits, and it's important not to dwell on that too much because the best ideas in my experience are ones that work not because they walk in off the street, looking like a fully formed television idea – they are glimmers of something, opportunities, a half-idea, a territory, an approach.

Then what I do, as a commissioning editor, is look to find a way into that idea myself, to help it along – to bring my own experience to bear on it and to learn something in the process. My best commissions are ones I undertake because I want to learn something from the production, execution and broadcasting of that show. If I feel, as I said earlier, that there isn't the opportunity for failure or scope for it to take me out of my comfort zone, then I'm much less inclined to give it a whirl.

It was made by an inexperienced director, Patrick Collerton, but was deeply heartfelt – so much so that Patrick had spent months nobbling the Commissioning Editor to make it, and even then had not been given a big budget. Collerton, a very artistic and creative director, as it turned out, followed the last few months of a young man dying of a rare genetic and excruciatingly painful disorder. His skin literally peeled off.

Not a lot was expected of the film, but towards the end of the edit it still wasn't working quite right. It was then titled *Jonny Pops His Clogs*. It was the first thing I had ever worked on outside the BBC, even preceding the first series of *Jamie's School Dinners*, so I needed to show that it could be perfect – this was to be the start of my return. I applied everything I have been talking about in this book to transforming this one film over just a few days. When I first saw it, a family row broke out. I often watch DVDs with my now eighty-nine-year-old mother – it kills two birds with one stone, and she is very perceptive about story. With my own films she would often say: 'Not up to your usual standard, dear.' But this time was different. After I had left she rang my sister. 'This can't be transmitted,' she told her. For the first time since I had begun showing my mother films, back with Tri-ang, she was shocked. She worried that the contributor was being exploited, and even described the film as almost like disability porn. Now of course Jonny was the opposite of exploited – he had wanted to make the film – but his warmth wasn't coming out. My aged ma wasn't being made to sympathise and care.

I had never known a film arouse such family argument before. Because I could see that it had some utterly brilliant sequences. But it was a real mix of contradictions:

- It had a strong CHARACTER, but he was hard to sympathise with.

- It was very OUT OF THE BOX and original, but was so gruesome it was hard to take.

- It had a natural story but it needed a NARRATIVE DRIVE.

- It had a totally amazing FRONT already, thanks in part to the talented and original commissioning editor, but although clever and original it wasn't quite working because it didn't make clear the big question.

- It had a lot of **L**OVE. Jonny had been filmed extensively at home, and in fact a key part would be him wanting to move into his own home, but this wasn't yet explicit from the front.

- It was a film that had extraordinary and moving **I**NTERVIEW material, but no commentary, other than the very neat idea of having the character narrating his own film, if this could be made to work.

- Worst of all my mother didn't **C**ARE.

In the cut I first saw, as the film opened you discovered that the character narrating it was lying dead in his coffin describing his family, who were looking on at his body. It had been a wonderful idea to think of starting at the funeral with Jonny introducing himself and the other characters in voice-over, and brilliant as executed.

SIMON DICKSON

Commissioning Editor, *The Boy Whose Skin Fell Off*

When that idea occurred to me, I got a little tingly feeling that I was doing something, albeit just for a minute at the beginning of a film, that might be different to what had been done before, and seemed to be an unorthodox way of opening a documentary. I knew even then, when I was relatively fresh to commissioning, that it felt like this was a different way of kicking off a film.

PATRICK COLLERTON

Director, *The Boy Whose Skin Fell Off*

The references discussed with Simon were Sunset Boulevard, The Big Chill, American Beauty. *It just seemed more interesting to get away from the long, slow decline to somebody's death, by starting with the death. Then in the cutting room the editor Nick Fenton spotted the lines designed to go over the funeral would go over the actuality scene* [of Jonny at home, first in the wheelchair, then in an open coffin on the bed, surrounded by his family] *and the material showed another possibility.*

So brilliant was the execution that the production had been carried away with the idea and wanted Jonny to narrate the rest of the film. A great idea, but there was a big problem: they had recorded potential narration in interview with Jonny before he died, which was also before the film had been cut, and certainly before I had got my hands on the structure – in other words, before they had found and remade the story in the cutting room. As we recut it still didn't quite work, and now that Jonny was dead there was no chance of rerecording it.

So there was no perfectly attuned commentary or timeline, nor yet for me a real articulated reason for watching. And there was some very gruesome material close to the start, straight after the main title – scenes of Jonny looking desperately ill, and describing the disease, which would be deeply upsetting for many to watch, and made it hard to see Jonny's lighter and loveable side. However, I am no magician. To make a film great there needs to be a lurking story, sensitive interview and well-shot pictures for me to work with, and despite my mother there was some extraordinary magic lurking within Jonny.

To get at it I got out my C.O.N.F.L.I.C.T toolbox, and set to work, with the help of a very talented team, an open film editor, a passionate director, inspired by commissioning editor, Simon Dickson.

SIMON DICKSON

Commissioning Editor, *The Boy Whose Skin Fell Off*

The director was passionate and idealistic, but he didn't know how to get over the finishing line and there I felt I could help him. He had an extra-ordinary relationship with Jonny Kennedy and some singular ideas that ranged from the batty to the genuinely inspirational. So I found it pro-vocative and pleasurable to work with him, and that relationship was one key factor in the success of the film. But, as is often the case, the production company were showing signs of not being able to see the wood for the trees. And I felt they were in danger of taking the film in the wrong direction – they were trying to take their unique material and meld it into the kind of film I'd seen before. They were trying to lean towards a feature-led slot and approaching everything in a slightly ponderous, dignified way. And I felt it would be a better tribute to Jonny Kennedy, and a better film, if the film was more assertive and more on the front foot.

We were worried about what might happen to their film if nothing was done.

- The **CHARACTER** was already there, and strong, but needed to be made more sympathetic. Giving him a clear quest would help this.

- The thinking **OUT OF THE BOX** was brilliant, but the film would be helped by removing some of the most gruesome bits, and too much information, especially early on. This would also make Jonny seem a more sympathetic character.

- The brilliant, surprising and arresting actuality opening, with Jonny's voice-over from the coffin, would needed re-editing to get the big question out, to begin the **NARRATIVE DRIVE**. With this accomplished, we still needed the smaller questions and answers to make each sequence really work.

- The **FRONT** needed to give us a route map of where we were going.

- In it we needed to pose the big questions, including what I call **LOVE** – personal things that make someone human: in this case Jonny setting up his own home.

- To achieve this we would need to write a totally new commentary for a narrator. Inevitably this would be the most difficult change. The **INTERVIEW** with Jonny would need to be recut for the extraordinary front, but this alone would never be enough to tell the story.

- Most of all we needed to make the audience **CARE**. To help with this we would need a new **TITLE**, a rigorous **TIMELINE**, and an adherence to the bigger **TRUTH** of Jonny. We set to work.

First we recut the end of the opening voice-over of the stunning front which used Jonny's words from interview before his death, and culminated in Jonny saying that the director was doing such a bad job that he, Jonny, had come back to remake and narrate the film.

'Hello, my name is Jonny Kennedy. I've come back in spirit because the people making this programme were making such a bollocks of it. I thought I'd come back and do it myself, so let's carry on and see part of my life.'

Unfortunately this made the big question whether Jonny could make the film better than the director. But he was dead, so he couldn't. And it was hard to change, as clearly Jonny couldn't record any more narration. So from what existed we put together an opening quest in Jonny's voice:

'I have come back in spirit, to tell you the story of my life and my death . . .'

We were lucky to be able to use the second phrase: it completed the stunning opening created by the rest of the team, which made the film. But changing Jonny's line was not sufficient. The front was now saying a bit more what the film was about, but it still didn't give any detail, or ask a strong question. So, being too late to record more with Jonny, and not having the right words from him, we wrote new commentary for a new narrator to immediately follow his quest, leading up to the pre-title. It spelt out the three things that Jonny wanted to achieve before he died that were within the material that the director had filmed, three things that would be achieved (or not) by the end of the film; a route map. He would learn to fly, move out of his parents' home and, most important, get to No. 10 Downing Street to persuade Tony and Cherie Blair to help raise funds to research for causes and treatment for the disease, epidermolysis bullosa.

What better than to persuade the most powerful politician in the country to help end the disease that is about to kill you – the very day before your death? All our lives are about what we have actually done with them, as we approach the moment of our death. It's a universal question, with the key elements: conflict, transformation, redemption. This needed writing into the film. It was ultimate, and needed saying.

Then we needed to work on the sympathy. We made the decision to ditch Jonny's narration through the rest of the film; narration needs to be precise, and here it was really needed to tee up the sequences as cut – and replace them with a commentary voice. It was tough for the director, because he had wanted it to be Jonny's view, but this can only work if you can rewrite your contributor's lines and rerecord them *after* the edit, as we have discussed earlier.

Straight after the title, in the original cut, Jonny described the horror of his disease on the radio. We were anyway slightly confused by lack of precise and motivating narration, and this was not helped by now feeling a bit miserable and unsympathetic. Although the radio piece described the disease, it was not engaging, and we did not need to know about the disease at the front – we needed to engage. So we moved up that lively actuality scene as Jonny went shopping for his own coffin, a scene full of humour that would make one care about the character, and even laugh a bit with him. Remember it was introduced by a short, tight commentary starting the timeline: '*First there's the coffin to sort out.*' The scene began with Jonny discussing the size of his coffin, and ended with him asking the coffin-maker to put a Heinz Baked Beans symbol on the edge of his coffin. '*And you'll be asking me why? There's no reason at all. I just want people at my funeral looking at my coffin saying, why is the Heinz Baked Beans stuck on the side?*' There's no reason . . . and you engage with him as a warm and lovely character.

This set the film's timeline going immediately, counting down through his last four months, and even putting captions listing 'WEEKS TO GO' to Jonny's death. Some people thought this was crass, but Jonny's death was what the film was about, and anything that helped the audience to understand what had been a difficult story seemed good to me.

So now we had sorted a front to the film, complete with a route map and question, and straight after the title we had started a timeline with a scene that got the story going humorously, with actuality to help us care. Then we had slotted each sequence into this big story from the beginning to the end, with small questions and answers that contributed to the whole. And because you cared you could take more of the gruesome disease as it went along, though never quite as much as had been there at the start. Even then, for some people it was still too much. Conversely, some of the team initially thought we had now softened the film, and had not liked adding commentary, but now we were all on side. We still, though, had two things for lively discussion: the length and the title.

The film had been ninety minutes, but ninety minutes is a very long time and despite some questioning we reduced it to a Channel 4 hour. It would make it pacier and less indulgent, and make the audience care more. Shorter is invariably better. So often directors want their films to be longer, but almost everything you throw out tends to be an improvement. Think how many Hollywood directors want their films to be three hours, but luckily for us the studios make them cut them to two hours, because even with all the money, scriptwriting and actors three hours is a very long time to sit through a movie. So is ninety minutes for TV.

Even a BBC hour, without the ad breaks to take it down to 47 minutes, can be long. And so finally the film was cut to a Channel 4 hour. It had been a fantastic team, with a great editor in Nick Fenton, and the response exceeded what many of us had thought possible. I was very lucky that the director had created some fabulous and original material to work with. Using the toolbox you can always make an adequate film out of weak ingredients, but you need some magic moments and characters, if you are to lift a film to greatness.

But there was still one thing wrong: the title. Directors get used to titles and persuading them to change them can be hard: they often think a title that might attract the largest audience is crass. But getting as many people to watch a film as possible is the point. As positioning and marketing swing into action, the title can make a big difference.

TITLES

The TITLE, the final T of C.O.N.F.L.I.C.T, is surprisingly important. It can make a huge difference to the audience's expectation of your programme, and whether they even come to it. The very first series I worked on, as an assistant producer, wasn't helped by its title. It included strong stories, such as *Billion Dollar Day*, which followed three young foreign currency dealers round the world for twenty-four hours as they gambled a billion dollars against each other, and the film about Robert Maxwell's purchase of the *Daily Mirror*, called *How to Win Newspapers and Influence People*. Despite the strong stories, and those good individual titles, the series as a whole didn't win through for one sad and simple reason. A bottle of champagne was offered round the department for the person who invented the best series title. And the best anyone could come up with, on the spur of the moment, was *Commercial Breaks*. Which made it sound like a series on ads rather than following exciting human business stories. It is a lesson I never forgot. If it doesn't say on the tin what you have got inside, you have lost half the battle.

It was basically untruthful – it sounded like a series on advertising and then didn't deliver on this at all. For that reason, I believe, it was never the success it should have been. I have been extra-careful with titles ever since – the Sir John Harvey-Jones series was originally called *Company Doctor*. I wasn't satisfied with this and we worked on a new title for months, until the executive producer's secretary came up with

Troubleshooter. It was brilliant because it summed up Sir John Harvey-Jones. He *was* the Troubleshooter. Troubleshooting was what he in fact did, and today it is how he is remembered. It helped make the series. *The Apprentice* works in just the same way. However, while *Jamie's School Dinners* tells you what is inside, *Jamie's Ministry of Food* doesn't. Is it surprising that, despite being very good, it got a lower audience?

The strand *Trouble at the Top* started off being called *New Broom*. I knew that was not right, and after months of mental anguish I realised that in my story the key was our hero's quest. And in order to have a quest there needed to be something to set it off. One Sunday morning on Hampstead Heath I thought back to *Troubleshooter*. In business it could be 'trouble'. *Trouble at the Top* suggested jeopardy, and it was certainly better than *New Broom*. I could also use it to brand more series from *Trouble between the Covers* to *Trouble at the Big Top*, hopefully making a short-run series feel bigger. More branding.

It is vital that the title sums up what is inside the tin. *Back to the Floor* delivered just what it promised, as did its successor *Undercover Boss*, or *Wife Swap* and *Britain's Worst Driver* or *Extreme Home Makeover*. The title *Blood on the Carpet* helped ensure the success of the series about business battles. You know a title has really worked when you read it in newspapers about other stories, and it continues to be used long after the series is over and forgotten. You still read stories about *Trouble at the Top* in business. Like anything in television, persevere and keep at it. Success is going for that little bit more in every detail and in every way.

One of the hardest tasks in factual television can be telling contributors about the title and persuading them to accept the best.

JO BALL

Commissioning Editor, Features, BBC

You haven't got a programme till you've got a title. It's chicken and egg: if you haven't got a good title it's probably not going to get commissioned, and if it is commissioned and you can't describe your film with a pithy compelling title, it's probably not very interesting. Your book wouldn't stand a chance on an Electronic Programme Guide. Conflict *is OK, but the subtitle sounds dull so why not tell the truth and call it* Confessions of a Pushy AP?

Sometimes contributors just don't, and you need to be brave and remember that, once the shoot is over, it is the audience you are working for. Sometimes it is hard even to tell them the final title, but you are the professional, not them, and it is vital that you go for the best one – they will not thank you afterwards if the audience is small. And that is the other key thing to remember all through the film – that contributors will in the end mind most of all if filming to which they have given so much time ends up being unsuccessful and unwatched. Contributors will try to stop you pushing them and getting the best sequence as you film, and then wish they had allowed you more when they realise the finished product would have been better for it. So you owe it to them to push and to make the best film – with the best title.

When we came up with the title *Trouble at the Top* and told company bosses who had been filmed, they weren't keen to be associated with the idea of 'trouble' within their companies. Nor were potential bosses for the next series, with whom we were negotiating for access, especially as they hadn't seen the success of the first, nor the title in daily use. But their worry was exactly why we had chosen *Trouble* – it would be a winner with the audience. I sold it to the bosses by telling them that we all overcome trouble, that is our job, and to seem heroic we must be shown surmounting obstacles. But it wasn't easy.

Blood on the Carpet was even tougher. Rocco Forte came to the office to see the film of his business battle as Granada, and its boss, Gerry Robinson, attempted to take over the huge hotel and catering group founded by his father – a very emotional film. I normally only show completed films with title and commentary, so it is harder to change and looks more complete. But this time I had left off the opening title sequence – a bloodthirsty shark approaching a boardroom table under the carpet. Even so, I knew Rocco would be worried by the film. Fortunately I had a bandaged foot, and – thinking out of the box – used it to good effect. After the viewing, while I was taking him to the lift, we were able to talk about gout (though that was not why my foot was so painful) and, as a sufferer from something similar, he was sympathetic (as I've recommended: find something in common). As I said goodbye and the doors were closing I said: 'And by the way, we are calling it *Blood on the Carpet*.' I saw a horrified face disappear behind the closing lift doors.

Simple titles can make a film. Call your film *Ice Cream Wars* and the audience know what they are getting, with a bit of humour added.

When for *Trouble at the Top* we followed the old Northampton shoe factory turning to fetish footwear for salvation, it just had to be called *The Kinky Boot Factory*. The feature film that followed, based on our documentary, used the same title, *Kinky Boots* – in fact maybe the title helped them to want to copy the documentary and make the feature!

TITLE SEQUENCES

It is not just the title you need to get right, but the title sequences as well. Many say that the title sequence and the film's packaging are not that important in TV. But try saying that to book publishers about their covers, or to detergent manufacturers about their boxes! If the title sequence is really to work, then you are going to have to work too – real obsession is involved as you hone down what your film is truly about for the graphic artists. Their remit has to be intensely focused.

In *Trouble at the Top*, by our third meeting with the graphic designers we ended up describing the series as a rollercoaster ride for bosses. Once we had this simple notion, we came up with a storyboard of a desk shooting out of an office and off on to a Blackpool rollercoaster. Shooting it was great fun; we had a desk mounted on a special motion control stage, and as it wobbled we back-projected the view shot from a rollercoaster carriage behind it and so, wobbling away, it appeared to race down the track and struggle back up again.

Similarly, we honed the concept of *Back to the Floor* down to bosses leaving their hallowed offices in the heavens and descending to the hell of the shop floor. The final storyboard showed blue sky with puffy clouds, then an area of the sky opening up like a lift door to reveal an interior whose doors look just like the sky. Into the lift goes the camera, 'B' for basement lights up, and the lift shoots down with us inside. When the doors open they reveal the flames of life on the shop floor below the heavens. As always, choice of music is vital. For my first series, *Troubleshooter*, we were getting near transmisson and couldn't find the right music. A fellow guest at a dinner party offered to help. It turned out he was Michael Nyman, and the music that created the right emotion helped to make the series and spawned a full-length piece. Luck again.

This process of honing down, articulating what the film is about for the graphic designers, can also help you focus for yourself what your story really is as you struggle to find it in the cutting room. It's a two-way process. The *Blood on the Carpet* titles were honed to the 'shark' entering the boardroom under the carpet. And that was what the series was about. Sometimes simple can be best, and titles can be much shorter. On *School Dinners* we had all sorts of complex notions, but came up with a simple old-fashioned café menu-board, where the words were written with white pegs on to the black board. We would show the original menu, and would then animate Jamie's changes. Once we had decided on this we agonised over just what menu items these should be, even changing one item after the titles were finished! I have tinkered and tinkered with title sequences, and I always try to attend the shoot. It's that important. Even after programmes have been delivered to the broadcaster, I have often insisted on re-editing titles – even just a few frames here and there. I even shortened the *Troubleshooter* titles and the Nyman music at the very last minute.

Sometimes titles can be even shorter. The beginning of the film can be so very arresting that just a simple caption can work best. This was the case in *The Boy Whose Skin Fell Off* – just some plain, simple words superimposed on the first shot of the film, lasting around three seconds. Again unusual, as most titles now come after a minute or two of cold open or pre-title. As a rule of thumb, written words in titles should last about twice as long as it takes to read them, captions within films about one and a half times.

Complete with the new title, narration, and all the other final changes, *The Boy Whose Skin Fell Off* was finished just as a new Head of Programmes arrived at Channel 4. He saw the finished film and was so convinced by it that he announced to the channel it was just the sort of film he liked, and decided to give it a prime-time slot – for once no subterfuge was involved. So the marketing team swung into action behind it. With a title like that, the wonderful opening speech from Jonny after he had died (which had not originally been my idea, let me say again, but another from the sharp commissioning editor and team), and a character one truly cared about, the film became about confront-ing death by making something out of life. Wonderfully for the time-line, and the story, the final hurdle was only surmounted with Jonny's journey to No. 10 Downing Street the day before he died.

We all try to make something out of our lives. In this film it was writ large as Jonny succeeded in getting the money to end the disease for others the day before he himself died. It portrayed a universal theme, redemptive, heroic, Shakespearean, a universal truth. I think Jonny would have been proud of it. It was also a film that was as honest as possible. That was partly why Channel 4 liked it so much. The film had achieved an audience share of 18 per cent – very high for a one-off serious factual programme. After it was transmitted a new Chief Executive arrived at Channel 4 from the BBC, just as the existing Chief Executive, Mark Thompson, headed back to the BBC to become its Director General. On arrival he stood up and said it was his favourite film of the year. It was very originally made, but luck had played its part, particularly with Jonny reaching No. 10 just before his death.

If you remember the requirements for getting on in television from Chapter 1, they were, in reverse order, cleverness, charm, hunger and luck – and luck remains most important. *Jamie's School Dinners* started three months late with my obsession to find a school, and editing delayed it even more. If I had started and finished the series on time it might have been a disaster, but it came out late just before the election, whose date we couldn't have predicted, so the government had to listen, and it turned out to be 'of the moment'. But although you can be lucky sometimes, and should remember your successes are not just from being cleverer – remember that you can't have luck all the time. I was unlucky that *Jamie's Great Italian Escape* came so soon after the *School Dinners* hit. In countries with a bigger gap between transmissions it was a big hit too, but it was too soon in the UK and could only be 'OK'. We can end up with a surfeit of Gordon Ramsay or any other star. One of the toughest tricks in television is not overmilking your golden calves. Kill a series while it is still ahead. *Fawlty Towers* only ever had two series, the original *Troubleshooter* the same. Yet all these years later people still remember individual episodes of both.

PARTIES AND AWARDS

Finally, after all this hard work, you get to the end and transmission. After all that effort, this can feel incredibly flat – like after exams but worse – so I strongly advise organising a transmission party and watching the film going out together. This does not have to be expensive – you can just do it in someone's house. Even if you are the assistant producer and no one else suggests it, organise something yourself. Without it everyone will probably feel miserable and flat. You may do anyway, for the next day reviews and audience figures will come in. Whatever the outcome, try to meet as many people as possible, both in your production company and, ideally, at the broadcaster, because that way you will be able to manage how it is being talked about, at least a bit, and also take some of the glory if there is any going.

There is one last thing. If you have applied all these tools, had a lot of luck (and not been shafted) you may get to a wonderful moment – the awards ceremonies. However good your film, it helps hugely if you have had the schedulers and marketeers on side. Adam Curtis's brilliant series *Power of Nightmares* might have been just another obscure current affairs series had it not been properly pushed. Try hard to get a repeat in late autumn just before the awards season – there's a greater chance that juries might see it, and a repeat signals that it matters more. Put in for as many awards as you can, even obscure ones. I won a fine vase in the Medicine in the Media awards. There can be an award out there for nearly everyone. There are hundreds of awards around the world for specialist areas from the Wincott Award for Business TV, to the Mental Health Media Award, to the George Foster Peabody Award for US TV Journalism. So try to find out what your programme might qualify for, if any, and persuade your bosses to apply if you can't.

If in doubt, find or encourage a new award if you can. *Back to the Floor* and *Blood on the Carpet* seemed unlikely to win BAFTAs for best documentary series – they weren't worthy enough. But they had invented a new popular factual genre. Luckily BAFTA did the same, and they won that features BAFTA for its first two years, followed in quick succession by *Naked Chef*, *Faking It*, *Wife Swap*, *Top Gear* and *The Apprentice*. All these winners had both entertainment and content – back to Chapter 1 again, for it is a heady mix that works.

Finally there is the thorny problem of who gets to collect the award on stage. My first experience of BAFTA was for my own *Troubleshooter*. Sir John was unable to attend, so my executive producer was called up to get it. But never be shy at these moments. Uninvited, I followed. When a surprised Griff Rhys Jones, who was hosting the award ceremony, asked me 'Who are you?' in front of millions of TV viewers, I said: 'I made it.'

At the National TV Awards for *Jamie's School Dinners* we were under strict instructions from the organisers, and from Jamie's company boss, that only Jamie should go up on stage if we won. When we did win, I grabbed the entire team, including the production manager, coordinator, and the boss – it is always best to take everybody whether you are supposed to or not – and raced up after Jamie to the stage, live on ITV, unfortunately tripping in my haste to catch up!

Success has many parents. *Jamie's School Dinners* was apparently invented by almost everyone who came in contact with it, from countless TV bosses to Jamie himself, and many who didn't. The only person who definitely did not come up with the idea is me. I am a craftsman – I just use ideas and make them work. I believe it is the best job in TV. For the most creative part of TV is not just the initial idea, as many commissioners think, but also making ideas *into* TV, transforming them, giving them clothes and creating heroes.

A programme, as it evolves, is like a living organism. You have continually to struggle to find a reason or motivation in order to make people care. When a film or series lacks that kind of inspiration, as with *Jamie's Great Italian Escape*, you have a real problem. I joined that series when it was well under way, but needed help on the eve of filming. The best premise I could invent was this: Jamie is shattered by the *School Dinners* experience, and is also going through an early but classic mid-life crisis. He has lived with Jules and worked without a break since he was sixteen, and is desperate to get away on the gap year he has missed.

It was only just before we set off that we discovered that he was taking a book-writing team along too, as well as our film crew. The demands of cookbooks, complete with photographs, and film crews with their need to create heroes, are very different. Jamie's time was, as usual, incredibly limited; fireworks were on their way as both needed lots of time and quite different approaches. Finally I was called down to Sicily. The following morning Jamie Oliver and Jules came into my hotel room on the small island of Marettima to say the filming was off, and I wondered which rule of television I had broken this time. And then as filming fell apart, a howling gale blew, boats were cancelled, it was too windy even for rescue helicopters and the stars were caught in the original tempest. And I remembered the most necessary rule of all in making television – don't panic!

After what seemed like weeks, but was just two days, the winds lifted, and we saw a ferry trying to brave the waves and make it into the tiny harbour. There was a jubilant scream as Jamie, Jules and the whole team raced to catch it. And then I remembered that perhaps you can make cooking shows without any reason at all, something Jamie had known all along, and I realised that I had broken the most important rule of all, the real secret of success: once you have learnt all the rules of factual television storytelling, ignore and break them.

Two weeks later we were somewhere unexpected. A bit more love, a bit less push and some lateral scheduling had saved the day. The cookbook was done and Jamie was being filmed by my now peaceful crew, all alone in a monastery cell, trying to stay silent. The crisis had made for stronger TV. Hold your nerve!

It's fun, if a bit scary at times, being a TV producer. Now it is time to let your material dictate your story, and do it in your own way, making your own rules. Good luck!

Appendix

THE HUNDRED RULES
OF TELEVISION

The Hundred Rules of Television

to help you through the film-making process

(and a TV career) from start to finish

1. Never take on something that has been successful.

2. Take on any disaster which has a chance of being saved.

3. To create winners, get different genres banging into each other.

4. Follow the crazy idea, if your gut tells you to strongly enough.

5. Never subjects, always stories.

6. Good stories often follow people under pressure through transformation, ideally to redemption.

7. Stories that take you into hidden worlds are useful too.

8. Pick a mythic story, and stick to it.

9. Dress these stories in new clothes as much as possible, but continue to tell the same story.

10. Success requires entertainment plus content.

11. Your subject and story should seem big, while being small enough to film.

12	Drama needs heroes and heroes need opponents.
13	Television reduces people so you need characters with the potential to be larger than life.
14	Be very suspicious of anyone who is too instantly keen to take part in your film.
15	The harder the time on the quest, the more the public will love the hero.
16	The more you can do to mark out and popularise your main characters the better.
17	Appeal to contributors' vanity.
18	Appeal to contributors to help you - or you'll be fired.
19	You can always find something in common with anyone so express interest in their interest.
20	Don't on first meeting give contributors the chance to say no.
21	Don't ask contributors to marry you too soon.
22	Appear to be well-meaning but slightly silly.
23	Getting contributors to trust you is the most important fuel in getting them going.
24	The more you can do to mark out and popularise your main characters the better.
25	Clear your mind of preconceptions, and do open-minded research.

26 The truth is in this research.

27 Time spent researching is the cheapest.

28 You can hardly ever start a film too late.

29 The script is a route map – a clear idea where you are going.

30 Often when it is wrong, it is right.

31 Choose a counter-intuitive presenter where possible.

32 Also if possible choose passionate experts.

33 Assemble the right team to do it.

34 Employ by recommendation.

35 Employ the inexperienced but hungry.

36 Find interesting theatres for your characters to perform in.

37 Build up the drama till your hero and villain meet.

38 You know it's right when you hear it two ways.

39 Narrative is small questions and small answers which all contribute to the big question and big answer.

40 Think of all dimensions of film-making simultaneously:

1 – Storytelling skills.

2 – Visual flair.

3 – People skills.

4 – Organisational skills.

5 – Journalistic and persuasive skills.

41 In filming as in medicine, morality is as important as technique.

42 Do not film too much.

43 Never film in offices. Find interesting locations.

44 Many of the best films are shot in limited time and space.

45 It doesn't matter what you don't film only what you do.

46 Don't judge while you are filming, try to understand.

47 Get a good film editor.

48 Trust your editor, and let the rushes tell their own story.

49 The best editing is done in the garden.

50 Show your film to other bright people and use their ideas.

51 Films do not need introductions, they need to get going, so get rid of the next ten minutes.

52 Instead, put a strong actuality scene straight after the subtitle.

53 Admit when you are wrong.

54 Add a twist or surprise.

55 Editing should be two steps forward, one step back.

56 If the presenter looks good, you look good.

57	Tell the presenter the best idea is theirs.
58	Make contributors look bad to look good.
59	Film contributors at home, and with their families.
60	It is not just presenters and contributors to keep happy, but your team.
61	To get on, you need, in reverse order, cleverness, charm, hunger and luck.
62	Manage your bosses' boss.
63	Executives are lonely, cultivate them.
64	Find something no one else is doing, and differentiate it.
65	If you want something, pretend you are leaving.
66	Brand yourself.
67	As a researcher, seek talented directors and help them rather than trying to make your own films too soon.
68	Always have your next film but one or next job but one planned.
69	Appear to overshare but don't.
70	Find friends or partners outside TV who won't let you talk about it all the time.
71	Take holidays – and long ones sometimes.
72	On location actuality is best.
73	Appear confused while being ordered and in control.

74	When in doubt, focus your contributors on three things you need from each actuality sequence.
75	The filming before and after a conversation can be best.
76	Interview is for emotion.
77	Silence, and the look that goes with it, can be the very best part of an interview.
78	Commentary should be in spoken language not written.
79	Humour helps in commentary.
80	Always reduce the commentary. Even at the record (especially if rewriting).
81	Write proposals leaving them wanting more.
82	Whatever is asked for, do the opposite.
83	Try to tell it in a couple of sentences and get the attention of everyone in the pub.
84	Making the film is only half the battle.
85	Chat up the schedulers, marketeers and publicity people, and take them to lunch.
86	Flatter the press and help them.
87	In publicity, timing and pictures are everything.
88	Make your own press publicity.
89	It is not the total audience size that counts, but it helps, especially the best for your kind of film.

90	You can never compliment presenters enough.
91	Time can be the greatest organising principle of a film.
92	Shorter is invariably better.
93	Titles matter enormously. Say on the tin what is inside.
94	The most obvious is often best.
95	Be true to yourself, and true to your presenter.
96	Check every fact inside out.
97	Turn from hungry young Turk to Grand Old Man in one pirouette.
98	If you are a film-maker who gets to manage, avoid gobbledygook and the latest fad.
99	Win as many awards as possible.
100	Don't panic.
	And, oh yes –
101	Once you've learnt the rules, ignore and break them.

INDEX